AF757195

Public Interest and Private Rights in Social Media

CHANDOS
SOCIAL MEDIA SERIES

Series Editors: Geoff Walton and Woody Evans
(e-mails: g.l.walton@staffs.ac.uk and kdevans@gmail.com)

This series of books is aimed at practitioners and academics involved in using social media in all its forms and in any context. This includes information professionals, academics, librarians and managers, and leaders in business. Social media can enhance services, build communication channels, and create competitive advantage. The impact of these new media and decisions that surround their use in business can no longer be ignored. The delivery of education, privacy issues, logistics, political activism and research rounds out the series' coverage. As a resource to complement the understanding of issues relating to other areas of information science, teaching and related areas, books in this series respond with practical applications. If you would like a full listing of current and forthcoming titles, please visit our website www.chandospublishing.com or email wp@woodheadpublishing.com or telephone +44 (0) 1223 499140.

New authors: we are always pleased to receive ideas for new titles; if you would like to write a book for Chandos in the area of social media, please contact Jonathan Davis, Commissioning Editor, on jonathan.davis@chandospublishing.com or telephone +44 (0) 1993 848726.

Bulk orders: some organisations buy a number of copies of our books. If you are interested in doing this, we would be pleased to discuss a discount. Please email wp@woodheadpublishing.com or telephone +44 (0) 1223 499140.

Public Interest and Private Rights in Social Media

Edited by

Cornelis Reiman

CHANDOS PUBLISHING

Oxford Cambridge New Delhi

Chandos Publishing
Hexagon House
Avenue 4
Station Lane
Witney
Oxford OX28 4BN
UK
Tel: +44 (0) 1993 848726
Email: info@chandospublishing.com
www.chandospublishing.com
www.chandospublishingonline.com

Chandos Publishing is an imprint of Woodhead Publishing Limited

Woodhead Publishing Limited
80 High Street
Sawston
Cambridge CB22 3HJ
UK
Tel: +44 (0) 1223 499140
Fax: +44 (0) 1223 832819
www.woodheadpublishing.com

First published in 2012

ISBN: 978-1-84334-693-7 (print)
ISBN: 978-1-78063-353-4 (online)

British Library Cataloguing-in-Publication Data.
A catalogue record for this book is available from the British Library.

Typeset by Domex e-Data Pvt. Ltd., India

Contents

List of figures and tables

Figures

Tables

Acknowledgements

The compiling and completion of this collection required the able assistance of several people to whom heartfelt thanks must be given. It was particularly warming for me to have many people of high standing respond positively to my call for assistance in relation to the preparation of this book.

Firstly, there are the authors of chapters herein, each of whom proved themselves to be particularly helpful in writing about their area of expertise, as well as collaborating in a professional manner. These contributors made the job of an editor an easy one.

Secondly, the people at Chandos Publishing were supportive, courteous and considerate throughout the term of the project that gave rise to this book. As such, special thanks must go to Glyn Jones, Jonathan Davis, George Knott and Vicki Hart.

Thirdly, those who are a fundamental part of the production process must be thanked, particularly Juliet Gardner for her sterling effort as copy-editor.

Preface

Generally, social media texts focus on specific aspects only, and do not provide overall guidance as to the issues and related remedies. Furthermore, other texts often deal with mass media issues (such as newspaper, television and radio), but these do not usually address Internet-driven social media.

When Chandos Publishing commissioned a series of books on social media, and its impacts and trends, I saw this as the opportunity for an overall guide to the key components of corporate and academic use, socio-political impact and legality.

I was spurred onward by the chief objective of the publisher in seeking practical – rather than theoretical – information that was easy to digest. This struck me as being ideal as an avenue to deliver current and relevant topics that had a broad, international appeal to people working in the area of social media implementation and usage.

Once the good people at Chandos Publishing agreed with my ideas for this book, I set out to secure the support of key authors who, from their particular perspectives, would give fresh commentary on social media. I was fortunate to receive an excellent response from some wonderful folk who provided me with very interesting contributions that added to my understanding of the social media phenomenon. I hoped that this would also be the reaction of readers who want to learn about social media in terms of planning for proper implementation at the organisational level, whether in the private, not-for-profit or public sectors, plus the ramifications of social media usage socially, cross-industry, locally and internationally, as well as currently and over time.

The intention of this book, therefore, is to capture key aspects of social media that are beyond online marketing, as is common, whether for products and services, and for people who promote themselves privately or professionally. Particularly, there is the issue of social media being a political tool, which has upset a variety of governments who saw it used effectively by common people seeking significant changes in how a country is managed. In addition, social media provides effective vehicles for connecting with larger audiences, as is very necessary in the not-for-profit sector where good causes require strong support.

This book provides thoughtful insight as to the utilisation and impact of social media, with chapters giving support for the title of the collection, being *Public Interest and Private Rights in Social Media*. As such, the contributing authors make available sound guidance regarding social media issues in various vestiges of society.

Specifically, learned and professional authors share their valuable expertise related to the use of social media in the corporate sector, the not-for-profit domain and academia, as well as highlight the rising influence of social media in garnering public and political opinion worldwide. Also, specific legal implications are addressed. Unique perspectives on social media usage as well as associated challenges for people in developed and developing countries alike are brought together. This edited book, therefore, presents chapters written by selected researchers, academics and practitioners who provide unique perspectives on social media usage, as well as its associated challenges.

The unique features of this book include:

- planning and operational perspectives;
- technological and non-technological perspectives;
- legal perspectives;
- international perspectives; and
- futuristic perspectives.

An added indication as to the fundamental characteristics of this book is provided by way of the target audience. Specifically, it is aimed at practitioners, academics and students in the areas of information science, management and systems, as well as communications and marketing. This book provides thoughtful insight regarding the utilisation, impact and future of social media. Accordingly, the target audience can be summarised by way of the following list:

- chief digital officers;
- chief information officers;
- chief technology officers;
- chief ethical officers;
- communications managers and other professionals;

- marketing managers and other professionals;
- information technology managers and other professionals;
- corporate governance professionals;
- managers and executives in corporate, government and non-government organisations; and
- academics and students of information science, information management, information systems, knowledge management and marketing.

As the title of this book indicates, particular attention is paid to public interest and private rights in social media. The collection of contributions from accomplished authors therefore provides guidance for a wide audience that, more and more, needs to be mindful about the proper processes that are necessary when engaged in the use of social media. Whether individuals, or as members of broad organisations, readers will gain considerable benefit from what practitioners and academics have offered in relation to intra-organisational concerns, as well as external factors, such as those generated by emerging laws and rising anxiety of some governments.

Chapter overview

Anyone who is reading this, and most of the people known to us, are an integral part of a large cohort in modern society that can still remember when any social media application had yet to take effect. The future is certain to be one full of excitement and promise, plus more than a few related challenges. This is indicated herein through the research and considered opinions expressed by people who share their perspectives of how social media affects the evolving, modern world, as well as how all of that can have an impact upon the future of people, privacy, politics and the promotion of humanitarian campaigns.

Understandably, there are many aspects of social media that can be intertwined in relation to particular topics upon which contributing authors have focused. The sequence of the following chapters, therefore, was contemplated in relation to interlocking themes, with the resultant sequence bearing no relation to the comparative importance of these contributions. In effect, the eventual progression of chapters arose from the telling of a story, whereby we commenced with an introduction to social media issues provided in the first chapter, which are related to the growth of the user population, what they do online and how this can affect others. Next, we see how legal implications arise, and why these might differ internationally. Then, we ponder what the ramifications might be at a deeper level within society and government. Thereafter, we review social media usage in the not-for-profit, academic and business sectors. This is followed by further guidance as to the proper implementation and management of social media strategies in any organisational environment. Finally, we conclude with a view of what is likely to arise from widespread social media usage in time to come, as is done in terms of future social discourse.

What follows are the chapters, presented in summary form, so as to show the related flow of themes herein.

The first chapter is by the Editor, Cornelis Reiman, entitled 'Social media growth and global change'. This initial part of the collection is introductory in nature, and with focus upon broad topics and effects arising from the phenomenon of social media. There is attention paid to the history of social media, the rising use of social media in relation to social and political activism, plus social media in the workplace, as well as legal implications of social media usage overall. Also, social analytics are introduced, which relies upon the vast amount of data that social media users generate.

It is well known that the United States of America upholds freedom of speech, having enshrined this liberty in the Constitution of that country. Yet there is a necessary history that must be understood for anyone to gain an appreciation of how judicial decisions relate to recent cases involving flash mobs and, more importantly, how such decisions can affect future outcomes of such cases. In this regard, Margot Kaminski, Executive Director of the Information Society Project at Yale Law School, presents a riveting chapter entitled 'Flash rob or protest movement: the First Amendment and regulating online calls to action'. This is a learned work, and one that is instructive, as much as it is educational.

Next, Kurt Ramin and Antje Meyer provide a much more global perspective of legal issues in 'World justice – the rule of law around the world'. This interesting chapter, as the title suggests, discusses the Rule of Law Index in considering the legal impact upon social media. The Index provides an intriguing analysis of what constitutes the rule of law in different countries, with attention paid to Germany, China and the

United Arab Emirates. In addition, the authors pose a pertinent question: social media – chance or challenge?

Appropriately, this prospect of challenges leads to the chapter by Florian Hadler and Gabriel Yoran, entitled 'Default metaphysics – social networks and the self'. This contribution, being rather philosophical yet incredibly edifying, brings together idealistic issues and technological ones that shape what we do in modern society, especially for anyone who uses the Internet. Accordingly, this is an extremely thoughtful work by two authors who have garnered great experience in the digital domain. They are practitioners, although with a profound insight.

The first contribution relating to the not-for-profit sector, the next section in our story, is by Marshall Sitten. His contribution is entitled 'A service-oriented approach to public sector social media strategy'. Directed specifically at public organisations, not-for-profit organisations and agencies of that ilk, this chapter focuses upon the critical issues that must be considered before any social media communications strategy is advised and implemented. The author is well versed in this area, having advised numerous entities of that type, and in that capacity. Actual examples help to identify what problems can exist, and how these can be overcome.

As might be known, public and non-for-profit organisations differ from private sector entities, and that must be taken into account when any social media initiative is planned and brought into being. Of particular importance is the need for any entity to be intimately familiar with the fundamental elements, as well as how these should be brought onboard to enhance communications, and increase engagement with key stakeholders.

The next chapter is 'Social media in the humanitarian space', by Claudia Gonzalez and Alan Rosenblatt, and also deals with the not-for-profit sector. Here, we see how the experience of seasoned practitioners shines in this chapter. In so doing, the authors identify what can be done with social media in pursuing humanitarian outcomes, and also indicate the reasons why. Among other things, a beneficial result is achieved through the presentation of excellent examples that identify ways by which humanitarian organisations can expand their reach into the general public, as well as into the global community. Whether the purpose is to broadcast the core message, engage with people in need, or interact with existing or prospective donors, the authors offer an instructive contribution to the collection.

This is followed by the work of Susan Bandias and Anthony Gilding whose chapter is entitled 'Social media: the new tool in business education'. The academic authors of this chapter talk of social media and social capital, and how these two concepts intertwine. In so doing, they present the various forms of social media that exist, and which of these are applicable to an educational setting, one with attention paid to business students. Considerable learning benefits are reported from the use of social media applications, as can be imagined when any interaction between students is facilitated appropriately.

Thereafter, academics Andrew Creed and Ambika Zutshi pose, and address, a question that is the heading of their learned contribution: 'Social media: does it generate the continuum of transparency in organisations?' This chapter is about the need for transparency in social media usage, which arises because there is a high chance that harm can be inflicted upon people and organisations. It is not the social media application that can cause damage, but how that application is used. This leads to the need for appropriate social media guidelines, as well as any other communication policies, to reduce the prospect of abuses through social media usage and interrelationships on the Internet.

Moving on from the not-for-profit and education sectors, and stepping into the more commercial domain, businessman Richard Messik provides a short but useful opinion piece entitled 'Social media: blessing or curse? – a business perspective'. This chapter looks at social media from the viewpoint of one who lives in the corporate sector. Richard suggests that social media applications have the capacity to replace email, which has dominated modern business communication for quite some time. This is an intriguing notion. Still, he cautions all who use any form of electronic communication to be careful as to what is sent and to whom. In addition, care must be taken about what is posted for broader consumption, such as when any public access is possible.

In relation to the implementation, management and measurement of social media applications, as well as outcomes, two contributions by measurement experts produce excellent details regarding what is needed to maximise efficiencies when pursuing communications strategies. Aptly entitled 'Improving the customer experience: how social media can make a difference', the next chapter is by Urs Gattiker. It is an account of necessities when engaging with a targeted audience for more beneficial outcomes. Urs indicates that much depends upon understanding the processes associated with crafting social media strategy and any ensuing implementation. In addition, it is critical that appropriate measurements are determined, as well as monitored and managed. These so-called actionable metrics are a critical component to achieving or exceeding expectations of any social media initiative, and are worth noting.

Similarly, Marshall Sponder addresses particularly pertinent issues in his chapter, entitled 'The uses and accuracy of social analytics data and platforms'. Marshall explores the issues and advantages of social analytics for public relations, branding, advertising and sales, which are relevant to all entities, whether they are commercial, not-for-profit or public organisations. Alternatives for the measurement of necessary data are discussed, and Marshall pushes the need for appropriate return on investment when considering social media usage. Again, we see the benefit of a seasoned practitioner sharing his experience, especially when he offers valuable advice on what works for organisations that seek tangible benefits in particular areas of their social media strategy. In relation to numerous elements that constitute the social media space, he asks, and answers, 'What works best?' He also indicates that the extent to which data is collected does cause concerns for some in relation to user privacy, which is a recurrent theme throughout this collection.

In amidst all of the discussion as to the usefulness of social media comes a forward-looking contribution from Russell Yardley, who provides us with the remaining chapter, which is eloquently entitled 'Altruism – a valuable dimension of the digital age'. Russell is another practitioner, with extensive experience as an executive, entrepreneur and investor in the digital domain. He provides a logical contribution, and one that seems appropriate as a concluding chapter in our journey together. Of particular interest here is the strongly proposed view that our future will be one wherein we will see more altruism through unselfish contribution to the greater good than is typical of socio-political scenarios to date. As the title of his chapter suggests, altruism is a possible, and valuable, outcome of what we already see in nascent form today.

Russell expands upon the commonly held view that altruism exists, although in small amounts, and that this can grow through the use of social media applications that link likeminded folk, as well as provide guidance regarding the character of possible partners and associates, which is presented in the form of an eternal digital history. Russell proposes, quite convincingly, that selflessness is sure to grow with increased use made of social media applications where productive connections can be made with progressively more ease. In addition, these new methods of networking will improve through viewing, and analysing, what contacts occur and how. Thus networking improves, and this provides the firmer and wider platform upon which selfless endeavours can stand. This unfolding reality will attract additional interest, and ideas, and shall become something of benefit for a broader audience and that this will, in some form, be of use to all of us.

Essentially, this book provides the invaluable opportunity to explore fascinating and very relevant topics that include: social media policy formulation in a organisational setting; the use of social media tools in academia and commerce; social media for public engagement and the pursuit of social good; blurred boundaries between personal and professional lives; the heightened feeling of transparency; working, learning and living with social media; and the use of social media professionally.

I do hope that readers find considerable value, and enjoyment, in the contributions that constitute this collection.

Cornelis A. Reiman
Bangkok, Thailand
February 2012

About the editor

Cornelis Reiman, PhD (Economics), is an international Board advisor and academic with extensive experience in the technological domain. He enjoys a number of exceptional professional qualifications in accounting, corporate governance, marketing and management, including FCPA (Australia and Singapore), FCIS and Chartered Accountant. He is also a Senior Member and Certified Professional with the Australian Computer Society. In addition to considerable business skills, he gained a sound IT background when working with IBM in technical, marketing, management and executive positions. Thereafter, he proceeded to apply his particular abilities by serving private clients as a management consultant.

Previously, he was President of an international economic development entity spanning the former Soviet Union, and before that he was based in Singapore. There he worked as a global Chief Technology Officer of a B2C and B2B entity, playing a pivotal role in establishing a premium e-university that pioneered social media in online classes that connected students internationally.

Earlier, Cornelis was Dean and Vice President of a university in Thailand. He also taught international business, management and economics to postgraduate students at Monash University in Australia, where he pioneered online learning in the Department of Management. Cornelis additionally consulted in the private and public sectors on issues such as computing, corporate management, strategic planning and business incubation. The global information technology provider IBM, and the former accounting services firm of Arthur Andersen & Co., employed him earlier.

More recently, he has advised boards and senior executives in relation to the use of technological platforms that improve efficiencies in production and, especially, business reporting, which is necessary for vital decision making.

Overall, his unique blend of skills and experience is evident in the manner by which the following collection of papers is forged in providing inquisitive readers, practitioners and scholars with a useful point of reference to address particular issues. It also presents a sound basis by which readers can explore even further what social media offers.

Email: *cornelis.reiman@gmail.com*

LinkedIn: *http://th.linkedin.com/pub/cornelis-reiman/0/926/903*

About the contributors

Assorted social media applications are designed to bring people together, and do so through numerous means, as well as for a variety of purposes. The collection of papers contained in this book, therefore, explore a variety of uses to which social media tools are put, and how this is best done. Essentially, the contributing authors were selected for the strength and clarity of their voice in relation to key elements that are as much a product of the social media momentum as they are a catalyst for more impetus in time to come.

Selected researchers, academics and practitioners provide unique perspectives of social media usage, as well as associated challenges and proven remedies. Those who contributed to this book are listed below.

Susan Bandias

Dr Susan Bandias is a lecturer in the School of Business at Charles Darwin University. Her area of expertise is in the disciplines of Management and Human Resource Management. She has a longstanding interest in the education applications of Information and Communications Technology (ICT) and has published widely in the areas of telecommunications issues and the social implications of ICT.

Susan is also very actively engaged in the development of online education and has extensive experience in distance education. She uses a range of social media including web conferencing tools, Wikis, RSS feeds, discussion forums and video conferencing extensively in the curriculum and is adept at exploiting the potential of social media to enhance the learning experience for students. Susan has lived in Darwin, Australia for over 20 years.

Currently, Susan is the Director of the Women's Board of the Australian Computer Society and takes an active role in encouraging and supporting women in the ICT sector.

Email: *Susan.Bandias@cdu.edu.au*

Andrew Creed

Currently a lecturer at Deakin University, in Australia, Dr Andrew Creed has qualifications and research interests in e-learning technologies in the field of management education, ethics and organisational behaviour. He is also an author of textbooks, multimedia learning objects and supplements for publishers including Oxford University Press, Wiley and Prentice-Hall. Previously, he was an adjunct Associate Professor in the online MBA programme at the University of Maryland University College, an instructional designer, writer and project manager for online industrial training toolboxes in the fields of food and meat processing, and office administration; he was also a consultant to government and not-for-profit organisations, in addition to being a mentor to hundreds of start-up entrepreneurs.

Email: *andrew.creed@deakin.edu.au*

Urs Gattiker

Professor Urs E. Gattiker, PhD, is an internationally renowned risk technologist, social media expert, author and blogger. In addition, he is both a founder and the Chief Executive Officer of CyTRAP Labs GmbH. This entity provides corporate governance and social media services to organisations worldwide. With his company's software My.ComMetrics.com (benchmark your blog – improve your social media resonance), he has developed the FT ComMetrics Blog Index for the *Financial Times* that ranks among the most successful blogs of the Global 500 companies.

He is also the author of several books, one of which is about social networking, entitled *The Internet as a Diverse Community* (2001). His latest book, *Social Media Audit: Measure for Impact*, is forthcoming in 2012 (see *www.SecURL.de/audit*).

Email: *Urs.Gattiker@gmail.com*
Website: *http://info.cytrap.eu*

Anthony Gilding

Dr Anthony Gilding has held a number of positions in academic development and management of support services related to online teaching and learning in several universities. This has included both large metropolitan and smaller regional universities. In addition, he has led projects on the redevelopment of courses and teaching practices across nearly all university disciplines and professional areas.

Dr Gilding has a longstanding interest in the way that technology can be used to improve the student learning experience through providing both students and teaching staff with more engaging and effective learning activities. Also, in relation to university teaching, he has assisted and guided teaching staff in the use of all the contemporary online tools and media.

Email: *gtony@y7mail.com*

Claudia Gonzalez

Claudia is Head of Marketing of the Global Fund to Fight AIDS, Tuberculosis and Malaria where she manages branding, marketing and social media. Previously, Claudia was the Head of Public Relations and Special Projects for two years at the United Nations High Commissioner for Refugees (UNHCR), the UN's refugee agency and, before that, spent almost eight years working with the World Economic Forum.

Claudia is a strategist with 15 years of experience in integrated communications, and specialising in social media, celebrities and branding. Earlier, Claudia was a diplomat for Mexico, her home country, having also been a press correspondent for a number of years in different countries.

Claudia's academic background includes a Master's from the London School of Economics on Media and Communications.

Email: *claudia.gonzalez@theglobalfund.org*
Twitter: *@claudiagonzalez*

Florian Hadler

Florian Hadler is co-founder and shareholder of aka-aki networks, a location-based social network. In addition, he is a consultant for concepts, creation and production of social media solutions, brand communication and apps for web and mobile. He acts as a European Commission expert for digital economy and innovation. He also teaches at the Berlin University of the Arts.

In his position as Creative Director at aka-aki networks, he has earned several international awards, including two Webby Awards in 2009 and a Lead Award in 2010. Together with Steffen Krämer, under their common association spotlab media, Florian also produces and directs documentaries, commercials, image spots and music videos.

Florian holds a Master's in Social and Economic Communications from the Berlin University of the Arts and is currently pursuing his PhD in the Media and Communication division of the European Graduate School in Saas Fee, Switzerland.

Email: *flohadler@googlemail.com*
Website: *www.flohadler.com*

Margot Kaminski

Margot E. Kaminski is a Research Scholar in Law and Executive Director of the Information Society Project at Yale Law School. She is a graduate of Harvard University and Yale Law School, in addition to being a former fellow of the Information Society Project. While at Yale Law School, she was a Knight Law and Media Scholar, as well as co-founder of the Media Freedom and Information Access Practicum. Following graduation from Yale Law School, Margot clerked for the Honorable Andrew J. Kleinfeld of the Ninth Circuit Court of Appeals. Also, Margot was a Radcliffe Research Fellow at Harvard, and a Google Policy Fellow at the Electronic Frontier Foundation.

Margot's research and advocacy work focuses on media freedom, online civil liberties, data mining and surveillance issues. She has written widely on law and technology issues for law journals, and the popular press. Furthermore, Margot has drawn public attention to civil liberties issues surrounding the Anti-Counterfeiting Trade Agreement and other Free Trade Agreements.

Email: *margot.kaminski@yale.edu*
Website: *www.law.yale.edu/intellectuallife/informationsocietyproject.htm*

Richard Messik

Richard is a chartered accountant with specific interest in technology and all aspects of cloud computing, as well as being the co-founder of RFM Associates – Cloud Computing Consultancy. It is noteworthy that Richard was an early espouser and innovator of cloud computing with the Easycounting online accounting system. In addition, Richard's decision to set up a cloud consultancy allows him to focus on this particular area, being his main area of interest, by offering education, advice and implementation, plus working with people who want to join him in thinking forwards, and never backwards.

Richard writes extensively on the subject of cloud computing and believes that business success depends very much on combining forward planning, ongoing development, cost-effective inter-office communication and central administration with all that technology has to offer.

Email: *rfmessik@rfmassociates.com*
Twitter: @*richard_messik*
LinkedIn: *http://uk.linkedin.com/in/richardmessik*

Antje Meyer

Antje Meyer studied law (*Magister Juris*) and graduated from Constance University, Germany. In Brussels and Strasbourg she worked with and assisted a European Member of Parliament with research, studies and speeches. In Frankfurt, New York, Hong Kong and Dubai she was employed by major international companies, such as PricewaterhouseCoopers, Allianz and Duane Morris.

Email: *antje.m.meyer@gmail.com*

Kurt Ramin

Kurt is a Director at AccountAbility and Global Head of Standards.

He is a pioneer in global reporting languages and standards, having previously been a director and advisor to the International Financial Reporting Standards (IFRS) Foundation at the International Accounting Standards Board (IASB) in London for over ten years. His work on behalf of the IASB involved introducing XBRL and IFRS to more than 70 countries.

During his tenure with the IASB, he served as the Global Chairman of XBRL and was a member of the EU Commission High Level Expert Group and the Brookings Institution Task Force on Intangibles.

Prior to joining the IFRS Foundation and its predecessor, the International Accounting Standards Committee (IASC), Kurt was a Global Capital Markets Group Partner at PricewaterhouseCoopers in New York. He holds MBA, CPA and CEBS degrees, and is a board member of several international organisations. He is a member of the American Institute of Certified Public Accountants (AICPA), Financial Executives International and other professional associations.

An accomplished writer and public speaker, Kurt has authored numerous articles on international financial reporting, XBRL and capital markets, and chaired global business conferences and summits. He has also lectured at Columbia University, and was a professor at the College of Insurance in New York.

Kurt currently serves as Treasurer on the Council of the International Union for Conservation of Nature (IUCN), the world's largest association of conservation agencies, headquartered in Switzerland.

Outside of work, Kurt likes biking, skiing and engaging with friends around the globe. In 2009 he bicycled on a 4000km goodwill tour from Rome to Mecca.

He is fluent in German and English.

Email: *kurt.ramin@gmail.com*

LinkedIn: *http://ae.linkedin.com/pub/kurt-ramin/12/2b1/636*

Alan Rosenblatt, PhD

Since 1993, Alan Rosenblatt has been at the cutting edge of digital politics. A frequent speaker and author on digital and social media, advocacy and politics, Alan is currently the associate director for online advocacy at the Center for American Progress, where he directs its social media and advocacy programme, having also pioneered social advocacy strategy for issue campaigns. Prior to joining American Progress in 2007, he was a political science professor at George Mason University (1991–2000), and then an Internet advocacy consultant at Stateside Associates, e-Advocates, as well as at his own firm, the Internet Advocacy Center, where he founded the Internet Advocacy Roundtable in 2005.

In addition to his day job, Alan is an adjunct professor at Georgetown, Johns Hopkins and American Universities, where he teaches graduate courses on digital political strategy and Internet advocacy. In addition to blogging at BigThink.com, he writes about digital politics and other musings at DrDigipol.Tumblr.com. Alan also posts an occasional article to TechPresident.com, HuffingtonPost.com and KStreetCafe.com.

Email: *arosenblatt@americanprogressaction.org*
Website: *http://ProgressLeague.org*
Twitter: *@DrDigipol*, *@ProgressLeague* and *@CAPAction*

Marshall Sitten

Marshall Sitten has been a communications strategy professional since 1998. He advises a broad portfolio of private companies, United Nations agencies and public sector organisations. Most recently, he performed work for World Radio Switzerland and the International Organizations MBA at the University of Geneva, a unique programme that trains managers for careers in the United Nations, non-profit and socially responsible business sectors.

Before co-founding Flashing12 Communications in 2006, he worked as consultant and Chief Technologist at TSD Communications, where he worked with clients such as the Center for Democracy in the Americas and the Center for Budget and Policy Priorities on how to use technology effectively as part of an overall communications strategy.

Marshall received a BA in Psychology from the University of Maryland in 1997, and received his MBA from the University of Geneva in 2009. Currently, in addition to his work with Flashing12, he is performing doctoral research in the area of Service Science for the HEG Geneva Service Lab, by studying the use of ethnomethodology and theatre-based re-enactment for the design and improvement of public sector services. Presently, he lives in Brooklyn, New York, with his wife Irene and their two cats, Laszlo and Nikita.

Twitter: *@marshallsitten*
Email: *marshall@flashing12.net*
Website: *www.flashing12.net*

Marshall Sponder

Marshall Sponder is a web analytics and SEO/SEM specialist with expertise in market research, social media and networking. As both an in-house team leader and consultant, he has used sophisticated analysis to optimise the social media marketing efforts of companies and brands, including IBM, Monster, Porter Novelli, WCG, Gillette, Pfizer, Warner Brothers, Laughing Cow, the *New York Times* and Havana Central.

Marshall is also a board member emeritus at the Web Analytics Association, and emeritus member of the Certified Institute of Public Relations Social Media Measurement Study Group (CIPR). He is the author of *Social Media Analytics: Effective Tools for Building, Interpreting, and Using Metrics.*

Email: *now.seo@gmail.com*
Website: *webmetricsguru.com*
Twitter: *@webmetricsguru* and *@smanalyticsbook*
LinkedIn: *www.linkedin.com/in/marshallsponder*

Russell Yardley

After graduating from the University of Melbourne, Russell joined IBM in 1978 and left in 1985 to establish his own company that developed technology-delivered training and decision support systems. Since then, Russell has developed multimedia and was an early developer of websites and Internet applications.

Over the past 26 years, the companies that Russell has led were often at the leading edge of multimedia and Internet development, such as creating one of the first online collaborative learning projects in 1995, and the first government portals at *www.vic.gov.au* in 1996. He has won many awards, including 'best employer' in Australia, awarded by the Australian Graduate School of Management and Australian Financial Review in 2000, as well as several Australian Internet design awards.

In addition, Russell participated as a member of the Austrade 2001 Australian UK eGovernment Mission and was selected for one of ten positions on the Australian European Hi-tech Tour of 2002. He has also judged the Telstra Australian Business Awards and the Australian Information Industry Association (AIIA) iAwards, and is currently on the national board of the AIIA. Furthermore, he is an advisor to several innovative, fast-growing businesses and is a director on several boards in both the private and government sectors.

Russell is a graduate of the Australian Institute of Company Directors Company Director Course. He is a respected speaker and advisor to boards on the impact of technology, as well as the importance of developing the capability of boards to discuss technology and its impact on how we work, learn and live in this connected world.

Email: *yardley@algonquininvestments.com*
Twitter: *@rmyardley*
LinkedIn: *www.linkedin.com/in/russellyardley*

Gabriel Yoran

Gabriel Yoran is co-founder of consumer privacy software company Steganos (which he started at the age of 17) and also of the location-based social network, aka-aki.

He is an expert in product design and consumer marketing with more than 15 years of related professional experience. He is also a member of the European Union Social Networks Group. Gabriel is a mentor at the Founder Institute, a global network of start-ups and mentors that helps entrepreneurs launch meaningful and enduring technology companies, and gives lectures on entrepreneurship, marketing and product design.

Products designed by Gabriel have earned numerous awards, including two Webby Awards, a Lead Award, and numerous Best Buy and Product of the Year awards in magazines like *PC World*. In addition, Gabriel is a regular speaker at industry events, such as the European Union's Future Internet Assembly, Webinale, World Usability Day, Web 2.0 Expo and the Mobile 2.0 Summit. In his spare time he occasionally writes for the Grimme Award-winning blog Riesenmaschine.

Gabriel studied Communication in Social and Economic Contexts and holds a Master of Arts from the Berlin University of the Arts.

Email: *gabriel@yoran.com*
Website: *www.yoran.com*

Ambika Zutshi

Currently a senior lecturer at Deakin University, in Australia, Dr Ambika Zutshi's qualifications include a Bachelor's degree in Environmental Sciences, a Master's degree in Environmental Management and a PhD. Her current research is focused in the area of corporate social responsibility, business ethics, the role of stakeholders in the Environmental Management Systems (EMS) and supply chain management. She has had articles accepted for publication in several journals, such as

Technovation, *Journal for Cleaner Production*, *European Business Review*, *Business Process Management Journal*, *Managerial Auditing Journal*, *Management of Environmental Quality: An International Journal*, *Australian Accounting Review*, *Alternative Law Journal* and *International Journal of Environmental and Sustainable Development*.

Email: *ambika.zutshi@deakin.edu.au*

1

Social media growth and global change

Cornelis Reiman

Abstract: Through a remarkably rapid rise in the availability and pervasive use of social media, the once-familiar face of interpersonal communication, product promotion, information dissemination, political activism and governmental concern has changed significantly.

Boundaries have blurred between personal and professional lives, as well as between nations, through international networks that bring people together as never before. It is vital, therefore, that all who implement social media strategies for organisations, or use it for personal purposes, are aware of what the digital world offers in the community, the political sphere and the workplace. Also, it is noteworthy that laws and enforcement alter in all instances to accommodate changes that are brought about by a new communications paradigm that has global ramifications. Plus, social media users generate a vast amount of data that can be mined for the purposes of social analytics.

Key words: social media, social media history, social activism, social media in the workplace, social analytics, legal implications of social media.

Introduction

The Internet is an exceptional development that has transformed economic activity worldwide, more so in some countries than others (McKinsey, 2011). However, in addition to that marvel, there are a vast number of applications that have changed businesses, as well as the lives of ordinary people. I think particularly of social media, and doubt that a day goes by without a news report on how social media applications are used for the betterment, or the detriment, of society. We can only be amused, amazed or appalled at the ingenuity of people who utilise new technological applications for their own purposes, or that of collectives with which they are associated. The sheer size and reach of social media is also remarkable. Consider some recent examples, as are presented below.

According to statistics released by Twitter, users of that social media application send over 350 million tweets per day, being the equivalent of a 15 million-page book. (Tsukayama, 2011; Morrison Foerster, 2011). A subset of that is expressed in the traffic related to one topic. For instance, in a very short timeframe, Sina Weibo, which is China's Twitter-like micro-blogging service, attracted more than one million posts related to a Japanese mayor who denied that the Nanjing massacre happened (Armstrong, 2012). Clearly, social media numbers are immense. Remarkably, music consumer research indicates that celebrities who bombard fans with Twitter updates are likely to have shorter careers than those who maintain an aura of mystique. Apparently, easy access to stars through social networking websites has made them less appealing and increases the likelihood of followers getting bored (Reuters, 2011).

With increased social networking involving children, a recent innovation is of benefit to parents. With the help of new software, parents can monitor offspring on Facebook without being 'friends'. The programme scans Facebook profiles, communications and 'friend' requests, and uses algorithms to identify potential bullying, sexual overtures, or talk of drugs, violence or suicide. This alerts parents to signs of trouble in a child's Facebook account without them being privy to content shared between friends (AFP, 2011a).

Furthermore, widespread use of social media applications has introduced new complexities to the legal and ethical environment of higher education. For instance, traditionally, social communications were considered to be private. However, with much of this information now published online and accessible by the public, more insight is available as to students' attitudes, opinions and characters (Cain and Fink, 2010). Even so, at all levels of education, from primary school to universities, educators use social media to enhance classroom discussion. Students can comment, pose questions (that can be answered by anyone) and feel free to voice their opinions (Gabriel, 2011).

Wherever social media is used, it is worth highlighting the need for prudence, care and discipline, and checking settings when posting. For instance, a teenage girl in Germany forgot to mark her birthday invitation as private on Facebook. When posted, mistakenly, her invitation could be seen by everyone on Facebook. This went viral, and 15 000 people confirmed their attendance. When her parents found out, the party was cancelled, their home was cordoned off and a hundred police were present, with four of them on horses. Still, 1500 guests showed up. Some were detained, and a few were injured (Grieshaber, 2011).

This raises the issue of how social media is affecting society, or large parts of it, and leads to the view that we are entering into a new paradigm that is changing behaviour and society. Particularly, there are many young people who are defined as being a part of a cohort called 'Generation C' – connected, communicating, content-centric, computerised, community-oriented and always clicking. This significant group of people is expected to stimulate economic growth, and encourage public and private invest in faster and more widespread communications infrastructure (Friedrich et al., 2011). Such is also expressed by Chappuis et al. (2011) in relation to digital consumers falling into distinct groups characterised by the types of digital experiences they prefer. These include:

- digital-media junkies – the people most likely to be early adopters of new technologies – often younger men;
- digital communicators – those spending more time on social networks – often women; and
- video digerati – those more likely to consume Internet-based video.

Obviously, segmentation of users is beneficial for marketing purposes, as well as for social scientists.

Such segmentation is also undertaken elsewhere, such as the humanitarian space, as was done by Edward G. Happ, who is the CIO of the International Red Cross and Red Crescent Societies (IFRC) based in Geneva, Switzerland. Also, he is Chairman of NetHope (*www.nethope.org*), a US-based consortium of 33 leading international relief, development and conservation nonprofits focused on information and communications technology (ICT) and collaboration. He provides wise words by suggesting that:

- technology capacity building for the vulnerable needs to be clear about audience and intention, and beware of unintended consequences;
- the most important participants on the team are the beneficiaries, and the most relevant technologies are the ones that beneficiaries adopt; and
- the prophets and the priests of technology can learn from each other, assuming both distance and proximity (Happ, 2011).

As might be apparent, social media applications offer very positive benefits for people, and organisations of all types. These arise in daily life for many users, even if only keeping in contact with selected friends and family members. Even so, there are negative elements, too. Incessant twitters from people full of self-importance, and streams of trivia, clog social media channels. As stands to reason, you can tell a great deal about a person and their values by what they post. This could be interpreted as a positive outcome. However, when any of that online activity goes too far, it is good to know that laws, and lawyers more so, are very much up to date with what must be done in situations where there is an obvious objection, or actual offence.

To state the absolute obvious, social media is an incredible event, and a wonderful experience, and this has had an impact upon a large proportion of the global population. As is generally accepted, social media is a wonderful marketing resource for generating brand awareness and connecting with prospective consumers and/or supporters. Also, these applications provide individuals, collectives and companies with a solid yet flexible platform that facilitates the crafting of valuable connections and lasting relationships. It is all about community, a sense of community and a community spirit. The issue, then, is what binds people to become part of a collective, and what keeps them together, such as to advance a common ideal, or share in a broader experiences that, in itself, is the social media community.

Essentially, communities can form for any number of reasons. For instance, there is a Facebook page dedicated to people who are called Phil, or Phyllis, Campbell. These people even arranged a convention in a tiny place called Phil Campbell in Alabama (Severson, 2011). In effect, any community is Web 2.0-based and user-driven, with communication provided by users creating and sharing content (whether text, graphics, pictures, audio or video) through computers or mobile technology, such as smartphones.

Fundamentally, accelerating technology facilitates the social media phenomenon by way of making access to others entirely transportable. In addition, this means that users of such electronic devices are contactable – constantly at that – thereby providing additional impetus to interactivity through social media. Simply, people are brought together, even when physically disparate. Of course, usually, people keep their connections within a particular social network, as provided by any one of the hundreds of so-called vertical social networking sites that are based on common interests of participants, such as books, music, online games, ethnicity or geography.

No matter what the social media bond is, all boundaries blur in terms of what traditionally had stopped people from communicating effectively in times past. Consider, here, that distance is now irrelevant as people can connect with others located in the next street or across the globe.

Time is immaterial, in that messages are sent, accessed by others and responded to in an asynchronous manner, meaning that such interactions need not occur in rapid succession, as occurs in face-to-face conversation, or in other forms of real-time communication, such as telephony or instant messaging.

In addition, social media applications allow for complete freedom of expression as no one is present who can obstruct them. As such, the transfer of ideas and opinions is effortless. That in itself can be a form of catharsis, as it could lead people to say more than is prudent, which can become problematic if others take offence.

Clearly, we live in a connected world, although not all people have Internet access. Figure 1.1 puts this into perspective.

As is generally agreed, each of us is related to anyone in the world through the oft-mentioned six degrees of separation. But you do not need to connect with everyone, even if that was possible. For instance, you have your immediate contacts, such as family, friends, business acquaintances and others. Then there are less necessary contacts, followed by the rest that constitute the remainder of the world's vast population.

> The Internet is becoming the town square for the global village of tomorrow.
>
> Bill Gates, founder, Microsoft

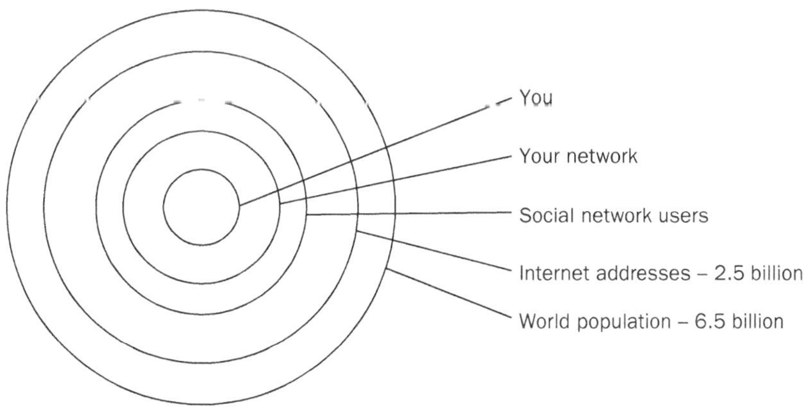

Figure 1.1 You and the rest of humanity

Source: Author's own composition

Some history

Before we continue on our journey together, we should have a look at what brought us here before we can explore more about the impact of social media on the lives of many worldwide. Table 1.1 provides some history as to how we have social media in such abundance today.

Table 1.1 The quick history of social media

Time	Event
1971	Email began – although in simple form through dial-up.
1978	Bulletin boards began with BBS (Bulletin Board Systems).
1978	Web browsers are born through Usenet.
1994	Geocities is founded, being a web-hosting service and, so, becoming one of the first social media applications. This business went public in 1998, was purchased by Yahoo! for $3.57 billion in 1999 when it was the third most popular website, and closed down in 2009.
1994	*theglobe.com*, another social media pioneer, allowed users to personalise their online experience, publish own content and connect with others who have similar interests. This business began with a record initial public offering of $850 million and, three years later, its market capitalisation had fallen to $4 million.
1997	AOL Instant Messenger was launched.
1997	*Sixgdegrees.com* was launched, and allows for profile creation and the listing of friends. The user base grew to 3 million in the first three months.
1999	Blogger – a blogging service – was launched, and was purchased by Google in 2003.
2002	Friendster was launched and pioneered the online connection. Membership peaked in 2008.
2003	MySpace was launched. It was bought by News Corp in 2005 for $580 million and was receiving more than 75 million visitors per month in 2008. It was sold in 2011 for $35 million.
2003	LinkedIn – a corporate social networking site – was launched.
2004	Facebook was launched, originally, as an application to connect students at Harvard University.
2006	Twitter – a text-based social media application – was launched.
2006	Yahoo! offered to buy Facebook for $1 billion. The offer was declined.

Table 1.1 The quick history of social media (*Cont'd*)

2008	Facebook overtook MySpace – on the basis of the number of unique visitors per month.
2009	Facebook hit 350 million members in December, and 400 million two months later in February 2010, and 500 million five months later.
2010	Facebook passed Google in terms of weekly web traffic.
2011	LinkedIn was launched as a public company with a valuation of $4.3 billion. That market value more than doubled in the first day of share trading.
2011	Twitter celebrated its five-year birthday – the social media giant was by now delivering 350 000 000 000 tweets per day.
2012	Facebook expects to launch with an IPO that is likely to be valued at $100 billion.

Source: Based on Morrison Foerster, 2011. Also, see Bennett, 2011 and Sundheim, 2011
Note: $ = USD

Certainly, history shows that there are successes and failures along the way. Still, what will remain, regardless of the names and owners of social media applications, is the vast number of users. Currently, as is reported generally, there are over 800 million Facebook users, more than 500 million Twitter users, over 135 million people in LinkedIn and so on. All of these numbers can only increase as the present Internet user base of 2.5 billion people continues to grow. Also, there is obvious, increasing interest in getting connected with friends, colleagues and anyone almost anyone else. As such, any Internet user has the avenue to connect with millions of people in over 200 countries. (For additional information, see *www.internetworldstats.com/stats.htm*.)

> We have technology, finally, that for the first time in human history allows people to really maintain rich connections with much larger numbers of people.
>
> Pierre Omidyar, founder, eBay

In fact, social media users, collectively, are larger in size than almost all countries, other than the People's Republic of China and India. This is a stunning and sobering reality as to the way of things in the digital age. Certainly, there are likely to be related consequences when many people can connect so very effectively, and share their various interests and ambitions.

Social media and social activism

Social media facilitates social change at a family level, as well as at a national level; this has been evident when protesters engage in rallying through electronic means. With the advent and rise of the Internet, for example, social activism is now more powerful, especially in terms of its potential and actual reach. As indicated, we are now able to connect with more people than was ever possible previously, and social media applications facilitate contact with people who have similar views regarding possible problems in society.

Also, via media reports, we have seen the sheer power of user-driven initiatives, such as people using Facebook and Twitter to raise money, assistance or other support for victims of natural disasters, and political unrest. Since early 2011, the same applications have played a prominent role in distributing public sentiment and galvanising demonstrations in Egypt, elsewhere in the Middle East and around the world. Governments fell or trembled, as much because of people power as because of the physical or economic oppression that prompted popular rebellion.

So it is that social media is linked to social upheaval. Occupy Wall Street led to Occupy Other Locations (Voigt, 2011). This movement provided the means by which concerned citizens, as well as radical elements, showed their dissatisfaction with the prevailing social, political and economic order. Yet, despite what often captures the attention of news reports, social activism need not be politically motivated. For instance, in China last year, a concerned citizen mobilised sufficient support to stop a truck from carrying hundreds of dogs that were destined for slaughter. In this case, the social medium used was Sina Weibo, being much like Twitter, and showed the emerging shift in attitudes with regard to addressing issues in a country that supports no animal rights, or protection, other than for wild animals (Xinhua, 2011).

Essentially, we see that social media is a powerful tool of protest and subversion that can connect and motivate people. Governments, especially in developing countries, are mindful of this particular issue, and this has led to reduced freedom of the press. Of course, the obvious response to electronic avenues of opposition is for governments to deny Internet access. In effect, we could say that social media applications – especially the ever-popular and effective Facebook, Twitter and YouTube – have become political tools with tremendous clout when wielded by the right number of users. It is no wonder, therefore, that less-than-open governments that are under pressure to change policies and relinquish powers are likely to react adversely to any protests.

If communications systems can be used to fuel and fan the flames of pro-democratic intentions, it is understandable that shutting down Internet access is an obvious remedy for nervous governments, as is curtailing phone usage for protesters. Egypt did this in early 2011 in response to an uprising of so-called people power. It is noteworthy that the impact of that five-day shut-down was a cost to the Egyptian economy of US$90 million (OECD, 2011).

Understandably, the Arab Spring, in the form of the continuing wave of civil uprisings in the Middle East region, continues to attract attention for any number of reasons, with social media influences being one. This is reflected in Figure 1.2.

As can be seen on the next page, Facebook surpasses Al Jazeera, the Arabic-language news network, as the most-quoted source at that time. Interestingly, there is an argument against the prevailing view that social media helped spur the protests in Egypt, as per research by a graduate student at Yale University. While Twitter posting, texting and Facebook wall-posting are great for organising and spreading a message of protest, it is suggested that social media can also spread a message of caution, delay and confusion (Cohen, 2011).

Social media reports, as in Figure 1.2, are now very much in the mainstream of media monitoring and media content analysis. Of course, such analysis is not limited to socio-political tension in the Middle East and North Africa. This is because protests, political agitation and government disquiet are common contributors to human history, and modern means now bring more of this to light, and faster too. For instance, activists in Belarus, in the former Soviet Union, claimed that an opposition group's page on a Russian social media site was blocked by the government to stop further protests and that other illegal actions were undertaken to prevent the protest actions called for on the Internet (BBC, 2011).

Of course, even to casual observers of current affairs, it will be of no surprise that social media has affected every political arena, positively and negatively. For example, over the past decade, politicians have used social media as a promotional tool. Assorted governments, even in tightly controlled Singapore, prepare for the general elections by making use of social media applications when reaching out to the electorate, as these can also serve as a platform to introduce new candidates (Mydans, 2011). It is worth noting, however, that new political candidates are not always primed as to the power of public scrutiny. So it is that personal details, such as photos, are circulated on the Internet, with this generating negative publicity.

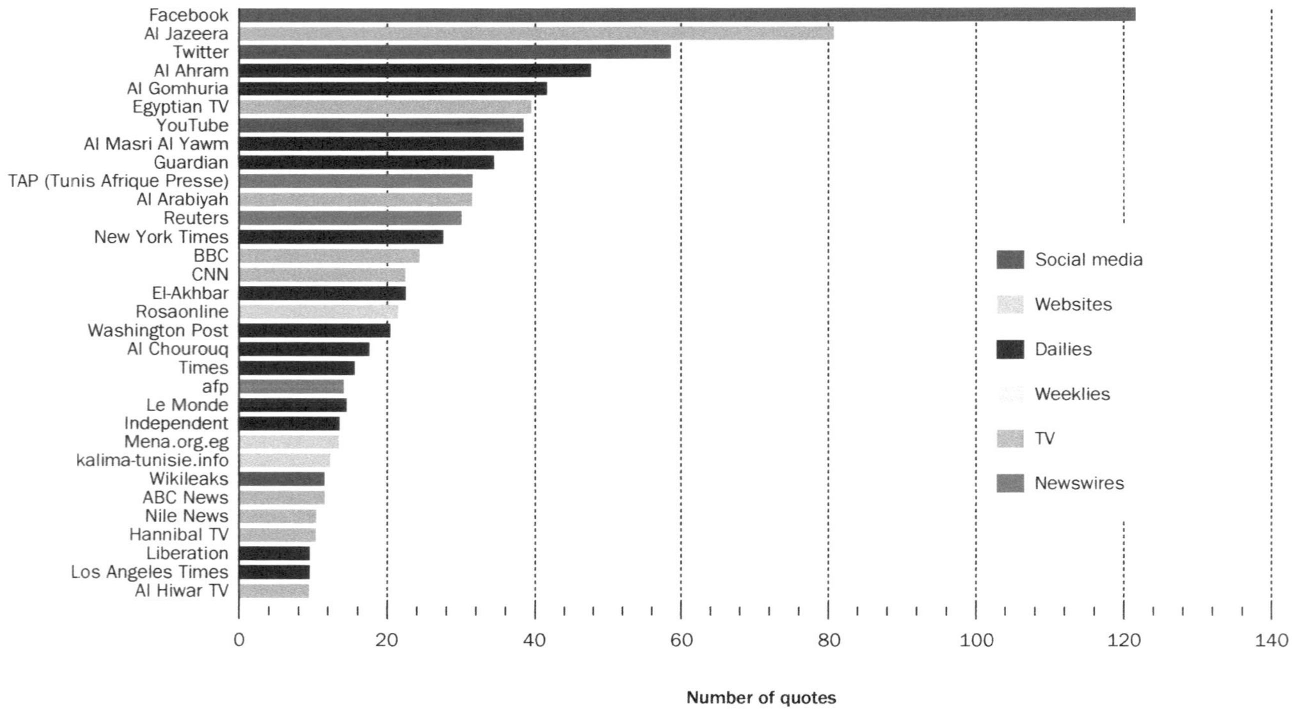

Figure 1.2 Indicators of change – Middle East and North Africa

Source: Media Tenor International, 2011

In relation to positive publicity, US President Barack Obama made history by taking questions posed to him on Twitter. In a virtual town hall meeting, with Twitter co-founder Jack Dorsey as moderator, Obama responded to live tweets as a new way of engaging directly with voters across the nation. Symbolically, 140 invited guests were in the room, with that number also being the maximum amount of characters that Twitter can handle per post (Norington, 2011).

Then, we find that technology and protests join together in political hacking, such as when an official Twitter account that was operated by Fox News posted malicious tweets claiming President Barack Obama had been assassinated (*The Australian*, 2011a). The issue of hacking is an unfortunate by-product of Internet success, and widespread social media usage. Following on from this, it is significant that the power of social media has attracted the attention of military agencies, especially in the wake of Arab uprisings that are generally accepted to be driven by Twitter and Facebook. Top military officers have expressed concerns about the apparent lightning pace of change in the Middle East, and social networks there are seen as an engine for protest against some long-time US allies.

This recent history has prompted the Pentagon, more specifically the Defence Advanced Research Projects Agency (DARPA), being the US military's high-tech research arm, to seek the help of scientists in determining how to detect and counter purposeful or deceptive messaging and misinformation on social media networks. The goal is to get ahead of the curve of events unfolding on new media and, thus far, DARPA has allocated US$39 million for the Social Media in Strategic Communication programme (*The Australian*, 2011b).

Social media at work

As is generally understood, social media can be used to promote a company, or other organisations, and its products or services. Additionally, social media can facilitate the way that an entity can interact with clients and the wider marketplace in which it operates. It is plausible that this can foster new views about product development and improvement.

Nevertheless, despite all of the possible benefits accruing to an Internet-connected entity, the popularity of social media applications, especially Facebook, has reached nigh on epidemic proportions, and that has bled into the workplace. Understandably, many employers are concerned about lost productivity, whereby social networking leads to social *not* working. In addition, there is the security of confidential information, as well as the security of systems, due to the possibility of viruses and malware. Plus there is the misuse of business assets for personal purposes, particularly related bandwidth depletion, and it seems to increase over time, especially when pictures are involved. So it is that social media usage at work can constrain business systems, and has a cost to the employer.

The usual Internet usage policies relate to non-work downloading, accessing unauthorised websites, as well as engaging in hacking and spam generation, or sending offensive emails and attachments. This can be extended to include social media access. For instance, a policy statement can be set to appear on a computer screen each time that a person signs on. Certainly, employees need to be made aware of any policy if it is to be adhered to, and if it is to be enforceable.

Complete blocking of access to various sites, if not the entire Internet, is a possible way to go, although this can be heavy-handed when employees, increasingly, require Internet access to do their work. The loss of productivity in such a situation is not limited solely to the likes of the aforementioned Egyptian government. Therefore, consider the need for more focus on what employees do with their time at work, as well as what they do with computing and telecommunications equipment that is available to them. Ideally, any policy that restricts Internet usage should be shared with employees, such as in the form of a signed declaration; it could also be appended to any employment contract.

> The more we use the internet, the more we use it for our direct personal or financial benefit.
>
> Christophe Jouan, CEO, Future Foundation

Monitoring and management, with regard to Internet access and usage, is advisable, as is enforcement if policy breaches are found. An alternative is to provide monitored access whereby connection with known sites (such as Facebook) leads to a report to management for possible follow-up with employees. Employment termination can be a consequence. Yet consider that social media access can be viewed realistically as a way to gain, and maintain, satisfied employees, thereby reducing the cost of hiring and training. This is also a way of retaining valuable corporate knowledge.

Whatever policies and restrictions are placed in relation to online social media access, it is quite obvious that phones and Twitter can be used if conventional IT avenues are closed. It can be concluded, therefore, that social media is an inevitable aspect of business life. (For more information on social media in the workplace, see Lurssen, 2010.)

Figure 1.3 provides thought-provoking detail as to the issues related to the use of social media applications in the workplace, with accessibility and control being paramount importance to any organisation.

While there is much to glean from this diagram, for the purposes of this chapter, it is evident that social media applications span much of the area, in terms of both scales that relate to accessibility and security, as well as structure. In the latter case, as can be seen, there is less emphasis on structure for social media applications and usage; this is understandable given that these, by their very nature, are user-driven and not a part of enterprise systems.

In seeking to increase engagement within the workplace, note that email is rapidly being replaced by social networks. Particularly, people are finding it easier to stay in touch using services such as Facebook, and this is now finding its way into the workplace. Similar to Facebook, an application called Chatter provides each user with a communications stream by which to see postings from other people within a work group (Grayson, 2011).

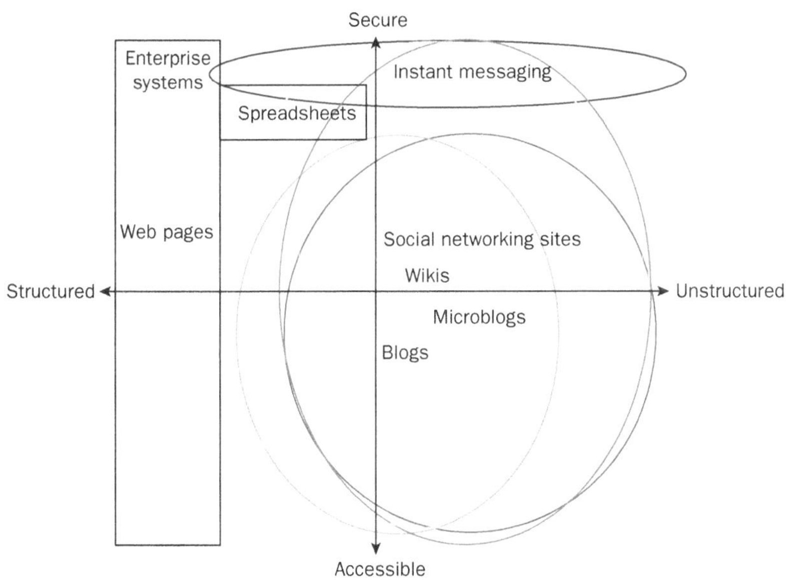

Figure 1.3 Web 2.0 tools in the workplace – accessibility, informality and control

Source: El-Sayed and Westrup, 2011

It is worth remembering that different benefits and issues arise when connecting with friends, colleagues and bosses. In the latter case, a boss could see more of a work-colleague's life than would happen otherwise. There is also the matter of how interrelationships should appear. Social media, in effect, adds insight that was not available before the advent of tech-connections. Private life and professional life can become one when all contacts are swept up in the same social media application. That is not healthy.

For some, such as teachers, schools are the workplace. There, faced with scandals and complaints involving teachers who misuse social media, schools are imposing strict guidelines that ban private conversations between teachers and their students on handheld phones and online platforms like Facebook and Twitter (Preston, 2011). Interestingly, if not understandably, given all that has happened with Internet access and social media in business circles, a recent development in the corporate sector is the rise of the Chief Digital Officer (RRA, 2011).

The matter of social media policies, as referred to earlier, is something that can plague executives, managers and employees alike. Of particular concern is 'getting the message across', which is necessary to reduce the chance of costly legal issues. As more companies and their workers tap into the world of blogs, Twitter and Facebook, employers are stumbling due to legal potholes related to social media (Borzo, 2011).

Social analytics

An accelerating development to come out of social media is that of social analytics, whereby services are provided by business enterprises that mine and assess social media data. Although these are mainly of interest to marketing professionals and brand managers, it is noteworthy that this niche service industry is based on ready access to the massive amount of data that is generated by users of social media applications, such as Twitter and Facebook. By evaluating social media streams, including the size of user networks, what is created and how other users respond to any such content, it can be determined who is influencing (or influenced by) particular topics, such as brands. For instance, see *klout.com*, *www.lithium.com*, *peoplebrowsr.com*, *www.radian6.com* and *www.sysomos.com*.

In addition to business-related analysis, social media usage is data-rich and can be mined for various other reasons. For example, Cornell University sociologists used language software to detect the presence of positive words in 509 million tweets from 2.4 million users in 84 different countries over a two-year period. This work has indicated, among other things, that people around the world are happiest in the morning. Positive peaks were also witnessed around midnight, and weekends, with assorted conclusions drawn as to work–life balance (Carey, 2011).

Of course, access to social media data and activity has number of consequences for users. For a start, there are legal implications, as the laws will vary from one jurisdiction to the next.

Legal implications of increasing social media usage

With the simplicity of Internet-based communication, and the means by which social media helps make that even easier, it is worth considering how little thought there might be in relation to creating content, and especially posting and sharing that content with others. This can have significant legal implications. For instance, consider people who cut and paste material without considering ownership issues, such as copyright. Then there is the additional problem of intellectual property rights, as must be considered in situations where there is a serious risk of violation. Trademark infringement is a similar issue. Or, all too frequently, there are people who fail to check whether something is factual before passing it on.

The personal character of a user also comes into play, such as whether they have standards that differ from others in the social media community, or people in the broader public who can access any content. For instance, someone might not think that another person will find their posting to be offensive, indecent or otherwise inappropriate. Worse still are people who use social media vehicles to harass others or spread maliciousness. This leads to two key points. One is the potential for defamation, or even action related to harassment or discrimination. The other is that social media applications invariably have a database that stores content and traffic, as can be accessed by aggrieved people in any related court case. Essentially, it pays to be prudent when engaged in social media activity, especially when a user is not familiar with everyone who has access to postings.

On that point, it is of particular interest that Europe is considering a new law that, if implemented, will force social media companies and others to obtain explicit consent from users about the use of their personal data. This will mean that, at the consumer's request, their data files are deleted forever. If this is not done, under the current proposal of the sweeping law, associated Internet-based companies will face fines for failing to comply once the law comes into effect, which could be in 2014 (Thierer, 2012; Ausloos, 2012).

Despite the European development, the issue of privacy is very much alive, in as much as whether any communiqué was meant for a select, vetted, known and fully understood group of users. Even so, others interested in possible problems, such as colleagues, fellow employees, employers and law enforcement professionals, could become involved in determining the validity of any posting. Again, prudence rules the day, especially when any right to privacy is eroded through the previously mentioned reality that content and messages are stored in social media systems, which can be accessed by other people who were not considered to be a part of the initial transmission.

Obviously, the critical issue is that of privacy, especially when personal details are accessible via social media applications. This raises the important question of what people are prepared to publish about themselves. Essentially, there is the risk that too much information, which can be confidential, is readily displayed in social media applications for others to see. This is not likely to be an issue if other users of the particular application, particularly those with direct access to personal details, are reliable and trustworthy – but that is not always the case. In addition, there is the added and obvious risk of hacking, as has happened on some social media sites, where details were stolen.

It seems that privacy is something that we cherish more so in the physical domain than in an electronic one where people readily give information about themselves, if only because they are prompted to do so through empty fields and related questions on social media web pages. Furthermore, there is the matter of magnification. For instance, a solitary tweet can have ramifications as it is read and resent, with this entertaining and informing a broader audience each time. The end result can affect the reputation of a person, company or brand in a very positive or negative way.

The new order driven by assorted forces of widespread social media usage has led to changes in relation to law and enforcement. Legal action is taken against respectable citizens for expressing their points of view online. Laws take people to task who use social media for malicious purposes. In each case, there is room for interpretation, resulting in new areas of law and precedents being set.

For instance, marketing, which is an avid user of social media, can have issues, such as protecting brands online. Traditional legal remedies, such as litigation, may not be the best way to protect your brand in the online stratosphere (see Lezaic, 2011). Although related not to a product but a person, implied meaning, such as of a tweet, can lead to legal action (Baird, 2011). More recently, in Australia, legal action against Twitter may result in a change of the defamation law in that country, which could have implications for social media sites too (Whiteman, 2012). On this theme, the government of Brazil is suing Twitter over posts that tip off drivers as to police roadblocks. The government contends users are 'directly endangering life, safety and property' (CNN, 2012b).

However, it is noteworthy that Twitter has said that it will delete users' tweets in countries that require it, doing so on a case-by-case basis. Note that users will be informed if their tweets are deleted, and that these tweets will still visible to the rest of the world. In effect, it is a form of censorship. However, examples of countries where tweets may have to be restricted include Germany and France, both of which ban pro-Nazi content. Twitter will operate in those countries but censor pro-Nazi tweets (CNN, 2012a).

With social media being communal, if not public, this has led to even stronger reactions to postings than those just mentioned. In the case of Mexico, for example, the drug war there has targeted, threatened and murdered, most viciously, people who post anything not liked by brutal criminals (AFP, 2011b). In that country, it is clear that technology plays a prominent role in describing and denouncing violence. For instance, Twitter users report gun battles and fiery road blockades. Also, a website lists victims' names and details of how they died, and a blog posts gory photos of gruesome killings and videos of drug lords' confessions (Shoichet, 2011).

On a lighter note, yet still one of concern, fraud experts call for Internet security to be taught in schools as children's identities are stolen via social networks. This is because children tend to post basic details about their lives on Facebook, such as their date of birth, school, name, email and photographs. In turn, this provides enough data for a criminal to apply for a credit card, loan or documents in the child's name. Essentially, children give too much of themselves away, and that will become a problem when the children reach 18 years of age and criminals fraudulently activate applications in the name of that person (Fraser and Tin, 2011).

While children do use social media willingly and readily, it can have an added downside from the goodness that is expected from the fostering of friendships. For instance, a teenage girl was too afraid to go to school after net bullies hijacked her identity, with this leading to an assault at a local shopping centre (Gilham, 2010). Elsewhere, a lawyer sued three girls who posted a mean-spirited video about his daughter on Facebook (NewsCore, 2011).

Social media users can also work together for good. For example, hundreds of witnesses to riots – triggered by an upset at a hockey final in Canada – responded to a police request. Social media users posted images of the violence online in a bid to identify those who were responsible. Along with law enforcement officials, Facebook groups urged people to identify the rioters (*Sunday Telegraph*, 2011).

Similarly, people have posted pictures online of people who have mugged them, ransacked their homes, or caused other injuries and crimes. This has led to the successful apprehension of perpetrators, as well as the return of lost property. For instance, a woman found her bike lock had been ripped out of a brick wall and her bike was missing. Quickly, she tweeted news of this loss and included a mobile phone photo of the thief that a neighbour had taken at the time of the crime. The bike rider was a social media manager, with more than 3000 followers and, less than five hours later, one of her followers spotted the thief and informed police, which led to her seeing the bike again (AP, 2011).

Given what is known of user demographics and habits, it is little wonder that social media is perceived as being an addictive technology, with Facebook having overtaken music as the number one way that young people define themselves. Remarkably, this has promoted politicians to insist that social networking sites enforce an age limit that denies access for children under the age of thirteen years (Brooks, 2010).

> You can have a Facebook page and invite a dialogue with users on an ongoing basis for years, if you so choose.
>
> Blake Chandlee, VP Europe, Facebook

In relation to emerging legal issues in social media, see Strutin (2011a, 2011b), Fraser (2009) and Ossian (2009). Also, if planning to go online, see Digital Business (2011).

Conclusion

Social media need not be confined to the use of prominent applications, such as Facebook and Twitter. Companies can create valuable connections with key stakeholders, including clients, customers, employees and suppliers, doing so in order to engage them in conversations that lead to business improvement.

With the rapid growth of technological advancement, as well as the related rise in creativity of application developers, we see the opportunity to expand personal networks beyond physical realms. The success of social media, as the name suggests, rests upon the prominence of user-led community-building. However, the rising trend is fed by socialising in some areas, as well as a more pointed purpose in others.

The pervasive tone is one of intent as to a person's actions, or the more strategic efforts of an organisation. How do social media users behave? How do organisations plan social media interactions in seeking a broader audience for their message, whether commercial or humanitarian?

There are additional questions to ponder. Does any social media application, or usage made thereof, fall within the rule of law? Alternatively, does any such activity sit within the bounds of social norms? In effect, the social media paradigm is a digital version of what transpires in the physical space. That is to say, people reach out, interact, communicate, promote, boast and preach. Yet we cannot forget that there is one distinct difference, which is that an audit trail remains, and can be agglomerated and stored for assorted purposes, whether this is for the benefit of marketers seeking emerging consumer preferences, or governments searching for untoward political activism and possible opposition.

What is obvious in all of this, and everything that we now see coming to us through social media, are the far-reaching implications of deep and widespread change in almost all aspects of our lives. As such, much depends upon what the vast community of social media users do when connecting with others, whether for pleasure or for business. An enticing question is the extent to which societal norms affect social media. Perhaps the opposite is true, in that the social media phenomenon will filter into society in ways that will have an impact upon standards of behaviour that we presently see as acceptable. This, of course, is for researchers to explore who, with the availability of existing data and related commentary, have a unique opportunity to assess how social media growth will lead to further global change.

References

AFP (2011a) Software helps parents track children on Facebook. [Online] 27 April. Available at *www.theaustralian.com.au/news/breaking-news/software-helps-parents-track-children-on-facebook/story-fn3dxity-1226045352917* (accessed 24 February 2012).

AFP (2011b) Drug violence critic beheaded. [Online] 10 November. Available at *www.theaustralian.com.au/news/breaking-news/drug-violence-critic-beheaded/story-fn3dxity-1226190793761* (accessed 10 November 2011).

AP (2011) Woman tracks down bike through Twitter. [Online] 26 May. Available at *www.theaustralian.com.au/news/breaking-news/woman-tracks-down-bike-through-twitter/story-fn3dxity-1226063096460* (accessed 26 May 2011).

Armstrong, P. (2012) Fury over Japanese politician's Nanjing Massacre denial. [Online] CNN, 23 February. Available at *http://edition.cnn.com/2012/02/23/world/asia/china-nanjing-row/index.html?hpt=hp_t3* (accessed 23 February 2012).

Ausloos, J. (2012) The 'Right to Be Forgotten' – Worth Remembering? *Computer Law & Security Review*. Available at *http://papers.ssrn.com/sol3/papers.cfm?abstract_id=1970392* (accessed 26 February 2012).

Baird, S. (2011) Associated Press Sued in Minnesota Over Krawczynski Twitter Tweet. [Online] 15 March. Available *at www.duetsblog.com/tags/social-media-legal-issues* (accessed 14 April 2011).

BBC (2011) Belarus: Lukashenko vows to quell 'revolution plot'. [Online] 3 July. Available at *www.bbc.co.uk/news/world-europe-14006365* (accessed 25 February 2012).

Bennett., S. (2011) A Short History Of Social Media (1978–2011). [Online] 17 August. Available at *www.mediabistro.com/alltwitter/history-social-media_b12770* (accessed 26 February 2012).

Borzo, J. (2011) Firings for Alleged Social-Media Infractions Sometimes Backfire on Companies. [Online] *Wall Street Journal*. Available at *http://online.wsj.com/article/SB10001424052748703954004576089850685724570.html* (accessed 25 February 2012).

Brooks, K. (2010) Policing the use of the internet by pre-teens is vital in today's virtual world. [Online] *The Courier Mail*, 13 October. Available at *www.couriermail.com.au/spike/columnists/policing-the-use-of-the-internet-by-pre-teens-is-vital-in-todays-virtual-world/story-e6frerfo-1225937758421* (accessed 3 October 2011).

Cain, J. and. Fink, J. (2010) 'Legal and Ethical Issues Regarding Social Media and Pharmacy Education. *American Journal of Pharmaceutical Education*, American Association of Colleges of Pharmacy, 74(10), 1–8.

Carey, B. (2011) Twitter Study Tracks When We Are. [Online] *New York Times*, 29 September. Available at *www.nytimes.com/2011/09/30/science/30twitter.html?_r=1&ref=global-home* (accessed 30 September 2011).

Chappuis, B., Gaffey, B. and Parvizi, P. (2011) Are your customers becoming digital junkies? [Online] *McKinsey Quarterly*, July. Available at *www.mckinseyquarterly.com/Business_Technology/BT_Strategy/Are_your_customers_becoming_digital_junkies_2839* (accessed 25 February 2012).

CNN (2012a) Twitter to delete posts if countries request it. [Online] 27 January. Available at *http://edition.cnn.com/2012/01/27/tech/twitter-deleting-posts/index.html* (accessed 24 February 2012).

CNN (2012b) Brazil sues Twitter over roadblock warning posts. [Online] 7 February. Available at *http://edition.cnn.com/2012/02/07/tech/brazil-twitter-suit/index.html?hpt=hp_t2* (accessed 8 February 2012).

Cohen, N. (2011) In Unsettled Times, Media Can Be a Call to Action, or a Distraction. [Online] 28 August. Available at *www.nytimes.com/2011/08/29/*

business/media/in-times-of-unrest-social-networks-can-be-a-distraction.html?_r=1&hpw=&pagewanted=all (accessed 29 August 2011).

Digital Business (2011) Planning to go online. [Online]. Available at *www.digitalbusiness.gov.au/planning-to-go-online/legal-issues* (accessed 14 April 2011).

El-Sayed and Westrup (2011) *Adopting Enterprise Web 2.0 collaborative technologies in business: The implications for management accountants.* Research executive summary series, Chartered Institute of Management Accountants, (7)1, 6, June.

Fraser, D. (2009) Legal Issues in Social Media With David Fraser. [Online]. Available at *www.slaw.ca/2009/01/26/legal-issues-in-social-media-with-david-fraser* (accessed 15 April 2011).

Fraser, K. and Tin, J. (2011) Fraud experts call for internet security to be taught in schools as children's identities are stolen via social networks. [Online] *The Sunday Mail (Qld), 2* October. Available at *www.couriermail.com.au/news/technology/kids-ids-stolen-from-social-networks/story-e6frep1o-1226155222825* (accessed 3 October 2011).

Friedrich, R., Peterson, M. and Koster, A. (2011) The Rise of Generation C – How to prepare for the Connected Generation's transformation of the consumer and business landscape. *strategy+business*, Spring, Issue 62, February.

Gabriel, T. (2011) Speaking Up in Class, Silently, via Social Media. [Online] 12 May. Available at *www.nytimes.com/2011/05/13/education/13social.html?_r=1&ref=global-home&pagewanted=all* (accessed 13 May 2011).

Gillham, A. (2010) Teenage girl scared to go out after internet bullies use her identity on Diva Chat. [Online] *Townsville Bulletin*, 4 August. Available at *www.couriermail.com.au/news/features/girl-scared-to-go-out-after-internet-bullies-use-her-identity-on-diva-chat/story-fn50ufcf-1225900878547* (accessed 3 October 2011).

Grayson, I. (2011) Social networking hits the office. [Online] *The Australian.* Available at *www.theaustralian.com.au/australian-it/cloud-computing/social-networking-hits-the-office/story-fn8lu7wm-1226048879132* (accessed 24 February 2012).

Grieshaber, K. (2011) Teen girl's Facebook party spins out of control. [Online] 6 June. Available at *www.theaustralian.com.au/news/breaking-news/teen-girls-facebook-party-spins-out-of-control/story-fn3dxity-1226069841511* (accessed 6 June 2011).

Happ, E. (2011) Stories from a cluttered desk. [Online] 2 April. Available at *http://eghapp.blogspot.com/2011/04/two-kinds-of-two-kinds-of-social-media.html* (accessed 24 February 2012).

Lezaic, M. (2011) Antisocial media? *Professional Marketing*, legal column, April–June, 35–6.

Lurssen, A. (2010) Social Media in the Workplace: Legal Issues, Business Policies. [Online] 4 November. Available at *http://scoop.jdsupra.com/2010/11/articles/media-coverage/social-media-in-the-workplace-legal-issues-business-policies* (accessed 26 February 2012).

McKinsey Global Institute (2011) Measuring the Net's growth dividend. *McKinsey Quarterly*, May.

Media Tenor International (2011) A New Era for Arab-Western Relations: Reducing the impact of stereotypes and recognizing indicators of change in order to prepare for the next step. Arab League Conference, Cairo, 6 April 2011.

Morrison Foerster (2011) A Short History of Social Media. [Online]. Available at *www.mofo.com/sociallyaware* (accessed 26 February 2012).

Mydans, S. (2011) In Singapore, Political Campaigning Goes Viral. *International Herald Tribune*, 5 May. Available at *www.nytimes.com/2011/05/06/world/asia/06iht-singapore06.html?hpw* (accessed 6 May 2011).

NewsCore (2011) Texas man sues girls for bullying his daughter on Facebook. [Online] 19 June. Available at *www.theaustralian.com.au/news/breaking-news/texas-man-sues-girls-for-bullying-his-daughter-on-facebook/story-fn3dxity-1226077835361* (accessed 19 June 2011).

Norington, B. (2011) Historic session as Obama tweets with voters. [Online] *The Australian*, 8 July. Available at *www.theaustralian.com.au/news/world/historic-session-as-obama-tweets-with-voters/story-e6frg6so-1226090128397* (accessed 8 July 2011).

Organisation for Economic Co-operation and Development (OECD) (2011) The economic impact of shutting down Internet and mobile phone services in Egypt. Available at *www.oecd.org/document/19/0,3746,en_2649_201185_47056659_1_1_1_1,00.html* (accessed 26 February 2012).

Ossian, K. (2009) *Legal Issues in Social Networking*. [Online] Institute of Continuing Legal Education. Available at *www.millercanfield.com/media/article/200120_LEGAL%20ISSUES%20IN%20SOCIAL%20NETWORKING.pdf* (accessed 26 February 2012).

Preston, J. (2011) Rules to Stop Pupil and Teacher From Getting Too Social Online. [Online] *New York Times*, 17 December. Available at *www.nytimes.com/2011/12/18/business/media/rules-to-limit-how-teachers-and-students-interact-online.html?_r=1&hpw* (accessed 18 December 2011).

Reuters (2011) Tweeting celebrities risk boring fans – survey. [Online] 14 May. Available at *http://au.news.yahoo.com/entertainment/a/-/entertainment/9431531/tweeting-celebrities-risk-boring-fans-survey* (accessed 14 May 2011).

Russell Reynolds Associates (RRA) (2012) The Rise of the Chief Digital Officer. [Online]. Available at *www.russellreynolds.com/content/leadership-and-talent-rise-of-chief-digital-officer-CDO* (accessed 25 February 2012).

Severson, K. (2011) In the Town of Phil Campbell, a Gathering of Phil Campbells. [Online] 17 June. Available at *www.nytimes.com/2011/06/18/us/18alabama.html?ref=global-home* (accessed 18 June 2011).

Shoichet, C. (2011) Latest battlefield in Mexico's drug war: Social media. [Online] *CNN*, 16 September. Available at *http://edition.cnn.com/2011/WORLD/americas/09/15/mexico.violence.internet/index.html?hpt=hp_t1* (accessed 16 September 2011).

Strutin, K. (2011a) Emerging Legal Issues in Social Media: Part I. [Online] 6 February. Available at *www.llrx.com/features/legalissuessocialmedia.htm* (accessed 26 February 2012).

Strutin, K. (2011b) Emerging Legal Issues in Social Media: Part II. [Online] 21 March. Available at *www.llrx.com/features/legalissuessocialmedia2.htm* (accessed 26 February 2012).

Sunday Telegraph (2011) Vancouver hockey rioters found on Facebook. [Online] *The Sunday Telegraph*, 19 June. Available at *www.theaustralian.com.au/news/breaking-news/vancouver-hockey-rioters-found-on-facebook/story-fn3dxity-1226077806139* (accessed 19 June 2011).

Sundheim, K. (2011) Where They Started, the Beginning of Facebook and Twitter: A Brief History of Social Media. [Online] 5 August. Available at *www.businessinsider.com/author/ken-sundheim* (accessed 24 February 2012).

The Australian (2011a) Fox twitter hacked with fake Obama assassination news. [Online] *The Australian*, 5 July. Available at *www.theaustralian.com.au/news/world/fox-twitter-hacked-with-fake-obama-assassination-news/story-e6frg6so-1226087614231* (accessed 5 July 2011).

The Australian (2011b) Social media is Pentagon's new battlefield. [Online] *The Australian*, 21 July. Available at *www.theaustralian.com.au/news/world/social-media-is-pentagons-new-battlefield/story-e6frg6so-1226098856796* (accessed 21 July 2011).

Thierer, A. (2012) Europe's 'Right to Be Forgotten': Privacy as Internet Censorship. The Technology Liberation Front, 23 January. Available at *http://techliberation.com/2012/01/23/europes-right-to-be-forgotten-privacy-as-internet-censorship* (accessed 26 February 2012).

Tsukayama, H. (2011) Twitter: Users send 200 million tweets per day. [Online]. Available at *www.washingtonpost.com/blogs/faster-forward/post/twitter-users-send-200-million-tweets-per-day/2011/07/01/AGEFBUtH_blog.html* (accessed 24 February 2012).

Voigt, K. (2011) Beyond Wall Street: 'Occupy' protests go global. [Online] *CNN*, October 7. Available at *http://edition.cnn.com/2011/10/07/business/wall-street-protest-global/index.html?hpt=hp_bn1* (accessed 8 October 2011).

Whiteman, H. (2012) Man takes on Twitter over 'hate blog'. [Online] *CNN*, 17 February. Available at *http://edition.cnn.com/2012/02/17/world/asia/australia-twitter-defamation/index.html?hpt=hp_t3* (accessed 17 February 2012).

Xinhua (2011) 1,000 dogs rescued on way to slaughter in southwest China, Want China Times, 17 October. Available at *www.wantchinatimes.com/news-subclass-cnt.aspx?id=20111017000070&cid=1103* (accessed 26 February 2012).

Websites

- *hi5.com*
- *twitter.com*
- *www.bebo.com*
- *www.facebook.com*
- *www.friendster.com*
- *www.internetworldstats.com/stats.htm*
- *www.linkedin.com*
- *www.mediatenor.com*
- *www.myspace.com*
- *www.zoominfo.com*

Flash rob or protest movement: the First Amendment and regulating online calls to action

Margot Kaminski

Abstract: The Internet, particularly social media, has been used for organising large groups of people in 'flash mobs' to accomplish everything from improvisational comedy to protest movements to theft. As states and local governments look to prevent harm from such activity, they run into First Amendment rights of expression and freedom of association. This paper explores existing US law on organising groups, and asks whether new concerns arise in the online context. It examines the tension between prosecution of conspiracy, a crime based on speech and protection of incitement of others to action. It concludes that states should link punishment to the imminence and likelihood of harm, not the medium used, and must carefully follow the First Amendment in determining whether speech is protected.

Key words: social media, flash mobs, rights of expression, freedom of association, criminal law, legal, case history, incitement, Brandenburg, new media, First Amendment protections.

Flash mobs

The past ten years have shown that the Internet is a highly useful tool for organising crowds. In the early 2000s, the phenomenon of the 'flash mob' emerged, when improvisational comedy groups started using public space for whimsical performative group gatherings.[1] The creation of flash mobs as they now exist, using social media to gather strangers for such an event, has often been credited to *Harper*'s senior editor Bill Wasik.[2]

The organiser of a flash mob would email, blog or use Twitter (a 'tweet') to send instructions to a specific group of people or the world at large, describing when and where to meet and what activity the group should do. A 'flash mob' has several features: the announcer usually does not know the full membership or size of the eventual crowd; the crowd is told the time, place and sometimes the purpose of the gathering; the crowd acts on the announcement with no apparent incentive, operating within parameters set by the announcer.[3]

At first, the flash mob served as comedic street performance, with groups meeting to shop en masse in a department store for a 'love rug', perch on a stone ledge in Central Park making bird noises, dance silently in public areas or freeze in place in crowded Grand Central Station.[4] Flash mobs have become so well recognised as performance art that mainstream advertisements now reference them.[5]

Unsurprisingly, groups started using flash mobs for political organisation.[6] These political protests are sometimes called 'smart mobs', a term coined by Howard Rheingold in 2002.[7] Howard Dean's presidential campaign proposed a flash mob in Seattle, and protesters staged a flash mob against Russian Prime Minister Vladimir Putin in St Petersburg.[8] In May 2006, a blogger used the software LiveJournal to propose a flash mob of ice cream eaters in Oktyabrskaya Square in Minsk, the capital of Belarus.[9] Police showed up and arrested ice cream eaters, and images of the arrests were circulated around the world.[10]

Flash mobs, more recently, were used by dissidents during the Arab Spring. In 2009, thousands of Iranians organised via Twitter to protest the elections. On 25 January 2010, more than 50 000 people gathered in Tahrir Square in Egypt, many informed through social media tools, such as Twitter or Facebook.[11]

Protest movements have taken place via flash mob in Europe and the United States, as well. In November 2011, members of the Occupy Rome movement expressed solidarity with Egyptians in Tahrir Square with a flash mob in front of the Egyptian Embassy in Rome, Italy.[12] Also, in August 2011, a flash mob gathered in Denver to dance to Lady Gaga's song *Born This Way* as a protest for marriage equality in the United States.[13]

As an organisational tool, the flash mob has notable benefits for would-be revolutionaries. The organiser is able to appeal to a wide audience, increasing the size of potential gatherings and protecting individual protestors with sheer numbers. The organiser usually does not know the scope of the audience, or their identities. So, if the organiser is detained, the gathering may still occur without them, and no membership list will be turned over to the authorities. Even so, authorities can often track where, and when, flash mobs will occur and arrest people. But sometimes, that's the point: the ice cream eaters of Belarus planned on circulating publicity about the inevitable arrests so as to show the overreach of the totalitarian state.[14]

The same tools that are useful for organising spontaneous performance art or starting a revolution are also useful for committing group crimes, and it can be hard for authorities to distinguish between the two. In cities across the United States, and during the UK riots in the summer of 2011,[15] social media has been used to organise flash mobs for more nefarious purposes.

'Flash robs', as they have been labelled, use flash mob tactics to overwhelm local police forces or shop owners by announcing the time and place of a potential robbery. In early 2010, flash mobs of young people turned violent in Philadelphia.[16] Other flash mobs resulting in arrests or injuries were reported the same year in Boston, South Orange, NJ, and Brooklyn.[17] In June 2011, 40 young men swarmed a Sears store in Philadelphia and stole thousands of dollars' worth of merchandise.[18] In July 2011, a flash mob robbed a Victoria's Secret store in Washington, DC.[19] Similar robberies or group violence have also occurred in Maryland,[20] Illinois,[21] Ohio,[22] Nevada,[23] Minnesota[24] and Canada.[25] Often the events are captured on surveillance video, and it sometimes appears that participants are posing for the camera.[26]

Frequently, coverage of these events assumes that they were started through social media. There has, however, been some pushback on this understanding. District of Columbia (DC) police have said that they have no evidence the group robberies in the DC area were organised through social media.[27] It also appears that some of the violence in Ohio was not started as a flash mob, though it may have been exacerbated by social media once the violence started.[28] Also, an investigation into one of the Maryland group robberies the media had termed a 'flash rob' found that the thieves had hatched their plan on a bus, not through social media.[29]

Whether or not this group violence is the result of social media, after a year of flash mob-associated violence, the term 'flash mob' itself has taken on a different connotation. 'Mob' is no longer a tongue-in-cheek term. It now means something closer to its original definition: 'a large or disorderly crowd; especially: one bent on riotous or destructive action'.[30]

Several governments have spoken of, or experimented with, shutting down, monitoring or regulating social media to prevent the harm that can result from flash mobs. In the UK, British Prime Minister David Cameron proposed limiting the use of social media.[31] Two men were jailed in north-west England for inciting disorder through social networking sites.[32] In San Francisco, police blocked cell phone service in the public transportation system, the BART, to prevent suspected protests.[33] In Philadelphia, the FBI has monitored social-networking sites for flash mob activity.[34] Philadelphia has also imposed 9 pm curfews on young people to prevent gatherings.[35]

In Cleveland, City Council members proposed an emergency ordinance, Section 605.091, 'prohibiting the improper use of social media to induce persons to commit a criminal offense'. The Cleveland Mayor vetoed the initial proposed ordinance and it did not become law.[36] In December 2011, however, Cleveland adopted a revised version of the ordinance that prohibited acts that incite riots, listing 'electronic media devices' as criminal tools.[37] The Mayor did not sign the revised ordinances, purportedly because they 'mirror state laws already in place'.[38] This new Section 605.011 bans inciting to riot, and adds computers and cellular telephones to a list of items that can be considered criminal tools when used illegally.[39]

If flash mobs and flash robs continue to occur, governments are likely to formalise their attempts to combat them. The question in the United States is: how much protection does the First Amendment afford?

The answer is complicated. From a US perspective, the organisation of flash mobs represents a classic First Amendment problem: speech entwined with action. More specifically, the problem is what to do about speech made by an individual that potentially inspires a large group to act. The Supreme Court struggled for much of the last century with how to address this dynamic, finally lighting upon the current doctrine of incitement in *Brandenburg v. Ohio* in 1969.[40]

The rise of flash mob activity in the past decade, however, will likely revive this debate in US courts, since new media appears (at first glance) to raise new problems. Attempts to penalise the organisation of flash mobs also reveal the underexplored tension between *Brandenburg*'s protection of speech to large groups, and criminal penalties for speech-based activity, such as conspiracy.

The history of incitement cases in the United States

The rise of flash mobs and flash robs has restarted discussion of the dichotomous nature of group organisation. On the one hand, flash mobs have the potential to be used for valuable political speech and political organisation, which many believe are at the core of the First Amendment.[41] On the other hand, flash robs can cause great damage, and governments are perhaps afraid of the power of uncontrolled group action.

The regulation of individual speech commanding group action has had a tortuous history in the United States. Over the twentieth century, the Supreme Court shifted from permitting the regulation of motivating speech as dangerous, to protecting it as fundamental to First Amendment values. This struggle reflects the paradox of verbal efficacy in this country: we value political speech highly, but the more effective that the speech is, the more dangerous it is and, thus, the more likely it is to be regulated.

The Supreme Court's approach to speech that advocates illegal action changed vastly over the course of the twentieth century, largely in response to the political backdrop of the times. The two central struggles have been over how to distinguish between abstract doctrine and incitement, and whether the advocated action must be imminent for the speech to be permissibly regulated.

The earliest cases involved the federal Espionage Act of 1917[42] and the Sedition Act of 1918,[43] and arose among widespread fear in the United States of the rise of Bolshevism in Russia. In 1919, the Supreme Court addressed advocacy of (or incitement to) illegal action for the first time in three cases: *Schenck v. United States*,[44] *Frohwerk v. United States*[45] and *Debs v. United States*.[46] In *Schenck*, a unanimous Court upheld the conviction of protestors who had distributed leaflets urging resistance to the draft, finding that the First Amendment does not protect words that are 'used in such circumstances and are of such a nature as to create a clear and present danger that they will bring about the substantive degree of evils the Congress has a right to prevent'.[47] The Court, famously, reasoned that the First Amendment 'would not protect a man in falsely shouting fire in a theater and causing a panic'.[48]

However, in *Frohwerk* and *Debs*, the Court looked not to 'clear and present danger', which requires a real immediate threat of danger, but to the speech's 'natural tendency and reasonably probable effects'.[49] This lower-threshold 'bad tendency' test eliminates consideration of how imminent the illegal action is, and can easily stretch to penalise advocacy of doctrine rather than action.

The Court again applied the bad tendency test to uphold convictions in *Abrams v. United States*[50] and in *Gitlow v. New York*.[51] In 1927, the Court in *Whitney v. California* used the bad tendency test to affirm the conviction of a member of the Communist Labor Party who had signed a resolution recognising the liberation of workers through organisation.[52]

Although the majority of the Court promulgated the bad tendency test through the 1920s, as early as 1919 a split began to form. Justice Holmes dissented in *Abrams* in 1919, insisting on a return to scrutinising a threat's immediacy under the clear and present danger test. Holmes wrote that speech should be protected unless it 'so imminently threaten[s] immediate interference with the lawful and pressing purpose of the law that an immediate check is required to save the country'.[53] Justice Holmes joined Justice Brandeis in a concurrence in 1927 in *Whitney*, concluding that speech advocating illegal action should not be regulated if it 'falls short of incitement and there is nothing to indicate that the advocacy would be immediately acted upon'.[54]

In the 1930s and 1940s, it appeared that the Court might shift to the clear and present danger test.[55] But, in 1951, the Court back-pedalled in *Dennis v. United States*.[56] The Court considered in *Dennis* 'whether the gravity of the "evil," discounted by its improbability, justifies such invasion of free speech as is necessary to avoid the danger'.[57]

The *Dennis* test does not mention imminence of the action, and the more 'evil' the speech is, the less the court needs to consider the probability of its actual occurrence. Justice Douglas dissented, emphasising the difference between abstract doctrine and incitement, and reiterating the importance of imminence.[58]

The Court took up the distinction between doctrine and incitement in *Yates v. United States*,[59] where it clarified that *Dennis* had not 'obliterated the traditional dividing line between advocacy of abstract doctrine and advocacy of action'.[60] However, the Court did not discuss whether imminence was required in *Yates* because it did not need to address the question.[61]

Several cases in the 1960s prefigured what is now the established doctrine on incitement.[62] Then, in 1969, the Court held in *Brandenburg v. Ohio* that government may not restrict advocacy of illegal action unless it 'is directed to inciting or producing imminent lawless action and is likely to incite or produce such action'.[63] *Brandenburg* is still the governing law.

Brandenburg addressed the conviction of a Ku Klux Klan leader under the Ohio Criminal Syndicalism statute, which made illegal 'advocat[ing] the duty, necessity, or propriety of crime, sabotage, violence, or unlawful methods of terrorism as a means of accomplishing industrial or political reform' and 'voluntarily assembl[ing] with any society, group, or assemblage of persons formed to teach or advocate the doctrines of criminal syndicalism'.[64]

The accused man had spoken at a rural Ohio Ku Klux Klan rally to 12 hooded figures, some of whom carried firearms. A Cincinnati television station covered the rally and broadcast portions of the speech that night. During the speech, the organiser stated that 'if our President, our Congress, our Supreme Court, continues to suppress the white, Caucasian race, it's possible that there might have to be some revengeance taken'.[65] He also announced a Fourth-of-July march on Congress.

The Court held that such speech was protected by the First Amendment, and explained that the statute 'purports to punish mere advocacy and to forbid, on pain of criminal punishment, assembly with others merely to advocate the described type of action'.[66]

At the core of *Brandenburg* is the recognition that the conversion of speech into action requires a meeting of minds between speaker and listener. To be held responsible for the actions of those listening, the speaker must, in fact, intend to cause the action: the speech must be 'directed' by the speaker to inciting action.[67] *Brandenburg* incorporates the listener's point of view too, by looking to whether the speech itself is likely to produce unlawful action. In other words, the listener must be able to clearly understand and follow through on the speaker's intent. Then, *Brandenburg* dictates that the state can regulate this meeting of minds only when the possible action is actually likely and imminent. In other words, there must be real danger, and physical closeness, between the speaker and the possibility of action. Even if a speaker intends to incite illegal action, and the listener understands the message, if the action is prevented because of circumstances, or is preventable because it is meant to take place at a more remote time, the state may not regulate the inciting speech.

At the Supreme Court level, it appears that the analysis of incitement ends with *Brandenburg*, and one case, *Hess v. Indiana*,[68] affirming it. In *Hess*, the appellant was convicted in Indiana under the State's disorderly conduct statute for shouting '[w]e'll take the fucking street later' or '[w]e'll take the fucking street again' at an antiwar demonstration.[69] The Court emphasised the importance of the recipient side of the *Brandenburg* evaluation, and held that since Hess's statement was not directed to any person, or group of persons, it could not be incitement and, therefore, was protected under the First Amendment.[70] The Court also emphasised imminence and likelihood, and the importance of the speaker's intent to incite.[71]

Thus, if flash mobs are to be regulated as incitement, the regulation must abide by the *Brandenburg* test. The speech being regulated must be intended to produce imminent illegal action; the speech must be likely to produce such action; the action must be imminent; and the action must be likely to occur. Any statute regulating flash-mob organising as incitement to illegal action would have to address the speaker's intent, how likely it is that an audience would understand the command, the imminence of the action and the likelihood of the occurrence of illegal activity.

This appears to be a high threshold to pass, as long as *Brandenburg* remains good law. But the inquiry does not end there. Some courts of appeals have exhibited discomfort with *Brandenburg*'s strictness, suggesting a tendency to limit its holding. This discomfort reflects an unresolved tension between the *Brandenburg* test and how speech is treated in criminal law, especially in aiding and abetting, solicitation and conspiracy.

How lower courts have dealt with *Brandenburg*

Since *Brandenburg*, multiple cases have come before lower courts addressing speech that could be analysed as incitement under *Brandenburg*. In a number of these cases, courts have avoided the *Brandenburg* standard.[72]

Some courts have sidestepped *Brandenburg*'s incitement test, instead placing the speech into other categories that have lower thresholds to regulation. The Ninth Circuit, for example, chose to analyse online speech as a 'true threat' instead of incitement. Sitting *en banc* in *Planned Parenthood v. American Coalition*,[73] the Ninth Circuit held that the public disclosure of the names and addresses of abortion providers on websites constituted true threats and, thus, were not protected speech. The Court distinguished *Brandenburg* by explaining that 'while advocating violence is protected, threatening a person with violence is not'.[74] Due to the fact that other abortion providers listed on posters had been killed after the posters had been released, putting a new individual's name on the 'wanted' posters constituted a true threat.[75]

As the Ninth Circuit chose to analyse these postings as true threats, rather than incitement, it did not have to address *Brandenburg*'s imminence or likelihood requirements. The dissent observed that the postings were merely intimidation, not true threats, because the speaker could not control the outcome of the threat.[76]

Other courts have avoided *Brandenburg* by finding an underlying crime, or analysing the speech as commercial speech, which has a lower threshold to regulation. For instance, the Third Circuit in *United States v. Bell*[77] held that it was permissible for the Court to bar a person from promoting and selling unlawful tax advice. The Third Circuit refused to analyse the unlawful tax advice as incitement to illegal activity, stating that the injunction 'should be grounded on aiding and abetting violations of the tax laws and on false commercial speech rather than on incitement of illegal activity'.[78] Similarly, the Eighth Circuit found in *United States v. Holecek* that the actual preparation of tax returns by the appellant took his speech, which had advocated violation of tax laws, outside of *Brandenburg*'s domain and into the actual commission of a crime.[79]

Courts of appeals have also recognised that, in spite of *Brandenburg*'s holding, speech can be prosecuted as aiding and abetting a crime, rather than inciting it. In *Rice v. Paladin*,[80] the Fourth Circuit held that the First Amendment did not bar a civil lawsuit against the publisher of a book of instructions on how to be a hit man. The publisher, Paladin, stipulated that it intended to attract and assist criminals, that the particular murderer followed instructions from the book, that it intended and had knowledge that the book would be used by criminals to plan and execute murder-for-hire, and that in publishing and selling the book it had assisted the particular murderer in these particular murders.[81] The Fourth Circuit recognised that speech that constitutes criminal aiding and abetting does not enjoy the protection of the First Amendment, and civil aiding and abetting is also not protected.[82] The Court reasoned with respect to *Brandenburg* that 'speech which, in its effect, is tantamount to legitimately proscribable nonexpressive conduct may itself be legitimately proscribed, punished, or regulated incidentally to the constitutional enforcement of generally applicable statutes'.[83] Thus, the 'provision of instructions that aid and abet another in the commission of a criminal offense is unprotected by the First Amendment'.[84] As such, the Fourth Circuit did not look to imminence, or to likelihood of action.

Conspiracy provides another loophole through which courts have escaped resorting to incitement analysis. Even though it is not in front of a court of appeals, *United States v. Stone*[85] is of interest because of its treatment of conspiracy. In *Stone*, the defendant was found to have conspired to use force, as distinct from having conspired to advocate the use of force. *Stone* distinguished between 'mere advocacy or conspiracy to advocate, which is subject to the *Brandenburg* test, and conspiracy to engage in otherwise unlawful, unprotected conduct, which is not subject to the *Brandenburg* test'.[86] Thus, the district court found that *Brandenburg* was not applicable. It concluded that because '[t]he gist of the crime of conspiracy is agreement to violate the law', it is 'both possible and permissible to charge that criminal statutes were violated entirely by means of speech'.[87] The court noted that '[n]umerous crimes under the federal criminal code are, or can be, committed by speech alone'.[88]

Stone builds on a line of cases in the Second Circuit concerning conspiracy and *Brandenburg*. The Second Circuit, in *Rahman*, explained that '[w]ords of this nature – ones that instruct, solicit, or persuade others to commit crimes of violence – violate the law and may be properly prosecuted'.[89] Furthermore, in *United States v. Rowlee*, the Second Circuit observed that conspiracy is not subject to a First Amendment defence, because the crime being punished is the act of conspiracy, which does not implicate speech.[90]

Conspiracy is a particularly fascinating paradox because it is a crime that intimately involves speech as part of the crime: you must show agreement. Speech is not merely evidence of the crime; it is part of the crime itself.

Criminal law: crimes and speech

These cases bring us to the post-*Brandenburg* paradox: while government regulation of incitement to lawless action must meet the *Brandenburg* standard, criminal law still penalises all sorts of speech that closely resemble incitement. Despite *Brandenburg*, then, states may be able to prosecute the organisers of flash mobs for aiding and abetting, or conspiring to violate the law, or soliciting illegal activity.

It is worth clarifying that, in the United States, state and local governments can regulate the presence of physical crowds[91] and any crimes committed within them. Crimes committed during a flash mob can be prosecuted against the individuals who commit them, and those who aid and abet those crimes. But, regulating the speech that causes the crowds to occur in the first place is a different matter, and conspiracy appears to reach substantially into *Brandenburg*'s territory and conflict with its holding.

Some crimes intimately involve speech. As discussed above, speech that instructs on how to commit a crime may be punishable as aiding and abetting.[92] Additionally, the crimes of solicitation and conspiracy involve speech. For instance, a person is guilty of solicitation under the Model Penal Code's definition if that person, with the purpose of promoting or facilitating the commission of a substantive offence, 'commands, encourages or requests another person to engage in conduct that would constitute the crime'.[93] Likewise, under the Model Penal Code, a person is guilty of conspiracy if they agree to commit an offence, attempt to commit an offence, solicit another to commit an offence, or aid another person in the planning or commission of the offence.[94] Thus, speech that constitutes an agreement to violate the law may be punishable as conspiracy, and speech that invites participation in an illegal activity may be punishable as solicitation.

Under *Brandenburg*, governments should not be able to specifically penalise the use of social media to incite illegal activity unless that activity is both imminent and likely. Despite *Brandenburg*, however, prosecutors may be able to prosecute the organisers of flash mobs for aiding and abetting a crime, conspiring to commit a crime or soliciting a crime. When a flash mob organiser gives clear directions of the time and place of a robbery, they might be seen to be aiding and abetting, or soliciting, that robbery. More disturbingly, when a flash mob organiser asks a group merely to gather, with no mention of any contemplated crime, prosecutors may still attempt to bring conspiracy charges against the organiser, and that is quite problematic.

This apparent paradox rests on two foundations: firstly, there is no First Amendment problem with the 'evidentiary use of speech to establish elements of crime or prove intent';[95] secondly, speech is an integral part of the core act, or *actus reus*, of crimes such as conspiracy and solicitation.

The Supreme Court has acknowledged both of these concepts several times since *Brandenburg*. In 1993, in *Wisconsin v. Mitchell*, the Court held that a racial bias may be taken into account during sentence enhancement, even though that bias is provable only through speech.[96] The Court observed that the First Amendment 'does not prohibit the evidentiary use of speech to establish the elements of a crime or to prove motive or intent'.[97] In 1982, in *Brown v. Hartledge*,[98] the Supreme Court recognised that the state may ban 'agreements to engage in illegal conduct', and the 'fact that such an agreement necessarily takes the form of words does not confer upon it, or upon the underlying conduct, the constitutional immunities that the First Amendment extends to speech'.[99] Similarly, 'solicitation to enter into an agreement... remains in essence an invitation to engage in an illegal exchange... and may properly be prohibited.'[100] The Court cited to a number of its previous decisions about commercial speech, where it had explained that the government may ban commercial speech related to illegal activity.[101]

The Court went on, in later cases, to make it clear that speech related to illegal activity may be regulated more generally. In *New York v. Ferber*, concerning child pornography, the Court observed that freedom of expression does not extend 'its immunity to speech or writing used as an integral part of conduct in violation of a valid criminal statute'.[102]

The Supreme Court's acknowledgement that some speech is coextensive with crime need not lead to a direct conflict with *Brandenburg*. Aiding and abetting through speech, while not yet addressed by the Supreme Court, appears to be restricted to giving highly specific instructions about how to commit a crime.[103] Solicitation of a crime also appears to require a high degree of specificity, as it is based on a deliberate request that a specific crime be committed.

Conspiracy, however, may be perilously broad.[104] Unlike *Brandenburg*'s queries about both the speaker's intent and the audience's understanding, and imminence and likelihood that the event will occur, the Model Penal Code version of conspiracy requires only that the person being prosecuted must have agreed to commit the crime, with no showing that anybody else has agreed to commit the crime with them, and no showing that the crime was likely to occur.[105] This unilateral approach is followed by many states.[106] The Model Penal Code also makes proof of an overt act unnecessary where the offence is sufficiently grave.[107] A person tweeting 'let's meet in Tahrir square to cause trouble for the cops' might be prosecuted for conspiracy to riot in states that follow the Model Penal Code, even if no other person has agreed to commit a crime, and the crowd never formed – and was never likely to form. All that would need to be shown was that the flash mob organiser agreed to riot.[108] It is worth noting, however, that many states now require an overt act in furtherance of the conspiracy, and some require a substantial step in furtherance of the conspiracy.[109]

Common law conspiracy, or the default conspiracy when a state does not have a conspiracy statute, requires proof of bilateral agreement:

agreement between two parties.[110] At first glance, this appears to be more favourable for the defendant, because a prosecutor must show that at least one other person agreed to commit the crime. A conspiracy at common law, however, need not be based on an express agreement, and a conspirator may be guilty even if they do not agree to every part of the substantive offence.[111] If a person tweets 'let's meet in Tahrir square to cause trouble for the cops', and somebody in fact shows up, that might be evidence of a conspiracy because showing up expresses agreement. Common law conspiracy may involve conspiracy to commit an act that is not itself illegal.[112] Common law conspiracy also requires only an agreement, with no overt act in furtherance of it.

As with the Supreme Court's earlier struggle with incitement, some of the expansiveness of the crime of conspiracy comes from fear of the nature of group activity. An early Kentucky case recognised that some actions that would not otherwise be criminal may be aggravated by the nature of group action. When done by individuals, these acts 'had only the essence of crime, but by means of the conspiracy, an unfair and mischievous advantage of the aggressors is recognised'.[113] The Kentucky court cited, as an example, the 'conspiracy to use violence, as a riot, which derives its indictability from the plurality of persons concerned'.[114] Government fear of group action, then, may have been muted by *Brandenburg*, but may continue to persist in the breadth of possible conspiracy charges.

Difficulties for *Brandenburg* posed by new media

Because flash mobs may appear highly threatening, there is a danger that courts will, increasingly, sidestep *Brandenburg* and analyse flash mob organisation as conspiracy. In part, this is because the new technology of social media, at first glance, appears to confront courts with new problems. With social media, people can contact larger groups than ever before, and do so instantaneously. Conversely, flash mobs may appear to be outside of *Brandenburg*'s scope because they can be organised far in advance. *Brandenburg* essentially limits regulation of incitement to control of the mob leader who is physically present and wielding the axe.

None of these features, however, should change the analysis under *Brandenburg*. Imminence can still be a requirement for regulation of incitement: if a flash mob is organised a week in advance, that would give police time to prepare for it, just as organising a riot through pamphlets in the past gave police adequate time to prepare. *Brandenburg*'s imminence requirement, thus, is still reasonable; it allows regulation of speech only when there is danger that illegal action is so imminent that law enforcement cannot otherwise counter the threat.

Likelihood of action should also remain part of the equation. Many calls for flash mobs are not likely to be followed, but if the organiser appeals to a group known to commit crimes via flash mob in the past, then the speech may exhibit a greater likelihood of incitement to illegal activity.

Another feature of the new media that counsels for preserving *Brandenburg* is that online communication is not ephemeral. The state can go back through records of communication and see how the organisation occurred.[115] It is easier to trace who in fact is aiding crimes, so the state should not overreach to get those who merely organise crowds.

In many ways, courts will be encountering the same problem with flash mobs as they once did with union organisers: the tension between conspiracy and incitement. The new media may have changed many things, but they likely have not changed the analysis under *Brandenburg*.

Other possible First Amendment protections

Despite the fuzziness of the interaction between *Brandenburg* and criminal law, courts should be reluctant to enforce regulation of flash mob activity. Flash mobs implicate not just the speaker's individual right to free speech, but also the association rights of both the speaker and the eventual gatherers. Freedom of association protects the 'right to associate for the purpose of engaging in those activities protected by the First Amendment – speech, assembly, petition for the redress of grievances, and the exercise of religion'.[116] The Supreme Court has recognised that the individual right to a protected activity creates a 'correlative freedom to engage in group efforts towards those ends'.[117]

It is noteworthy that freedom of association has been used to shield members of a group from prosecution for activities done by other members. The Court recognised in *NAACP v. Claiborne* that states cannot impose liability on non-violent protesters merely because of their association with those engaged in violence.[118] 'For liability to be imposed by reason of association alone, it is necessary to establish that the group itself possessed unlawful goals, and the individual held a specific intent to further those illegal aims.'[119]

In this regard, flash mobs should be governed by *NAACP v. Claiborne*. If this proves to be the case, individuals who do not actually commit the crimes should not be held liable for them unless the group itself can be shown to possess unlawful goals, and the individual can be shown to wish to further those aims. This standard would apply to the organiser of the mob as much as the individual appearing in response to the organisational call. Essentially, the organiser should not be held liable for crimes committed during the flash mob unless the group itself possessed unlawful goals, and the organiser, as an individual, intended to further those aims. More work is necessary to determine how this standard interacts with current state anti-riot laws.

Conclusion

The 'right of peaceable assembly is... equally fundamental' as the right of freedom of speech.[120] The potential of inspirational speech to be beneficial or harmful is far from a new dilemma in the United States. As governments contemplate how to handle the phenomenon of flash mobs, courts should keep in mind the fundamental expressive value of group organisation recognised by the Supreme Court.

Mobs, after all, are not just disorderly crowds. The word 'mob' can also refer to 'the lower classes of a community'.[121] Controlling crowd behaviour, on the one hand, may protect the body politic from violence produced by mob mentality; but, on the other hand, it may control which socioeconomic classes are permitted to participate in speaking and organising. That result is fundamentally anti-democratic in nature.

Thus far, flash mobs have not been handled with these principles in mind. One flash mob organiser pleaded guilty to misdemeanour shoplifting and conspiracy charges.[122] A Maryland Delegate plans to introduce a bill charging each member of a flash rob with stealing the total value of all merchandise stolen by the group.[123] Rather than analysing flash mob organisation as conspiracy, or holding individuals accountable for group action, courts should apply both *Brandenburg* and *Claiborne*, and look to:

30. Merriam-Webster.
31. *http://blogs.ft.com/fttechhub/2011/08/cameron-threatens-to-block-rioters-from-social-media*
32. *http://edition.cnn.com/2011/CRIME/08/16/maryland.flash.mob*
33. *http://techcrunch.com/2011/08/15/bart-shuts-down-cell-service-to-thwart-rumored-protests-gets-actual-protests*
34. *www.nytimes.com/2010/03/25/us/25mobs.html*
35. *http://edition.cnn.com/2011/CRIME/08/16/maryland.flash.mob*
36. *http://blog.cleveland.com/metro/2011/12/flash_mob_ordinances_become_la.html*
37. *Ibid.*
38. *Ibid.*
39. *http://blog.cleveland.com/metro/2011/12/cleveland_again_targets_social.html*
40. 395 US 444, 447 (1969).
41. *See Mills v. Alabama*, 384 US 214, 218–219 (1966) ('Whatever differences may exist about interpretations of the First Amendment, there is practically universal agreement that a major purpose of that Amendment was to protect the free discussion of governmental affairs. This of course includes discussions of candidates, structures and forms of government, the manner in which government is operated or should be operated, and all such matters relating to political processes.'); *see also Monitor Patriot Co. v. Roy*, 401 US 265, 271–272 (1971) ('[T]he First Amendment was "fashioned to assure the unfettered interchange of ideas for the bringing about of political and social changes desired by the people" ') (citation omitted).
42. Pub. L. No. 65-24, 40 Stat. 217 (1917).
43. Pub. L. No. 65-150, 40 Stat. 553 (1918).
44. 249 US 47 (1919).
45. 249 US 204 (1919).
46. 249 US 211 (1919).
47. *Schenck v. United States*, 249 US 47, 52 (1919).
48. *Ibid.*
49. *Debs v. United States*, 249 US 211, 216 (1919).
50. 250 US 616 (1919).
51. 268 US 652 (1925).
52. 274 US 357 (1927).
53. 250 US 616 at 630 (Holmes, J., dissenting).
54. *Whitney v. California*, 274 US 357, 376-77 (Brandeis and Holmes, JJ., concurring).
55. *DeJonge v. Oregon*, 299 US 353 (1937) and *Herndon v. Lowrey*, 301 US 242 (1937); *Bridges v. California*, 314 US 252 (1941).
56. 341 US 494 (1951) (plurality opinion).
57. *Ibid.* at 510.
58. *Ibid.* at 581–91.
59. 354 US 298 (1957).
60. *Ibid.* at 315.
61. *Ibid.* at 324–5.

62. *Noto v. United States*, 367 US 290 (1961); *Bond v. Floyd*, 385 US 110 (1966); *Watts v. United States*, 394 US 705 (1969) (per curiam).
63. 395 US 444, 447 (1969) (per curiam).
64. Ohio Rev. Code Ann. § 2923.13 (1919).
65. *Brandenburg*, 395 US at 446.
66. *Ibid.* at 449.
67. *Hess* at 329; the speaker's 'words were intended to produce, and likely to produce, the outcome.
68. 414 US 105 (1973) (per curiam).
69. *Ibid.* at 107.
70. *Ibid.* at 108–9.
71. *Ibid.*
72. At the same time that courts of appeals have struggled with aiding and abetting and inchoate crimes such as conspiracy, the portrayal of violence by the media is clearly protected. In *Video Software Dealers Ass'n v. Schwarzenegger*, 556 F.3d 950, 961 n.15 (9th Cir. 2009), *aff'd Brown v. Entm't Merchs. Ass'n*, 131 S. Ct. 2729 (2011), the Ninth Circuit explained that *Brandenburg* probably precluded the regulation of violent video games as incitement. The Ninth Circuit noted that multiple district courts had rejected the incitement-to-violence rationale for video game regulation. The Supreme Court affirmed the Ninth Circuit's decision, in *Brown v. Entertainment Merchants Association*, 131 S. Ct. 2729, 2733-34 (2011). The Supreme Court noted that violent-speech regulation does not follow obscenity regulation, and states may not 'shoehorn' regulation of portrayals of violence into regulation of obscenity. *Ibid.* at 2734.
73. 290 F.3d 1058 (9th Cir. 2002) (en banc).
74. *Ibid.* at 1072.
75. *Ibid.* at 1086.
76. *Ibid.* at 1089 (Kozinski, J., dissenting).
77. *U.S. v. Bell*, 414 F.3d 474 (3d Cir. 2005).
78. *Ibid.* at 481.
79. *U.S. v. Holecek*, 739 F.2d 331, 335 (8th Cir. 1984).
80. 128 F.3d 233 (4th Cir. 1997).
81. *Ibid.* at 241.
82. *Ibid.* at 241–2.
83. *Ibid.* at 243.
84. *Ibid.* at 245.
85. *U.S. v. Stone*, 2011 WL 795104, at *7+ (E.D. Mich., 12 January 2011).
86. *Ibid.* at *8.
87. *Ibid.* at *9 (quoting *United States v. Rahman*, No. S393 Cr. 181, 1994 WL 388927, at *1–*2 (SDNY 22 July 1994)).
88. *Ibid.* at *8.
89. *U.S. v. Rahman*, 189 F.3d 88, 117–118 (2nd Cir. 1999).
90. *U.S. v. Rowlee*, 899 F.2d 1275 (2nd Cir. 1990).
91. See, e.g., *Snyder v. Phelps*, 131 S. Ct. 1207, 1218 (2011) (noting that a group's 'choice of where and when to conduct its picketing is not beyond the Government's regulatory reach – it is "subject to reasonable time,

place, or manner restrictions" that are consistent with the standards announced in this Court's precedents').

92. See, e.g., *Rice v. Paladin*, 128 F.3d 233 (4th Cir. 1997).
93. Model Penal Code § 5.02(1).
94. Model Penal Code § 5.03(1).
95. *Wisconsin v. Mitchell*, 508 US 476, 489 (1993).
96. 508 US 476, 489–90 (1993).
97. *Ibid.*
98. 456 US 45, 55 (1982).
99. *Ibid.*
100. *Ibid.*
101. *Hoffman Estates v. Flipside*, 455 US 489, 496 (1982); *Central Hudson Gas & Elec. Corp. v. Pub. Serv. Comm'n*, 447 US 557, 563–64 (1980); *Pittsburgh Press Co. v. Pittsburgh Comm'n on Human Relations*, 413 US 376, 388 (1973).
102. *New York v. Ferber*, 458 US 747, 761–62 (1982)(citation omitted).
103. *Rice v. Paladin.*
104. Peter Buscemi, *Conspiracy: Statutory Reform Since the Model Penal Code*, 75 Colum. L. Rev. 1122 (1975) ('Conspiracy, even in its modern formulations, advances the moment of criminal guilt and permissible official intervention to a point considerably earlier than that allowed by the law of attempt.').
105. *Ibid.* at 1135–6.
106. *Ibid.*
107. MPC § 5.03 (5).
108. Definitions of 'riot' vary greatly from state to state, with differences in the number of people and amount of force or violence required. This example operates on the type of riot statute that refers to obstruction of justice as part of a group, such as Ohio's anti-riot statute.
109. Buscemi, *supra* n. 104 at 1156.
110. *Ibid.* at n. 67.
111. *Salinas v. United States*, 522 US 52, 63 (1997).
112. Peter Buscemi, *Conspiracy: Statutory Reform Since the Model Penal Code*, 75 Colum. L. Rev. 1122, 1129 (1975).
113. *Commonwealth v. Donoghue*, 63 S.W.2d 3, 5 (Ky. 1933).
114. *Ibid.*
115. *See* Wasik, *supra* n. 2 at 77 (noting that police use the digital trail left behind by social media to map the source of a flash mob).
116. *Robert v. U.S. Jaycees*, 468 US 609, 618 (1984).
117. *NAACP v. Alabama*, 357 US 449, 461–3 (1958).
118. 458 US at 924–6.
119. *Ibid.* at 920.
120. *Brandenburg*, n. 4.
121. *Ibid.*
122. *http://online.wsj.com/article/SB10001424052970203752604576643422390552158.html*
123. *www.dispatch.com/content/stories/national_world/2011/12/19/flash-rob-thieves-like-locusts-clean-out-store.html*

3

World justice – the rule of law around the world

Kurt Ramin and Antje Meyer

Abstract: Critical issues associated with legal structures and processes determine the extent to which countries have the capacity to deal with topics that affect the expectations of governments and societies. So it is that rule of law can be seen as an impediment to the dissemination of information, as can be facilitated by social media applications. In this regard, of particular interest is the Rule of Law Index that was developed and administered by the World Justice Project. This index offers the means by which strong comparison can be made between countries in terms of similarities and differences as to the rule of law. Specific examples in comparative analysis undertaken show the basis for varying treatment of liberties, as seen in containment of Internet usage, specifically due to the effectiveness of social media in rallying people to support particular causes. The more that such causes are in contrast to government interests, the more likely is it that the rule of law will be applied to thwart possible or actual opposition. Some countries, clearly, have more legal capacity to do so than do others. Accordingly, the Rule of Law Index helps to explain why that is so. It is an emerging question, then, as to whether social media provides a chance for development, or a serious challenge to some countries.

Key words: social media, legal implications, rule of law, Rule of Law Index, World Justice Project, Germany, China, United Arab Emirates.

Legal implications of social media

One of the most interesting aspects of the Internet age is the legal implications of social media. As is generally understood, laws were developed and influenced by culture, religion and the natural obsession of humans to attain power to control, as well as to gain insight in relation to other people. Similarly, the digital age has also influenced laws. Privacy of employees versus the rights of employers, utilising and protecting intellectual property, such as music, copyrights and trademarks, in addition to the movement of data, are just some of the broader issues we are facing in modern society. In addition, and conversely, the development of social media is influenced by the law.

In this chapter we will explore how the law, which in stark contrast to the Internet is still pretty much controlled within borders, adjusted to the Internet age. Clearly, any areas of professional, social and industrial activity are now guided by global standards, such as accounting and business reporting standards by International Financial Reporting Standards (IFRS), technical standards by ISO and electrical standards by IEEE. In relation to global legal standards, however, these are still very much in their infancy and it is, therefore, difficult to look at what the legal implications of social media are on a global scale. Even so, the World Justice Project (WJP) explores legal situations for major countries and this credible effort is ideally suited to show what the implications might be for the inroads that social media is making in various countries.

The rule of law

As societies of the world grow closer together, the laws are expected to converge. Will there be justice around the world? Certainly there should more justice as we learn more from each other through social media, and as we travel virtually around the globe. For instance, intellectual property will be shared, and managed universally as we improve the use of all assets, physical or otherwise. So in that regard, as well as in others, we can imagine that the rule of law will continue to govern at a local level and that, overall, the rule of law will find common denominators when international comparisons are made, and as commonalities are pushed to new frontiers by mutual judicial and legislative interests.

It is worthwhile pondering a very pertinent question at this point. Particularly, what is the current status of world justice? Can we even measure and compare different levels of justice? In reply, the Rule of Law Index is noteworthy. Specifically, it is a new tool that is developed and administered by the World Justice Project (WJP) to measure countries' adherence to the rule of law in practice. It is heralded as being a multidisciplinary, multinational movement to advance the rule of law for communities of opportunity and equity. In addition, this work provides new data regarding a variety of dimensions as to the rule of law. Essentially, the index currently covers 66 countries. (See *www.worldjusticeproject.org*.) On the following pages, we will take a look at three countries in more detail: Germany, China and the United Arab Emirates (UAE), selected especially because these three differ in terms of size, governance, religious foundations and average income levels. Accordingly, these are representative of many others captured by the index.

So, let us start with the rule of law definition.

In its basic form, it is generally held that the rule of law is the legal maxim that no one is above the law. Essentially, all people and any institutions are subject to law that is applied and enforced in a fair way. That is to say, legal and governmental decisions are made by applying known principles and laws, and this is done with minimal discretion in their application.

Yet different people have differing opinions about what the rule of law means. Two major ideas have achieved general acceptance, with these being a formalist and a substantive definition. While formalists do not make a judgement about the justness of law itself, they define specific procedural attributes that a legal framework must have in order to be in compliance with the rule of law. From the substantive perspective, this is not enough. Substantive conceptions require certain substantive rights that are said to be based on, or derived, from the rule of law.[1]

Despite shades of difference in the related definition, the Rule of Law Index initiated by the World Justice Project analyses the rule of law around the world from a practical perspective. It is designed to offer a detailed and comprehensive picture of the extent to which countries, in each case, adhere to the rule of law in practice.[2] The Index, therefore, considers practical situations in which a rule of law deficit might affect the daily lives of people. For instance, are the laws stable and comprehensible to members of the general public? Do people have access to public services without the need to pay any related bribe? Do individuals and entities have equal access to justice?

In 2011, as suggested earlier, 66 countries participated in global polls conducted by the WJP in which 2000 experts, and over 66 000 other people, responded. The data collected by the WJP was analysed and then organised in the form of country reports, tables and figures. See Table 3.1 for countries referenced in the 2011 survey, as well as the related methodology which follows.

Table 3.1 Countries indexed in 2011

Country	Region	Income level
Albania	Eastern Europe & Central Asia	Upper middle income
Argentina	Latin America & Caribbean	Upper middle income
Australia	East Asia & Pacific	High income
Austria	Western Europe & North America	High income
Bangladesh	South Asia	Low income
Belgium	Western Europe & North America	High income
Bolivia	Latin America & Caribbean	Lower middle income
Brazil	Latin America & Caribbean	Upper middle income
Bulgaria	Eastern Europe & Central Asia	Upper middle income
Cambodia	East Asia & Pacific	Low income
Cameroon	Sub-Saharan Africa	Lower middle income
Canada	Western Europe & North America	High income
Chile	Latin America & Caribbean	Upper middle income
China	East Asia & Pacific	Lower middle income
Colombia	Latin America & Caribbean	Upper middle income
Croatia	Eastern Europe & Central Asia	High income
Czech Republic	Eastern Europe & Central Asia	High income
Dominican Republic	Latin America & Caribbean	Upper middle income
El Salvador	Latin America & Caribbean	Lower middle income
Estonia	Eastern Europe & Central Asia	High income
Ethiopia	Sub-Saharan Africa	Low income
France	Western Europe & North America	High income
Germany	Western Europe & North America	High income
Ghana	Sub-Saharan Africa	Low income
Guatemala	Latin America & Caribbean	Lower middle income
Hong Kong SAR, China	East Asia & Pacific	High income
India	South Asia	Lower middle income
Indonesia	East Asia & Pacific	Lower middle income
Iran	Middle East & North Africa	Upper middle income
Italy	Western Europe & North America	High income
Jamaica	Latin America & Caribbean	Upper middle income
Japan	East Asia & Pacific	High income
Jordan	Middle East & North Africa	Lower middle income
Kazakhstan	Eastern Europe & Central Asia	Upper middle income
Kenya	Sub-Saharan Africa	Low income
Kyrgyzstan	Eastern Europe & Central Asia	Low income
Lebanon	Middle East & North Africa	Upper middle income
Liberia	Sub-Saharan Africa	Low income
Malaysia	East Asia & Pacific	Upper middle income
Mexico	Latin America & Caribbean	Upper middle income
Morocco	Middle East & North Africa	Lower middle income
Netherlands	Western Europe & North America	High income
New Zealand	East Asia & Pacific	High income

Table 3.1 **Countries indexed in 2011 (*Cont'd*)**

Country	Region	Income level
Nigeria	Sub-Saharan Africa	Lower middle income
Norway	Western Europe & North America	High income
Pakistan	South Asia	Lower middle income
Peru	Latin America & Caribbean	Upper middle income
Philippines	East Asia & Pacific	Lower middle income
Poland	Eastern Europe & Central Asia	High income
Romania	Eastern Europe & Central Asia	Upper middle income
Russia	Eastern Europe & Central Asia	Upper middle income
Senegal	Sub-Saharan Africa	Lower middle income
Singapore	East Asia & Pacific	High income
South Africa	Sub-Saharan Africa	Upper middle income
South Korea	East Asia & Pacific	High income
Spain	Western Europe & North America	High income
Sweden	Western Europe & North America	High income
Thailand	East Asia & Pacific	Lower middle income
Turkey	Eastern Europe & Central Asia	Upper middle income
United Arab Emirates	Middle East & North Africa	High income
Uganda	Sub-Saharan Africa	Low income
Ukraine	Eastern Europe & Central Asia	Lower middle income
United Kingdom	Western Europe & North America	High income
United States	Western Europe & North America	High income
Venezuela	Latin America & Caribbean	Upper middle income
Vietnam	East Asia & Pacific	Lower middle income

Source: World Justice Project Rule of Law Index 2011

Note: In 2012, more countries, expected to be in excess of 100, will provide data for the next report.

The WJP Rule of Law Index methodology in a nutshell

The production of the WJP Rule of Law Index may be summarized in ten steps:

1. The WJP developed the conceptual framework summarized in the Index's nine factors and 52 sub-factors, in consultation with academics, practitioners, and community leaders from around the world.
2. The Index team developed a set of five questionnaires based on the Index's conceptual framework, to be administered to

experts and the general public. Questionnaires were translated into several languages and adapted to reflect commonly used terms and expressions. These instruments were piloted in six countries in 2008.

3. The team identified, on average, more than 300 potential local experts per country to respond to the qualified respondents' questionnaires, and engaged the services of leading local polling companies.
4. Polling companies conducted pre-test pilot surveys of the general public in consultation with the Index team, and launched the final survey.
5. The team sent the questionnaires to local experts and engaged in continual interaction with them.
6. The Index team collected and mapped the data on to the 52 sub-factors.
7. The Index team constructed the final scores using a five-step process:
   a. Codified the questionnaire items as numeric values.
   b. Produced raw country scores by aggregating the responses from several individuals (experts or general public).
   c. Normalized the raw scores.
   d. Aggregated the normalized scores into sub-factors and factors using simple averages.
   e. Produced the final rankings using the normalized scores.
8. The data were subject to a series of tests to identify possible biases and errors. For example, the Index team cross-checked all sub-factors against more than 60 third-party sources, including quantitative data and qualitative assessments drawn from local and international organizations.
9. A sensitivity analysis was conducted by the Econometrics and Applied Statistics Unit of the European Commission's Joint Research Centre, in collaboration with the Index team, to assess the statistical reliability of the results.
10. Finally, the data were organized into country reports, tables, and figures to facilitate their presentation and interpretation.

Source: World Justice Project Rule of Law Index 2011

The challenge was to formulate a set of principles that would constitute a definition of the rule of law. Since we are living in different constitutions, political systems and cultures, as well as having different religious and ethical backgrounds, it was essential to establish standards and norms that enjoy broad acceptance across countries, and incorporate both substantive and procedural elements. The result of this serious consideration was a set of eight indicators. Effectively, there are eight principles to measure how legal systems function in relation to prevalent political powers and to individuals of each state. These are:

1. limited government powers;
2. absence of corruption;
3. order and security;
4. fundamental rights;
5. open government;
6. effective regulatory enforcement;
7. access to civil justice; and
8. effective criminal justice.

Each of these is addressed in turn in summary form below.

Limited government powers

Government powers should be defined by fundamental law. It measures not only to what extent they are limited by legislature and judiciary, but, if the government and its officials are limited by independent auditing and review, also if they are sanctioned for misconduct. It also includes non-governmental checks.

Absence of corruption

This factor deals with the question as to whether government officials use, or do not use, public office for private gain. Bribery, improper influence by public and private interests, and misappropriation of public funds or other resources are analysed. This includes the executive branch, police and military, as well as the judiciary and the legislature.

Order and security

Order and security focuses on how the government assures the security of persons and property in terms of whether crime is effectively controlled and civil conflicts are limited. This includes also terrorism, the absence of violence and vigilantism.

Fundamental rights

Fundamental rights have to be protected. Although the discussion about what rights are – and always will be – in progress, and may never be fully resolved, the Universal Declaration of Human Rights[3] builds the framework for this index. This principle requires governments to respect core human rights that are established under international law and are most closely related to the rule of law.

Against this background, the right to life, freedom of thought, religion and expression, equal treatment and absence of discrimination, the right to privacy, freedom of assembly and association, as well as fundamental labour rights, were identified as a minimum of human rights that should be guaranteed.

Open government

People are able to abide by law if they know what the law is. On the one hand, the law must be comprehensible, clear and explained to the public in plain language. This factor includes the basic necessity not only to publish the law, but also to make laws widely accessible to the general public.

On the other hand, it is determined whether the people have the possibility to take part in the process of making laws. This means, among other criteria, that official drafts and information are available, that proceedings are held with timely notice and are open to the public, and that people have the right to petition.

Effective regulatory enforcement

This factor measures the extent to which government regulations are fair and effectively enforced. Such regulations should be applied without improper influence by public officials, or by private interests. It covers the adherence to administrative procedures that are consistent and predictable.

Access to civil justice

All people should have access to civil justice. Legal advice and representation should be affordable. It requires the system to be free of discrimination, corruption and improper government influence.

Effective criminal justice

Here, effective criminal justice means that the crimes are investigated effectively and adjudicated in a timely manner. The criminal justice system should be impartial, as well as free of corruption and improper government influence.

These measures allowed for more exploration as to the results inter-regionally, as is the purpose of the next section.

Rankings of the rule of law by regions

The average ranking sees Europe and North America ahead of most other regions. Surprisingly, the greatest weakness in Western Europe and North America appears to be related to the accessibility of the civil justice system, especially for low-income segments of the population. This is likely to change as electronic systems and monopolistic powers of the legal profession are improved in this region.

See Table 3.2 on the next page for related details.

Now, let us have a detailed look at three very different countries that exemplify how different political and cultural systems perform in this report. As indicated earlier, the three countries chosen for this purposes are:

- Germany;
- the United Arab Emirates; and
- China

Each if these is considered below, with particular attention paid to Germany in order to provide an understanding as to the details that are available in the *WJP Rule of Law Report 2011*.

Table 3.2 Average rankings by region

Factor	Sub-Saharan Africa	East Asia & Pacific	Eastern Europe & Central Asia	Western Europe & North America	Latin America & Caribbean	Middle East & North Africa	South Asia
1. Limited Government Powers	51	30	50	9	39	39	48
2. Absence of Corruption	52	26	40	13	44	38	58
3. Order and Security	58	21	29	14	53	34	65
4. Fundamental Rights	52	32	33	12	35	56	48
5. Open Government	60	26	40	11	36	41	54
6. Regulatory Enforcement	53	32	38	11	38	29	58
7. Access to Civil Justice	43	41	34	10	38	28	62
8. Effective Criminal Justice	46	24	38	12	50	39	40

Source: World Justice Project Rule of Law Index 2011

Germany

As might well be expected, Germany is one of the top performers in this report. To a great extent, the government is accountable. Fundamental rights are well protected, and corruption is very low, with this resulting in a high ranking for Germany of 6th out of 66. See the following report extracts for particular details.

In the first instance, Table 3.3 below shows the ranking of Germany in relation to the eight factors that are fundamental to the construction of Rule of Law Index.

The table displays the featured country's aggregate scores by factor and the country's rankings within its regional and income level groups. The table is organised as follows.

- The first column lists the first eight factors that make up the Index.
- The second column displays the country's aggregate score for each of the eight factors.

Table 3.3 Germany in the WJP Rule of Law Index

Germany						Berlin, Hamburg, Munich
Income High **Region** Western Europe & North America **Population** 82m (2010) 74% Urban 8% in three largest cities		**WJP Rule of Law Index Factors**	**Score**	**Global Ranking**	**Regional Ranking**	**Income Group Ranking**
	Factor 1:	Limited Government Powers	0.81	6/66	4/12	6/23
	Factor 2:	Absence of Corruption	0.83	12/66	6/12	12/23
	Factor 3:	Order and Security	0.88	9/66	5/12	9/23
	Factor 4:	Fundamental Rights	0.84	6/66	5/12	6/23
	Factor 5:	Open Government	0.73	11/66	7/12	11/23
	Factor 6:	Regulatory Enforcement	0.77	8/66	5/12	8/23
	Factor 7:	Access to Civil Justice	0.79	2/66	2/12	2/23
	Factor 8:	Effective Criminal Justice	0.78	9/66	5/12	9/23

Source: World Justice Project Rule of Law Index 2011

- The third column displays the country's global ranking for each factor.
- The fourth column shows the country's ranking within its region.
- The fifth column shows the country's ranking among countries with comparable per capita income levels.

The index points out that the German civil justice system, ranking 2nd of 66, is nearly free of undue influence. In addition, access to the civil justice system is affordable, and courts are reported to be efficient. Due to the possibility of legal aid, even people with no income have access to the civil justice system and can afford legal advice.

The following graphs provide additional details in relation to the WJP assessment of Germany. Particularly, these graphs present the scores for all WJP Rule of Law Index sub-factors for Germany.

The four graphs in Figures 3.2 and 3.3 show the country's disaggregated scores for each of the sub-factors that compose the WJP Rule of Law Index. Each graph shows a circle that corresponds to one concept measured by the Index. Each sub-factor is represented by a radius running from the centre of the circle to the periphery. The centre of each circle corresponds to the lowest possible score for each sub-factor (0.00) and the outer edge of the circle marks the highest possible score for each sub-factor (1.00). Higher scores signify a higher adherence to the rule of law.

As per the key to each graph presented in Figure 3.1, the country scores are shown with a thick line that features small squares. The graphs also show the average scores of all countries indexed within the region (by way of a line that features small triangles) and all countries indexed with comparable per capita income levels (represented by a thin line that features small squares). As a point of reference, the graphs also show the score achieved for each sub-factor by the top performer among all 66 countries indexed (being a small dot close to the end of each radius).

Firstly, we see the scores for what constitutes accountable government, as well as security and fundamental rights.

Secondly, we see the scores for what constitutes open government and regulatory enforcement, as well as access to justice.

Nevertheless, equal access to justice can differ, even in high-income countries. This is shown in Figure 3.4 wherein a comparison is made between Germany and the United States of America.

While in Germany income plays no significant role in filing a lawsuit in court to resolve a dispute, it seems that in the United States only the Americans with a high income use the court system. Most of the people with low income take no action and are discriminated against.

These sub-factors are available for each country and provide a deeper look as to why these countries are listed as they are in relation to the behaviour of government, fundamental rights of individuals and access to the justice system.

Figure 3.1 **Key to graphs**

Source: World Justice Project Rule of Law Index 2011

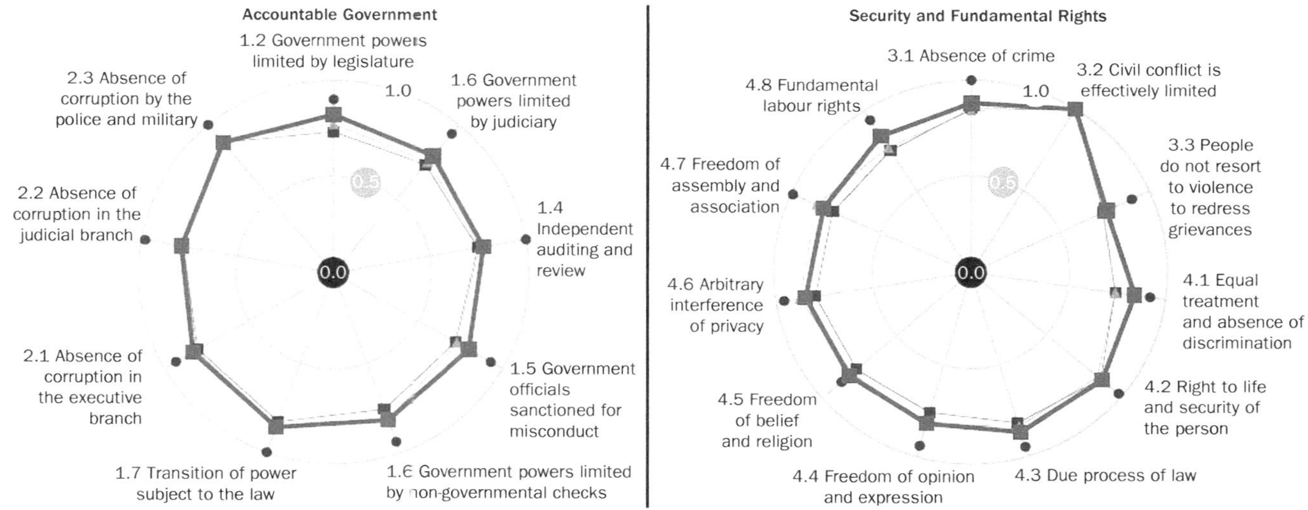

Figure 3.2 Accountable Government/Security and Fundamental Rights – Germany

Source: World Justice Project Rule of Law Index 2011

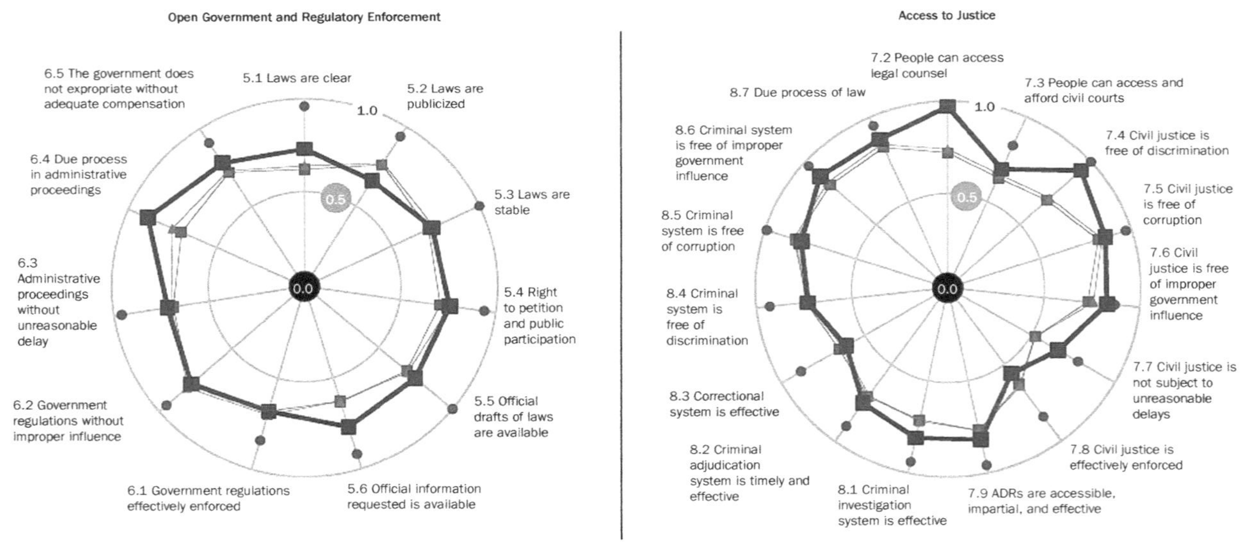

Figure 3.3 Open Government and Regulatory Enforcement/Access to Justice – Germany

Source: World Justice Project Rule of Law Index 2011

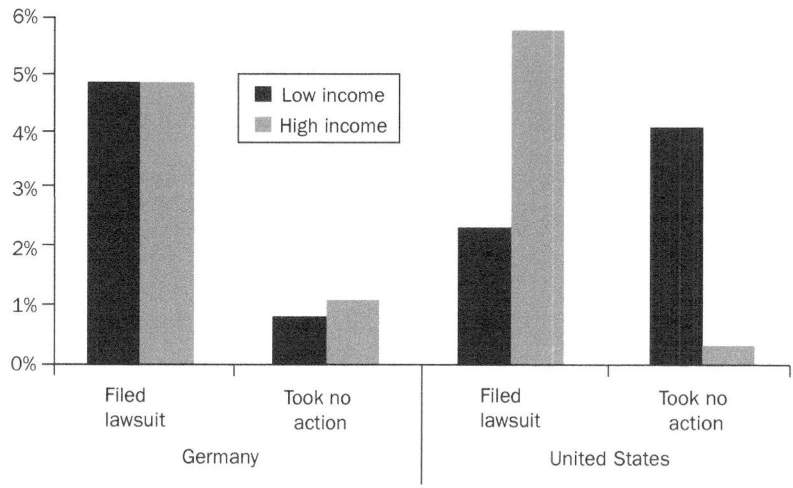

Figure 3.4 **Access to Justice: Germany and the USA**

Source: World Justice Project Rule of Law Index 2011

The United Arab Emirates

Compared to other countries in this region that took part in the Rule of Law Index survey, the United Arab Emirates (UAE) has the highest scores in most dimensions, ranking 1st. When considering the related results globally, the UAE performs much better than expected in terms of absence of corruption, order and security, regulatory enforcement, access to civil justice and effectiveness of criminal justice.

Although fundamental rights are still limited in the UAE, including freedom of religion and assembly, labour rights and freedom of opinion and expression, it is apparent that the civil court system works in an efficient manner. It is also evident that courts and public institutions in the UAE are well developed and relatively free of corruption.

This report also shows, quite strikingly, that crime in the UAE is effectively investigated and adjudicated in a timely manner. In fact, the criminal justice system of the UAE ranks fourth out of all countries.

See Table 3.4 for more detailed results related to the UAE.

Table 3.4 **The United Arab Emirates in the WJP Rule of Law Index**

<table>
<tr><th colspan="3">United Arab Emirates</th><th colspan="4">Dubai, Sharjah, Abu-Dhabi</th></tr>
<tr><td>Income
High</td><td></td><td>WJP Rule of Law Index Factors</td><td>Score</td><td>Global Ranking</td><td>Regional Ranking</td><td>Income Group Ranking</td></tr>
<tr><td rowspan="8">Region
Middle East & North Africa

Population
5m (2010)
78% Urban
56% in three largest cities</td><td>Factor 1:</td><td>Limited Government Powers</td><td>0.60</td><td>28/66</td><td>1/5</td><td>20/23</td></tr>
<tr><td>Factor 2:</td><td>Absence of Corruption</td><td>0.83</td><td>13/66</td><td>1/5</td><td>13/23</td></tr>
<tr><td>Factor 3:</td><td>Order and Security</td><td>0.90</td><td>6/66</td><td>1/5</td><td>6/23</td></tr>
<tr><td>Factor 4:</td><td>Fundamental Rights</td><td>0.53</td><td>51/66</td><td>2/5</td><td>23/23</td></tr>
<tr><td>Factor 5:</td><td>Open Government</td><td>0.57</td><td>21/66</td><td>1/5</td><td>18/23</td></tr>
<tr><td>Factor 6:</td><td>Regulatory Enforcement</td><td>0.73</td><td>12/66</td><td>1/5</td><td>12/23</td></tr>
<tr><td>Factor 7:</td><td>Access to Civil Justice</td><td>0.68</td><td>11/66</td><td>1/5</td><td>11/23</td></tr>
<tr><td>Factor 8:</td><td>Effective Criminal Justice</td><td>0.84</td><td>4/66</td><td>1/5</td><td>4/23</td></tr>
</table>

Source: World Justice Project Rule of Law Index 2011

China

China does well among lower-middle income countries in most categories, and is the second-best performer among the comparable, and commonly grouped, BRIC economies (Brazil, Russia, India and China). It is reported that China has seen major improvements in the quality, effectiveness and accountability of its legal institutions. Security is high, ranking 25th, and the criminal justice systems ranks 2nd among its income-related peers. However, enforcement of regulations is relatively ineffective, ranking 43rd globally and 8th among lower-middle income countries. Yet the civil court system is relatively accessible and speedy. But judicial

Table 3.5 China in the WJP Rule of Law Index

<table>
<tr><td colspan="3">China</td><td colspan="4">Beijing, Shanghai, Guangzhou</td></tr>
<tr><td rowspan="9">Income
Lower Middle

Region
East Asia & Pacific

Population
1,341m (2010)
45% Urban
3% in three largest cities</td><td></td><td>WJP Rule of Law Index Factors</td><td>Score</td><td>Global Ranking</td><td>Regional Ranking</td><td>Income Group Ranking</td></tr>
<tr><td>Factor 1:</td><td>Limited Government Powers</td><td>0.53</td><td>37/66</td><td>11/13</td><td>7/16</td></tr>
<tr><td>Factor 2:</td><td>Absence of Corruption</td><td>0.60</td><td>31/66</td><td>9/13</td><td>3/16</td></tr>
<tr><td>Factor 3:</td><td>Order and Security</td><td>0.81</td><td>25/66</td><td>9/13</td><td>2/16</td></tr>
<tr><td>Factor 4:</td><td>Fundamental Rights</td><td>0.40</td><td>64/66</td><td>13/13</td><td>16/16</td></tr>
<tr><td>Factor 5:</td><td>Open Government</td><td>0.54</td><td>26/66</td><td>7/13</td><td>2/16</td></tr>
<tr><td>Factor 6:</td><td>Regulatory Enforcement</td><td>0.50</td><td>43/66</td><td>12/13</td><td>8/16</td></tr>
<tr><td>Factor 7:</td><td>Access to Civil Justice</td><td>0.52</td><td>44/66</td><td>8/13</td><td>6/16</td></tr>
<tr><td>Factor 8:</td><td>Effective Criminal Justice</td><td>0.61</td><td>25/66</td><td>8/13</td><td>2/16</td></tr>
</table>

Source: World Justice Project Rule of Law Index 2011

independence remains an area where more progress is needed. Also, indicators of fundamental rights are weak, including labour rights ranking 61st out of 66, freedom of speech ranking 66th globally and freedom of assembly also ranking 66th.

See Table 3.5 for more detailed results related to China.

Rule of Law Index and social media

A question that naturally arises here is: how do we relate WJP Rule of Law Index factors to rights in social media and open access to the Internet? Since the Internet is run mostly by privately owned entities, corruption does not seem to play a significant role. However, we can consider that fundamental rights and access to civil justice seem most important.

Now, consider a few appropriate comparisons. For instance, due to governmental powers, China ranks nearly at the end of the scale (being 64th out of 66 countries for that indicator) and the close relations to religion places the UAE at 51 out of 66.

Access to civil justice is fairly good in China, and the UAE ranks highly. Germany, as mentioned before, is number two in this category, well ahead of the frequently so-called 'superior' justice system of the USA (which is only ranked in 21st place out of 66 countries).

Lastly, who has the most efficient criminal justice system? For this indicator, Norway is rated number one and Hong Kong is in the number two position. Also, note that China ranks at number 25, Germany is in 9th place and the UAE (where 56 per cent of people live in the largest three cities) has an amazing 4th place result. All of these countries, generally, allow Internet access.

We could ponder whether access to the Internet plays an important role for any country on its way to a level of world justice, and if the reverse is true, whereby a low level of social justice is commensurate with low Internet access. In relation to this issue, give some thought to places like North Korea and Cuba where access to the Internet is very limited. There, the justice systems are the least developed parts of society and, in this day and age, it is surprising how single countries are still able to stop citizens from accessing the wonderful world of knowledge and international relations provided by the Internet and social media applications.

Consider also that Internet censoring seems to have roots in selected chapters of history, as well as in other issues of immense sensitivity. For example, Germany bans open comment on relatively recent history pertaining to German involvement in World War II, as well as to child pornography, which transcends time. Also, China is allergic to news about its connection with and affection for Tibet, and the UAE protects Islamic religion, as well as commercial interests associated with newly created phone companies there.

Of course, ideally, the blocking and filtering of Internet-based information will be reduced and the global community can participate in open discussions on any topic. But this aspiration needs the participation of everybody, including governments, religious leaders and lastly (but by no means least) the open-minded people who jump national firewalls in a well-meaning and diligent effort to improve their nation's circumstances through striving for equality and world justice. This intellectual movement, then, will have a driving effect on the rest of the world's legal system, as it is too focused on individual ownership of physical assets, as well as maintaining (inadvertently or otherwise) greed and disrespect for other global citizens.

Social media – chance or challenge?

Over two billion people now have access to the Internet. However, as that access increases, restriction is sure to increase too. Several reports stress that in the last few years, a growing number of governments are moving to restrict the free flow of information on the Internet. For instance, in 15 of 37 countries examined in the *Freedom of the Net Report 2011*, governments were actively engaged in the blocking of politically relevant information on the web. In detail, this means the blocking of websites for undefined periods, restricted user access, extensive surveillance and user registration, as well as the building of legal frameworks for filtering political content. In addition, private entities that fail to comply with these draconian regulations are sanctioned.

In China, more than 400 million people have access to the Internet. Nevertheless, it is the most censored environment for communication via the web. Chinese authorities have established a very sophisticated system of censoring, monitoring and manipulation. Hundreds of thousands of people are employed to control content. More than 60 000 websites were shut down in 2010 because of so-called 'harmful materials' and 350 million articles, videos and photographs were deleted. The most systematically censored topics included criticism of top leaders, independent evaluations of China's human rights record, violation of minority rights in Tibet, Xinjiang, the 1989 Beijing massacre and dissident initiatives.

Interestingly, cyber attacks, politically motivated censorship and government control over Internet infrastructure did not only emerge in China. For example, Internet freedom is classified as non-free in countries such as Iran, Burma (Myanmar), Saudi Arabia, Belarus, Cuba, Ethiopia, Bahrain, Thailand, Tunisia and Vietnam. New Internet restrictions around the globe are partly a response to the explosion in the popularity of advanced applications, such as Facebook, YouTube and Twitter, through which ordinary users can easily post their own content, share information and connect with large audiences. While serving mostly as a form of entertainment, over the last two years these tools have also played a significant role in political and social activism.

In countries with substantial censorship of political and social issues, such as China, Iran or Saudi Arabia, human rights defenders and pro-democracy reformers use the Internet to connect with each other and to build platforms to communicate more effectively to a broader audience, as well as among themselves. In restricted countries, such as those mentioned above, journalists need to be trained in the gathering of information and resources to facilitate public access to information that otherwise and in other places is readily available. For example, *Gozaar*, an online magazine that is supported by Freedom House, serves as an interactive, inclusive space for the discussion of human rights and democracy in Iran. Moreover, there exist hundreds of circumvention tools to avoid the government-endorsed restrictions. To date, those tools are relatively unknown to the general populace. A major aim for many who seek greater equality, fairness and justice will increase the awareness of such tools among the general populace.

All things considered, it can be said that social media applications function not only as a so-called watchdog in relation to the abuse of government powers, corruption and avoidance of human rights. Social media also gives power to people in some countries who have little opportunity to participate in a democratic manner. Accordingly, social networking platforms are, and will be, essential tools to report and discuss rule of law abuses, mobilise support and make such issues visible. Therefore, it is more than probable that social media will play a significant role in defending private rights.

Conclusion

Regarding future legal consolidation, let's take a look from a different perspective, with specific attention paid to products and services, finance, non-moveable physical assets, global communication and people.

Advertising and promotion for **products** and **services** are one of the most important drivers for the development of the Internet. Standards and laws are developing at a very fast rate and on a global scale. Related access to the Internet is not too restrictive. Associated abuses deal with the transfer of intellectual property, infringement of copyrights and outdated customs laws.

Movement of **financial assets** is still restricted by governmental regulation, protection and tax laws. Through credit card and international payment systems, the infrastructure is in place to reduce the legal burden when using the Internet for such transactions. Related legal issues circle around security and abuse for personal gain.

Non-moveable physical assets, such as the use and ownership of property, have deep roots in legal systems around the globe. This includes the use and misuse of natural resources, such as water, air and earth.

Here, social media has the largest opportunity to drive improvement to influence global actions that are supported by global legal agreements.

Global **communication** will be further enhanced by improved software and communication tools, as well as telecommunications equipment, with all of this being owned and operated mostly by private enterprises. This will reduce the power of governments and force these institutions to create legal structures on a larger, regional basis. This will be of increased benefit to people.

Also, the use of social media will speed up the movement of **people** around the globe. Due to language, cultural and religious differences, there is relatively little cross-border employment at this time. Here, social media has its largest challenge, but this is also an opportunity to bring related legal systems and justice closer to a common denominator.

References

Bekri, D., Dunn, B., Oguzertem, I., Su, Y. and Upreti, S. (2011), *Harnessing Social Media Tools to Fight Corruption*, Department of International Development at the London School of Economics and Political Science MSc Development Management, May.

Craig, P. (1997), 'Formal and substantive conceptions of the rule of law: an analytical framework', *Public Law*, 467.

Deibert, R. (2000), 'International Plug 'n Play? Citizen Activism, the Internet, and Global Public Policy', *International Studies Perspectives*.

Kelly, S. and Cook, S. (eds) (2011), *Freedom On The Net, A Global Assessment Of Internet And Digital Media*, Freedom House.

Sheppard, N. (2009), 'The government is monitoring Facebook and Twitter', *News Busters*, *http://newsbusters.org/blogs/noel-sheppard/2009/12/14/government-monitoring-facebook-twitter* (accessed on 30 March 2011).

United Nations General Assembly Resolutions A/RES/61/39, A/RES/62/70, A/RES/63/128.

World Justice Project (2011), *World Justice Project Rule of Law Index*.

Zomerman. M. and Lyer, A. (2009), 'Introduction to the Social and Psychological Dynamics of Collective Action', *Journal of Social Issues*, 65, 4.

Websites

- *alkasir.com*
- *freemorenews.com*
- *opennet.net*
- *www.freedomhouse.org/uploads/special_report/99.pdf*

- *www.gozaar.org*
- *www.irz-stiftung.de*
- *www.reuters.com/article/idUSTOE6BT01T2101230*
- *www.seasawe.net*
- *www.transparency.org*
- *www.wikileaks.ch*
- *www.wordpress.com*
- *www.worldjusticemap.org*
- *www.worldjusticeproject.org*

Notes

1. Craig, P. (1997) 'Formal and substantive conceptions of the rule of law: an analytical framework', *Public Law*: 467.
2. WJP Rule of Law Index 2011, p. 7.
3. Universal Declaration of Human Rights adopted by the United Nations General Assembly in 1948.

4

Default metaphysics – social networks and the self

Florian Hadler and Gabriel Yoran

Abstract: The fundamental issues of social media are the ways that people relay something of themselves to others and how this shapes society. Plus, increasingly, there is the breadth of social media reach, and the depth of what is kept in terms of related history of a person, captured constantly by postings and connections. As a consequence, much can be gleaned about people, especially as to their networks, actions and opinions. This leads to an additional matter of the concern generated when the massive amount of personal and socialised data is accessible, not only by befriended users of social media applications, but by government agencies, as is done for the purpose of pursuing political objectives. This gives social media a rather less than fresh and innocent appearance to any who see past the vast popularity of seemingly innocuous interchanges between old friends and new acquaintances met online.

Key words: social media, normalised differences, personalised data, socialised data, Rousseau, Latour, Guattari, Deleuze, Foucault, communication, governmentality, ubiquity of technology, data austerity, archiving, sociality, apparatus, defaults.

Normalised differences

Existing discourse on so-called social networks, let alone social media, often ignores the ideological implications that the usage of these terms imply. *Social* as well as *network* and, of course, *media* are concepts that are very controversial in their respective scientific disciplines, such as sociology, anthropology or philosophy. One cannot claim a clear and stable definition for any of these but must, rather, acknowledge their specific operational objectives when applying the terms to phenomena, such as web-based services, user-generated content, ubiquitous computing, viral marketing (which is another euphemistic expression) and other topics of economic interest. Nevertheless, for the purposes of this paper, the three terms are set out in turn below.

- *Social* in one of its primal denotations – *socius* – is participation, or association. But its function regarding society and sociality is quite obscure. The term was, and still is, used in the same sense as by Jean-Jacques Rousseau in his political theory. The concept of socialism eventually gave the term its specific meaning, so that sociology turned to notions like being sociable and co-extension. Bruno Latour (French sociologist of science and anthropologist, and an influential theorist in the field of science and technology studies) has been trying to establish a new notion of the term 'social', being one that focuses not on the connective character of the term, but towards that *which is to be connected* through all kinds of links and connectors.
- *Network* is a metaphor used for a relational view of phenomena, one that points to structuralism and post-structuralism and its conceptions of the world, not as an essential sum of objects, but as an ever-changing network of relations, as an ensemble, most noted in the term *rhizom* by French philosophers Guattari and Deleuze. The truncated term *net*, since then, has evolved into the most powerful paradigm of contemporary thought and it informs not only philosophy but all associated humanities.
- *Media*, at last, is a term that could not be more obscure – deriving from the Greek term *metaxy*, it unfolded its initial power in the Aristotelian epistemology *Peri Psyches*. Since then, it has experienced a never-ending, inflationary usage and currently covers everything from all kinds of mass communication technologies to clothing, cars, gestures, language, parapsychological phenomena, books, mobile devices, computers, publishing houses, network channels, advertising and many more things besides.

By operating within economic conditions, these three terms not only often reveal hidden ideology, but also execute their metaphysical programme by creating the environment in which the subject finds itself. Consider that the templates for our virtual identities are predefined by the services that we use. For instance, we have different services for different means. Private, erotic, professional and other interest-based communities offer separate spaces for our virtual communications and dialogues, either in writing, or in pictures, in links or in sound, in video or in any other kind of communication. Each of these channels demands a certain behaviour, which reflects its audience and acts according to the shared conventions and codes of that particular cohort.

There is rarely a thing that the so-called social networks are not supposed to facilitate, as can be seen from radical changes in communication, commerce, marketing, politics and even the 'Facebook revolution'. Is there anything that these social networks are not able to do? Also, what does it mean if actual revolutions are named after commercial web-based services? Who coined this term? What media were used in the revolutions preceding the Arab Spring uprising, and why did these not develop the same brand awareness? What does the term 'social' even mean in this context?

It is worth contemplating that the rampant usage of the term 'social media' demands a more detailed look as to its contexts and conditions. In so doing, we must be aware of the fact that social networks reflect communication according to the terms and conditions of privately held or publicly traded companies. These conditions, filters and restrictions tend to hide themselves and develop a hidden agenda that not only affect the aforementioned aspects of society but, first and foremost, affects the subject itself and the way that it interacts with others. These influences on concepts of identities are completely underestimated and unrecognised if one continues to use the term 'social media' in a strictly commercial sense.

We need to remember, at the same time, that each and every aspect of our behaviour within these so-called social networks is subject to commercial exploitation. The sheer fact that services costing hundreds of millions of dollars per year to maintain are being offered for free to the user suggests that the users themselves are the actual products being sold. Therefore, customer satisfaction cannot be measured by how quickly the user gets their needs fulfilled, but by how long and how often the user indulges in social networking. There is a reason why Internet strategists strive for so-called 'stickiness' when designing 'social' user experiences. Bluntly speaking, social networks manipulate their users to produce relevant content in order to build addiction. The users are the squeezed fruits which provide the juice that keeps the economy of attention running. The 'fight for eyeballs', known from classical media such as television, and still used for online campaigning with banner ads along the top of web pages, has become a fight for identities in at least two perspectives: on the one hand, we have the identity construction of the subjects themselves, that is performed in specific web-based services; on the other hand, we have the digital fingerprint, that is the behavioural patterns and preferences of the users. The more precise such a fingerprint is, the better it is for advertisers to target these users.

The irony of such individual approaches to advertising is that it only works for huge populations in which each individual is identical in terms of their differences. This might seem counterintuitive. However, these differences are normalised and standardised in order for users to be clustered into target groups and, therefore, no real differences exist within each cohort, other than settings that the user can adjust according to their self-construction. Consequently, any difference is anticipated and transformed into strategic intentions. So it is that the single usage proposition no longer exists, and the product itself anticipates its misuse. Although MySpace might not be the best current example of a successful social network, it nonetheless established the paradigm of user-generated usage. The re-appropriation of the profile pages, and their decoration with html snippets, was based on a simple error in the source code. Even so, this turned out to be their most promising proposition – at least for some years. Still, the unique selling proposition is no longer stable as it is a product of the users' projections whereby the services are mere platforms, or screens, on which the wishes of the users are projected and then recorded.

The omnipresence of the *like*, *share* or *+1* button all over the web is just the tip of the proverbial iceberg, with these representing only the visible ends of vast tentacles of the most prominent social networks – specifically, tracking, targeting and analysing user behaviour throughout the whole web. It is noteworthy that this behaviour is not only tracked by the particular service; it is also, in parts, visible to the so-called 'social graph' of the user, appearing in the so-called 'stream' and, therefore, is a fundamental part of the juicy addiction for which these services aim. The stream is not just a naturalised algorithm as it has become the personal river, where one can think while watching the waves; to all intents and purposes, it is conceived as a place. Social networks have successfully constructed a virtual ontology, one that suggests a topological structure of a 'where to go to' to connect with friends. Overall, social networks are perceived in a gross misconception as public places. On the contrary, these networks are not. They are secretly individualised filter bubbles; they are apparatuses of governmental power relations in a Foucaultian sense. These functions are hidden in naturalising metaphors such as stream, tweet and cloud, disguising their very essence and their technology, and luring the user into their realm. Once inside, the user is prompted to formulate their existence, according to the templates offered by the service. The identity of the user is structured by default.

Submitting subjects

> Whatever we may wish in the future, we can no longer live in Euclidian space under electronic conditions, and this means that the divisions between inner and outer, private and communal, whatever they may have been for a literate culture, are simply not there for an electronic one.
>
> Marshall McLuhan, Canadian educator, philosopher, and scholar

When entering the realm of social networks, we are confronted with three main paradigms, each one embodied by one of the leaders of the three most influential technology companies today. Google's Eric Schmidt suggests that if someone doesn't want anyone else to know what they are doing, then they shouldn't be doing it in the first place. Facebook founder Mark Zuckerberg suggests that one identity for each user is enough and that it should be the real one. Furthermore, Apple founder, the late Steve Jobs, suggested that one does not have to understand how technology works in order to use it and, in stark contrast, the more obscure the function of any technology is for the user, the better it adapts to their daily behaviour. In this regard, the Human Interface Guidelines from Apple propose the simulation of physical characteristics, such as balance points for screen designs and textures, that appear haptic, tactile and tangible in order to integrate more seamlessly with the user's real-world interactions.

These statements are the very essence of governmentality – the user is conceived as the ideal citizen, one whom governs themselves with the aforementioned social technologies to become transparent, addressable and morally adjusted. This is no longer achieved by repression or state institutions. On the contrary, the users themselves are acting in a democratised Panopticon, in a prison where the guards are inhabitants at the same time. Consider, therefore, that the pressure to put every part of one's life online leads to self-governing behaviour that constantly scans the user's behaviour for *postability*: 'Would what I am doing here receive positive feedback? Would it resonate with my peers?'

Individuals are reproducing Schmidt's dictum: Those who have nothing to hide can share everything. So it is that the tyranny of transparency is linked to a type of self-leadership that takes users towards decent behaviour by the means of Google and Facebook. For instance, the user's friends are their most respected and feared judges. Exposing actions, preferences, attendances and locations to the judgement of peers and, in return, commenting, liking and judging their online activities, is crucial to the economy of attention that keeps the social services running. We find here the technology of the self, described not only by Michel Foucault in his famous and oft-quoted 'discipline and punish', but also by Norbert Elias in his 'Civilizing Process – Sociogenetic and Psychogenetic Investigations'. Elias speaks of a *Zivilisationskurve* (civilisation graph), marked by the ever-growing internal self-regulation and anticipation of the other that renders institutional control instances more and more obsolete. Also, it is Jean Baudrillard's 'Transparency of Evil' which manifests itself in social networks: Sanctioning non-transparency, secrecy or silence is wished for politically – and realised in these services. In this regard, contemplate the pertinent musing of Baudrillard, who stated:

> When everything tends towards the visible, as is the case in our world, what becomes of the things that were once kept secret? They become occult, clandestine, maleficent: what was merely secret – or, in other words, given to be exchanged in secrecy – becomes evil and must be abolished, exterminated.

At this juncture, it is worthwhile to contemplate a definition of an authoritarian variation of democracy, as proposed by Fareed Zakaria, the renowned journalist, author and commentator, in which democratically elected politicians cut back on civil rights. What follows is that, with current illiberal security apparatuses, tracking is the new statistic and means of measurement and the basis of control. Every subject, on its own, needs to be placed under surveillance because every one of them could be the next Mohammed Atta, in the case of the Egypt Revolution, or Anders Behring Breivik, who perpetrated mass race-related killings in Norway.

It is no longer the statistical average, nor the Foucaultian security apparatuses, that creates the normative power of the 'average citizen', which modern nations once strived for. On the contrary, in an enormous effort of reversal of evidence called *telecommunications data retention*, every citizen is considered to be a potentially dangerous subject. People become loaded biomass, the energy signature of which must be uncloaked in due time. What started with the fingerprint in English colonies at the end of the nineteenth century – the developing of the anonymous population into addressable subjects starting with the identification of recidivist criminals – has now become a default for each and every citizen.

Consider that governmentality links self-leadership with techniques to lead others. Successfully conveying the feeling to be at the mercy of free-floating data is such a link. Also, as we now know, social networks create leadership by educating subjects to submit information willingly. In addition, such subjects produce a plethora of information that was entered voluntarily and that no longer needs to be recorded by government-backed secret services.

With the rise of technologies, such as smartphones, tablets and other mobile devices, this vicious circle of control and exposure integrates deeply and intimately into the everyday life of social media users. Recent products from Apple use the same metaphorical field of naturalisation that we already know from social services. For instance, Apple computers imitate breathing with harmonic standby lightning, and the iPhone 4 has a so-called retina display. These products are not bodily functions. Yet they demand to be treated as organic implants that need to be taken care of not only in form of providing nutrition, such as in the form of electricity, but also in providing attention. The selling proposition is no longer the product itself, but the virtual environment it provides (the 'ecosystem', as the industry calls it, in another naturalistic metaphor), as well as the possibility of connection, communication and interaction through all kinds of apps.

With the ubiquity of technology, it is no longer just the users' behaviour on the web that is tracked and analysed. There are also the physical whereabouts, routes and encounters of the user. Predictive behavioural targeting becomes localised. Spaces that were once conceived as private become hybrid as the user is constantly connected via a virtual umbilical cord. Classic concepts of privacy (which, by the way, is a rather young phenomenon) become obsolete as we enter the so-called digital age.

Being traded

Foucault's governmentality concept describes, among other things, a power structure in which power is exercised by *gentle means*. Social networks like Facebook act 'governmentally': their technology is the power of defaults. The microphysics of power manifests itself in the interface of social networks. Their defaults – that is, their design, and their ontology (like the dominant 'sharing with everyone') – act as a gentle means of power over the subjects.

The so-constructed 'social' subjects share data almost reflexively: 'I must tweet that' has become common practice, just like the 'checking in' at certain locations where users share their whereabouts with friends.

Facebook's triumphal procession through the private lives of over 800 million people will force the thinking of governments about Facebook becoming governmental technology, and it should not be a surprise, therefore, that the larger social network providers already have entire internal departments dedicated to cooperation with federal law enforcement institutions. There is hardly a case that does not take the online existence into account: claims of responsibility are found online, online correspondences lead to supporters and accomplices, tracking of locations via mobile devices leads to surveillance and arrests, and so forth.

The basic mechanisms of this technology are described by Georg Franck's 'Economy of Attention', which states:

> All of us are captivated by the question of how we are received by others. We can't stand not playing any role in someone else's consciousness. The human soul already begins to suffer if it does not play a leading role in another. It takes permanent damage and ends in bitterness when it does not receive ample attention to a minimum. And it is the highest of its delights to bathe in the other's attention.

Related to this particular notion, social network services, such as Facebook and Twitter, make transparent their presence in the consciousness of another person. This is what makes them so successful as a form of governmental technology: They promote transparency through their interfaces, and reward users with attention.

Following on from the preceding commentary, the power technology of data protectionists is the largely unsuccessful recursion on the economic principles of money. Data protection authorities lose influence because they have never produced a 'data market'. They simply try to limit it. Bloggers who integrate Facebook's 'Like' button should be reprimanded by the will of the German Data Protection Officer Thilo Weichert (formerly Head of the Independent Centre for Privacy Protection) because they transfer personal data into the United States without the user's consent. Absurdities of this kind are piling up, and the reason is the lack of a structured data market. In contrast to the regulation of world trade, including the elimination of tolls and the establishment of double taxation treaties, no equivalent exists for this ensemble of technologies of power in the data market. But social networks are 'administrative apparatuses' of the digital world. Hence, the real world and their economy, in actual fact, is the economy of attention. It is this economy that needs to be politically structured and, eventually, regulated.

It stands to reason therefore that politics today means aligning everything in such a way that the economy works. The conflict between privacy advocates and modern information processing runs along these lines: the latter is a prerequisite for the modern economy; the former is being seen as an economic impediment. From this pertinent perspective, data protection appears as critique of capitalism. Essentially, capitalism and data protection are diametrically opposed and, for now, it seems that the social networks have won. In addition, it can be seen that capitalism has entered the most delicate ramifications of the soul – the subject voluntarily charts their identity by mapping these ramifications into databases, driven by the urge not to be forgotten, and by the desire to resonate. This behaviour, inevitably, will change the not-yet-designed 'data market' to an identity market, in which subjects, in due course, are objects as well: that is to say, they do not only trade, but are also being traded.

Instead of limiting data transfer, as governments try to today, they will be forced to establish an economy of identities, using the economy of money as a blueprint. But this will be difficult since, in contrast to privacy advocates, private individuals have understood that even though data is a currency, its nature is different from that of money: some data, for instance, is more valuable the more widespread it is. This data creates added value to the soul in Franck's sense. Sharing of personal or even private data is a crucial technology of a subject's identity construction. Radical privacy advocates do not understand why individuals spend their data lightly. They do not believe that it is a good investment.

Attempts to educate users as to the benefits of 'data austerity' did not succeed. Individuals spend their data generously for the immediate return of attention.

Although the economy of data may have similarities to that of money, the consequences are quite different: for example, if I am too generous with money, I am poor at the end. However, if I am generous with data, I get attention. A liberal data market would reflect this and help regulate it. In contrast, any attempts to regulate the data market by keeping its currency 'data' scarce will fail for as long as individuals do not value their personal data as they value money. Basically, this asymmetrical valuation of personal data is Facebook's arbitrage.

Archiving the self

The exposure of one's activities through social networks does not only affect the immediate perception of the self through resonating with the other. It also builds an archive of the past, being one that remains available for later reference. Thereby, the self encounters itself through the mirror of its past activities – the ground-breaking effect of this enhanced sense of self surpasses the recording of real-life events, as became possible with the advent of handheld video cameras, and other technological developments in the late twentieth century. The user does not only have partial outtakes of their life, but a chronological timeline that reflects their behaviour and experience in different aspects – friendships they made, comments they received, content they shared, pictures and videos they were tagged in, places they had been, articles and other content they had read, companies for which they worked, projects done, products, companies, celebrities and other stuff that they liked, events that they had attended, and many more to come.

All of these entries refer to other content, as well as other people, and can be expanded infinitely. A user's life – or at least the increasing part of their life that is reflected online – rolls out like a map in front of them. This map is inter-stratified with economic interests, with targeted advertising and brands, companies and products that integrate seamlessly into the so-called stream of the user's history. The former personal memories are externalised and much more precise, reliable and comprehensive than is possible through personal recollection alone. Yet, at the same time, it is corrupted by commercial means. The life of a user becomes a collection of already structured and weighted entries, and thereby the user sees their own self as that of another – they have the same perspective of their online existence as do their contacts who can view the same content. Thus, a user gains a supposedly holistic view of their life in the same way they view the life of others. By instantaneous archiving of the user's existence, essentially, the self becomes the other in an externalised memory, doing so by projecting their identity on the templates of the social media services in use.

Attention as apparatus

It is an appropriate time to ponder. Do we remember a society that was not online? Are we able to make appointments outside of the services that provide access to our contacts? Would we remember the birthdays of our friends if we weren't constantly reminded through pop-ups and notifications? What were the conditions of 'staying in touch' before it was automated? Do we unlearn to make a simple phone call to keep up with what another person is doing? What happens to the people that are no longer in our online circles? Do they really cease to exist? Are we able to emancipate ourselves from our online existence and lead an offline life? Do we need to log our important events in order to remember them? Has the automated archive replaced our personal memory? Every technological evolution leads to the oblivion of ancient practices by offering an apparently more promising and efficient way of solving problems and fulfilling needs.

Clearly, social networks normalise identities and make them consumable. The notion of the media becoming an apparatus (or 'dispositif') in Foucault's sense is underlined by every 'Like' button integrated, by every tracking pixel placed on websites all over the world. A 'Facebook revolution' can only come into existence by overcoming these specific mechanisms.

Data protectionists try to protect consumers from data-processing corporations, which is what social networks are. But all they do is set up yet another apparatus to patronise individuals: the noble notion of privacy today holds as much water as do appeals of Christian churches to stop the commercialisation of Christmas. Individuals have long been governing themselves by way of the gentle means of default interfaces that structure their social life. Instead of remaining private, they trade themselves – and each other – in an economy of attention.

Social networking has transformed the subject into an object, which is being constructed and deconstructed, based on the way that it is traded, and by confronting the self with its otherness. The arrival of social networking, in this sense, might be capitalism's finest hour.

As inferred earlier by way of a probing question upon which to reflect, it is hard to imagine a way back to an 'offline sociality' that successfully deprives itself of aforementioned economic mechanisms. Also, one might doubt if the once-offline sociality really is a goal towards which one should aim. In the end, social networks provide sociality for deprived individuals, whether all situated locally, or scattered across the globe. These evolving networks provide resonance for individuals who are disconnected from their peers in real life. The social networks upon which we have focused provide solace for the lonely, give comfort for the needy and offer feedback for the insecure. But although social networks provide all these utopian promises, one should become aware of one's own economic potential. In other words, living up to the requirements of the economics of attention means knowing one's value. So it is that the obstructive, naturalising metaphors must give way to the economic underpinnings of today's sociality. There is a price to pay, and you had better know how much it is.

There is no doubt that the defaults of sociality have changed, as have the conditions of self-perception. Social networks change the default of our sociality. Still, not being there is not an option.

A service-oriented approach to public sector social media strategy

Marshall Sitten

Abstract: Organisations that employ a marketing-driven, broadcast-oriented communications strategy have chosen a path of minimum relative risk. However, organisations that actively impel a service-oriented approach to social media will achieve a higher level of engagement. Even so, it must be understood that there are important risk factors to consider when executing a social media strategy, just as there are issues that must be addressed. From related experience in the provision of strategic and operational advice, it is apparent and necessary for organisations, especially those in the public, not-for-profit and social sectors, to plan for a service-oriented approach. Also, this must be implemented with diligence and dedication to ensure that each organisation gains the necessary benefits of proper communications. In addition, possible problems must be foreseen, and addressed with proper remedies to ensure that that the 'voice' of an organisation has enough capacity to do well in the all-important job of interacting with a growing, demanding and giving online community.

Key words: social media, service orientation, public sector, strategy, organisations, communications, online community, not for profit, customer satisfaction, competitive advantage, service science, platforms, tools, audience, risk, resources, research, posting, curating, community management, campaign, measurement.

Introduction

Quite rapidly, social media has become an essential part of the communications toolkit for private sector companies of all sizes, from local restaurants and boutiques to large multinational corporations: Facebook for customer engagement; Twitter for announcements and PR; Groupon and Foursquare for deals and location-based services... the list goes on. Basically, the managers and drivers of brands have learned how to adapt their existing communications efforts – previously unidirectional, broadcast-oriented campaigns – into sophisticated, long-term engagement strategies that can improve customer satisfaction, increase sales and offer a significant competitive advantage.

For public sector and non-profit organisations, however, social media can prove to be a much more difficult tool to adopt. Limited resources, in terms of time, money and knowledgeable staff, can severely hamper an organisation's ability to create and execute a proper and effective social media campaign. In addition, political obstacles, conflicting organisational priorities and excessive risk aversion can stand in the way of developing a coherent communications strategy. Since it is much more difficult to measure the progress of a public sector organisation's communications goals (such as increasing issue awareness, changing constituent behaviours and raising more funds from individual donors) compared to those of a private sector company (such as increasing sales, improving market positioning and influencing brand perception), public sector organisations have a much more difficult time in justifying the necessary investment in social media, particularly given the aforementioned severe resource constraints.

Despite these challenges, it is clear that there is no longer a question of 'if' public sector organisations should begin using social media – it is only a question of 'how'. Organisations like UNICEF, Amnesty International and others have established a powerful presence on Facebook and Twitter, and have been able to engage with new audiences in ways that were not possible in the days before social media; but success of this kind requires more than just a Facebook account, a Twitter feed and an energetic college intern or two. Communications success of this type requires a new approach to communications thinking.

At Flashing12 Communications, we advise non-profit organisations, public sector organisations and United Nations agencies on how to use social media and other technologies as part of an overall communications strategy. Often, we have been called upon to assist organisations that are just starting to embrace social media for the first time, or are struggling with adapting social media into existing communications infrastructure. Regardless of the size, sector or focus of these organisations, we are frequently asked the same three questions (or some variant thereof) by client organisations that are expanding their use of social media. Specifically:

1. What social media platforms or tools should we be using?
2. How much do we need to commit, in terms of risk and resources?
3. How do we measure success?

Our approach to answering these questions is heavily informed by a practice known as *service science*, an interdisciplinary, human-centred method for designing and improving services. Since social media platforms differ from traditional communications tools in their dependence upon direct and indirect interaction with friends, followers and constituents, the use of these platforms more closely resembles a service interaction than a broadcast medium. Consider that social media-based audiences no longer respond to blunt-force pleas for donations via Facebook, nor are they as likely to respond to a call to action simply because it arrives in their Twitter feed. Users are demanding more reciprocal relationships with the groups to which they subscribe, and seek two-way interactions that provide them with value.

According to Professor Emmanuel Fragniere, of HEG Geneva's Service Lab, the key component of the service relationship is the notion of 'co-production', with this being the process through which both the service provider and the service consumer work together to create value. For example, the expertise and experience of the travel agent is combined with the desires and preferences of the vacationer to create the perfect holiday getaway. A similar principle applies to the use of social media by organisations: by providing something of value to the user (whether it is expertise, information, or some other tangible or intangible offering), the user is more likely to increase their responsiveness to, and connection with, the organisation.

We will attempt to illustrate this method by applying our service-oriented approach to answer the three questions stated above.

What social media platforms or tools should our organisation be using?

When we discuss the adoption of social media platforms with our clients, often we find ourselves talking about the so-called 'big names' – Facebook, Twitter and YouTube – and then moving on quite quickly to how (not whether) to adopt those platforms. Many organisations rush to assume that participation in these platforms is both necessary and desirable and, in the process, often ignore the smaller platforms, such as Quora, Pinterest, Google+ and others, while committing themselves to unsuccessful or even damaging efforts on the larger networks. Frequently, this reflects platform-centric thinking that works backwards from identifying social media tools that are successful for other organisations with different audiences. As should stand to reason, this approach might not meet the needs and preferences of their own followers.

A service-oriented approach to social media assumes that a key part of the organisation's strategic priorities is to provide value to its audience. With this assumption in mind, the most important questions to ask, in the first instance, when choosing what platforms to adopt are:

1. Who are we, and what do we want to achieve?
2. Who is our audience, and what do they want?
3. What do we have to offer our audience?

We will look at the three questions and address each one below.

Who are we, and what do we want to achieve?

Hopefully, this first question can be answered by the organisation's own mission and vision statements. Social media will offer little help to an organisation that lacks a clear vision or a coherent organisational strategy. But this question is worth revisiting during this process – possibly by way of a formal communications audit – as it will offer the organisation an opportunity to reflect on whether its existing communications infrastructure serves its mission and strategy, and whether any internal adjustments need to be made before proceeding to a new way of doing things.

Who is our audience, and what do they want?

Usually, there is a gap between what managers of an organisation think they know about their audience, and what is actual and true. In the old days of primarily unidirectional, broadcast-style communications (for instance, printed mailings, TV and radio advertising, online ads and email blasts), organisations could be somewhat forgiven for falling out of touch with who their audiences are, and how they live. But in a landscape where competition is fierce – whether for gaining attention, engagement or donations – organisations can no longer afford to make false assumptions about the very people that they are trying to reach. This is to say that taking a 'megaphone' approach to reaching core audiences is problematic in modern times.

Essentially, effective use of social media demands an approach that is based on co-production in bringing together the needs and goals of the organisation with those of the organisation's constituents so as to create value for both parties. As suggested earlier, few organisations – particularly in the non-profit, social or public sectors – have sufficient resources to make use all of the major social media platforms aggressively and comprehensively. Furthermore, to do so blindly – without knowing what platforms are the best fit for their organisation and their membership – could prove to be a waste of time and manpower.

So how does an organisation learn more about its audience? Constituent research is not a task that can be done once, then checked off the 'to do' list; it is a continuous process, and very much a way for an organisation to check in with its membership periodically. It is also a process that has both quantitative and qualitative components, and that uses both formal and informal techniques. Consider the most basic – yet still very effective – components of a constituent research effort. Three simple queries need to be considered, as follows.

Who they are

What does the organisation know about the most basic demographic characteristics of its membership? Age, gender, geographic location, job sector, job position, interests and years involved with a current issue are just some of the vital details that can help to shape a social media strategy. This information can be gleaned from new member registrations, website sign-up forms, event registrations or even surveys. Questions should be simple, straightforward, and return facts as answers, rather than receive opinions.

What they think

Reaching out for the opinions, suggestions and even criticisms from membership can be a painful task. Even so, it is absolutely necessary to do so (in this regard, Best Buy CEO Brian Dunn recently referred to feedback as 'a gift you don't always care to open'). Website polls, email surveys, and 'man on the street' survey research at events and other gatherings can offer key insights into what the organisation's constituency cares about. This form of feedback can alert the organisation's leadership to upcoming trends or burgeoning threats. Best of all, the simple act of asking these questions lets the audience know that the organisation cares to hear the answers.

What they do

How many new members registered this year compared to last year? How many of these new registrations were the result of referrals from existing members? How much money was raised this year? How many new visits were there to the website? Did any of them check out the news alert page that was set up? There are several measureable indicators of member behaviour, some which require no more than Google Analytics, Hootsuite or other web dashboard software. Some types of metrics require a little more spreadsheet digging, but the chances are that organisations have a great amount of useful information lying around that can describe what its members actually *do*, regardless of what they may say they do or say that they want to do.

Once an organisation has explored at least these three types of information about its members, it can ask (and hopefully begin to answer) more meaningful questions about how it can best serve its members by using social media. Analysing cross-sections of the collected data can reveal opportunities for expanding into new social media platforms, or abandoning platforms that aren't producing results – for example, surveys that suggest a demand for a mobile app combined with weak Facebook traffic data. Collecting and analysing information over time can reveal trends or patterns, or show the effects of particular campaigns or one-time phenomena. To provide additional context, conducting short, semi-directed interviews with individual constituents can offer different – and sometimes deeper – levels of insight into how, when and why an individual member interacts with the organisation.

When any entity takes the time to learn more about its user base, it has a much better idea of what tools and platforms to deploy. If the audience wants – and can commit to – a high level of engagement and interactivity, then Facebook might be the right call. If the organisation's membership is interested in curated photo content, then Pinterest might be a better use of resources. However, if a constituency looks to the organisation for breaking updates on a particular issue or service, then Twitter may be the best choice. Consider the case where one of our United Nations clients discovered that the reason a particular social media campaign in Ukraine was failing to achieve results was that the target audience had very little access to the Internet via computers and, instead, used mostly mobile phones and SMS messaging. Basically, without knowing who the audience is, and what they want, organisations run the risk of making costly, wasteful assumptions that will have a negative effect on critical decisions.

What do we have to offer our audience?

When organisations first begin to embrace social media, the temptation is extremely strong to use these tools purely as a way to mobilise audiences and 'get them to do things'. Share with your friends! Retweet this to your followers! Give money! Post your own photos from last week's rally! 'Like' us! This type of behaviour reflects the leftovers of broadcast thinking – for example, send them flyers, email newsletters, as well as calls-to-action, and hopefully they'll react. In stark contrast, a service-oriented approach to social media forces organisations to look beyond a loudspeaker-and-audience model to one of genuine give and take, and thereby authentic engagement through the generation of shared value.

In addition, once an organisation has taken the time to learn about its audiences, it can then look back over its assets to see how it might be able to provide value to its audience through using social media. Often, its audience is composed of various different stakeholder groups, sometimes with wildly varying interests; knowing what these interests are, and what content your organisation has to offer to each, is the key to selecting the right social media tools for the job.

Of course, it is not always that simple. There can be structural, political or organisational obstacles to providing certain kinds of content to constituents. For example, one of our clients, a Geneva-based United Nations agency, had rolled out its Facebook page and Twitter feed shortly before hiring us, having not had much of an idea beforehand of how these new tools were to be used. The organisation was feeling pressure to establish a presence on these platforms. However, there was no existing strategy, or formal policy, for how to proceed – nor was any new staff capacity allocated for the task. The job of setting up and maintaining these streams was laid at the feet of those who already had a full range of other responsibilities within the communications department.

When we began working with the people at that agency to develop a strategy for making the most out of the new platforms for community engagement, we learned that their personnel faced a major obstacle: They were forbidden from retweeting, reposting or sharing any content that did not originate with (or was not solicited by) the United Nations. This meant that one of the key advantages to social media – indeed, a key part of the 'social' nature of social media itself – was off-limits to them. Clearly, this restricted the use of their Twitter feed to that of a loudspeaker with which they could 'announce things' and 'denounce things', but really very little else could be done with that medium.

With the set of assets and limitations uncovered in the process of our review, Facebook seemed to offer a more appropriate set of options. In order to work around the most significant obstacle, we looked carefully at who comprised their existing user base on Facebook, and what they were doing. We found that most were silent, and not very involved. But an active minority was posting personal stories, questions and opinions related to first-hand experiences with human rights and discrimination around the world. These members were looking to the organisation, not just for things like announcements and press releases, but for answers and expertise – with these being two things that this particular UN organisation was uniquely positioned to provide. Accordingly, our final recommendation was for the organisation to focus primarily on Facebook, as well as to give their audience access to the entity's vast store of knowledge and expertise in pertinent issues through scheduled Facebook Q&A sessions with UN experts, through themed awareness campaigns, and also through the periodic posting of case studies, plus stories, that prompted real discussion and engagement.

What do we need to commit to, in terms of risk and resources?

The costs of running a social media campaign, comically, are almost lopsided. For instance, it costs literally nothing to create a Twitter, Facebook, YouTube or any other kind of social media account and begin posting. It also costs nothing to envision a grand social media 'strategy' consisting of a coordinated network of Twitter feeds, Facebook pages, blogs and user-submitted video galleries, with all of these components powered by a few energetic (and unpaid) interns and loyal volunteers who do the work of posting, tweeting, curating content and managing the small empire of online communities.

This utopian notion of a cheap, sustainable social media strategy is corrected by the high cost of labour and risk associated with deploying a sustainable social media engagement strategy. The benefits of using social media for communications are fairly clear: broaden it to reach new audiences, to deepen relationships with existing audiences, to wage campaigns and to respond quickly to events, as well as to raise funds in ways that were never possible before with traditional media channels. However, the tradeoffs are less easy to calculate, and can carry much greater consequences for the organisation. For instance, just witness the landscape of half-abandoned Facebook pages, dormant Twitter feeds and campaigns-gone-wrong that ended up costing more in damage control than any benefit that any of these vehicles could have offered.

Without a doubt, organisations should think about the costs and risks of expansion into greater social media engagement as though designing a service, rather than as rolling out an additional, simple communications campaign. This is because social media creates complex relationships and interactions between the organisation and its audiences, which is the very benefit, and also the danger, of using it. Consider, here, how posted content provokes reactions, produces unexpected consequences and generates network effects that can incur costs and outcomes for the organisation far beyond what was ever planned at the beginning of a campaign.

Resources – knowing what it costs to get what you want

What does it take to run a Facebook page or a Twitter feed? How much time, how many people and what kinds of skills are required to run a crowd-sourced fund-raising drive or an online contest? Every organisation, every campaign and every set of tools used requires a different level of allocation of time and manpower.

While there is no easy back-of-the-napkin calculation, it is at least possible to describe and discuss some of the different – and most essential – lines of work that are involved in various levels of social media implementation in order to offer a rough estimate of the minimum amount of capacity required to do so.

Research and monitoring

Social media is a powerful research tool; for issue-based advocacy organisations, it is essential to keep abreast of trending topics and influential contributors via Twitter, to monitor discussions on Quora or to follow the comment threads of similar (or opposing) organisations on Facebook. Social media monitoring via tools such as TweetDeck, Radian6 and HootSuite can serve as an important feedback mechanism that offers a glimpse into the things that people are saying about your organisation, the effectiveness of your ongoing campaigns, and the current events and discussions relevant to the issues about which you care.

Just as an individual might punctuate the work day by scanning headlines of news websites, organisations should periodically browse through and search social media sites in order to identify the leading topics and influencers in their particular sector. In addition, an organisation should continuously monitor the progress and feedback of its own currently running campaigns, and analyse web traffic and the click-through rates of posted links and ads, as well as measure the relative uptake and distribution of the organisation's own content by other users or organisations.

It must be said that the task of monitoring and researching social feeds belongs to everyone with a communications responsibility and function within an organisation, as it should also belong to anyone holding a senior management position. The reality, unfortunately, is that much of the monitoring work is tasked to just a few individuals (or even just one person) who, usually, is or are the same individual(s) responsible for maintaining the rest of the social media functions. That can lead to obvious overload, and ineffective outcomes.

Posting and curating

The second most basic social media functions include posting new content and curating new or existing content. Virtually everyone reading this chapter has published at least one piece of content to at least one social media platform – be it a comment, a blog entry, a tweet or a Facebook posting – so we do not need to spend much time on the particulars here. Still, it is important to consider that in most organisations, posting a single piece of content usually means following up with cross-postings on other social media platforms. For example, an announcement about a major event would need to be posted on Twitter, Facebook and the organisation's blog. This can be facilitated – and, to some degree, automated – through the use of social dashboards like HootSuite. Even so, effort still needs to be put into packaging the content for each of the targeted media.

Content strategy and curating, however, is how organisations apply service thinking to what, otherwise, would be flat delivery of compiled content. Suppose that you are the social media manager for an animal rights organisation. You represent a variety of different stakeholders, including veterinarians, pet owners, animal control workers and public health officials (not to mention the animals themselves!). Your organisation compiles a variety of content types, including research, photographs, case studies, videos and opinion essays, with these being original and collected from other sources. If all of this content was simply published to the web and social media in the order that it was released (which is generally how blogs work), it would lack context, priority or any of the added value that comes from meaningful filtration. In comparison, newspaper publishers curate news stories so that the most important events of the day are located at the very beginning of the publication; the rest of the stories are also curated meaningfully into sections that are easily located by the reader. Content curating for social media works along the same principle and is the process through which organisations apply their expertise and implicit knowledge, via social media, as a service to their audiences. (Note that two very useful resources for learning about content curating strategies are Beth Kanter's excellent blog (*www.bethkanter.org*) and the book *Essentials of Content Strategy* by Erin Kissane.)

Both content publication and curating require time and talent. While most people are able to learn how to post content to social media platforms, effective content curating requires a highly organised person with at least a basic understanding of content strategy. Once started, the process of content curating itself is an ongoing process linked to publication that requires little additional effort. Even so, the process of developing the initial content strategy that will guide the principles of curating (what types of content the organisation is interested in posting, how it is organised and displayed, and the rough editorial schedule) is periodic and can take days, or even weeks, at a time.

Community management

So, your organisation has a well-organised set of social media channels, a blog and even a mobile app. You have decided on a content strategy, and have started posting content. Now what? If your organisation is taking a broadcast-only approach to social media, posting content and moving on to the next item, then there's not much else to discuss – it is a low-input, low-output approach that is likely to yield a relatively low level of engagement. But if your organisation is interested in deepening engagement with its audiences, and broadening its reach, then additional effort must be spent on interacting with the communities that it has created on social media platforms.

One of our clients, an international NGO focused on early childhood education, had recently received survey feedback stating that its membership was looking for more interactivity from the organisation's social efforts than was provided just by press releases and fund-raising appeals. In moving the efforts of this entity towards a more service-oriented approach, we slowed down their editorial calendar slightly, and gave their social media coordinator enough time to go back over the comments and activity from earlier postings. Then the coordinator began acting as an intermediary for audience Q&A, seeking expertise from her colleagues, and responding to user questions and comments as the 'voice' of the organisation. This led to much more active discussions and participation by existing members, and even led to more of the organisation's postings, tweets and blog articles being shared with non-members than had ever occurred in the past.

Community management can be every bit as resource-intensive as new content creation. Still, it can also be every bit as important. When there are so many automated news readers and content aggregators out there, why spend time going to an organisation's Facebook page? The difference is in the notion of added value, of interactivity and participation. In a word, it is all to do with service.

Crowd-sourcing, contests, apps and other campaigns

Thus far, we have not explored an exhaustive list of activities – far from it. There are many other ways of deploying social media that are well beyond what was mentioned above. Many of these other tactics – such as video streaming, online crowd-sourcing, Facebook and mobile application design, to name a few – require expertise and commitment beyond that which most organisations in the public and social sectors can be expected to maintain internally. But since events, campaigns and crises do occur, it is important to plan and budget ahead of time for when that kind of competency and capacity are needed.

Risk – understanding the tradeoffs of social media

At Flashing12, generally, we are of the opinion that for organisations employing social media, more commitment to engaging with the public is better than less. Of course, there are exceptions, but we believe that the more users feel they are obtaining something of unique value from the organisations they support, the more authentic and stronger is their attachment to those organisations. Nevertheless, the benefits of engaging with the public come bundled with some very real risks, and it is critically important that organisations understand and accept those risks prior to proceeding.

Organisations that employ a marketing-driven, broadcast-oriented communications strategy have chosen a path of minimum relative risk (assuming the organisation itself is relatively non-controversial). The organisation creates all of its own marketing materials, and is able to control its message more tightly. It can choose not to respond to controversy by refusing press conferences or declining to give interviews. It does not have to defend itself in its marketing materials.

On the other hand, organisations that engage actively in a service-oriented approach to implementing social media are exposed to a far wider set of risks in exchange for a much higher level of engagement. For instance, think about the fact that disparaging or even slanderous comments can be left on the organisation's Facebook page. Also, discussions among commenters, or contributors, can spiral out of control and cross over into other media, and even into the mainstream press. It could take only a single misstatement or misconstrued remark made by the organisation on one of its social feeds to spark coordinated campaigns by angry members. You can imagine that an angry, torch-wielding Facebook mob can result in irreparable damage to an organisation's reputation.

A few rules of the game are as follows:

- Some people are not going to like you (nor 'Like' you).
- Eventually, you will be misunderstood, and that's OK.
- Control is something you have already decided to give up.

One of the first risks that an organisation must accept when entering the social media ecosystem is that, with each layer of interactivity allowed by the digital world, an organisation must relinquish an additional level of control. For example, one of our clients was struggling with a Wikipedia page that it had set up to address an extremely controversial matter of international political affairs. Wikipedia benefits from its strong brand recognition, search-friendly design and huge user base. However, as the name suggests, it is a wiki and user-fed, and is particularly vulnerable to acts of vandalism, as well as other unproductive mischief. In this particular case, our client's page was repeatedly altered by someone who had a specific political agenda to include factually incorrect assertions and inflammatory rhetoric. Thereby, the organisation's goal of publishing its content on something that was deemed to be social 'neutral territory' was subverted by the very attributes which drew them to use Wikipedia as a platform in the first place.

Another major risk factor to consider is how to handle online feedback. It is easy to handle positive feedback (when we're lucky enough to receive it). Yet what about criticisms? What about accusations? In some cases, answering an angry commenter can show that the organisation is willing to listen to its users, to collaborate and even to admit fault, if at all necessary. In other cases, responding to a comment, or providing too much information, can feed a fire instead of extinguishing it. Some consumer brands, such as the online shoe retailer Zappos.com, has a policy of attempting to answer and resolve every comment or question on its Facebook page, and doing so regardless of how negative (or even incoherent) the feedback might be. This gives its customer base the constant and strong feeling that the Facebook page is a real service community and one that is truly customer-focused. Other organisations, such as political and advocacy associations, might see excessive risk in responding to user comments – and, in some cases, might shut down commenting altogether to prevent the spread of damaging narratives or coordinated campaigns by any related opposition.

With the Internet, social media traffic moves at a blindingly fast pace. A bad story or opposing campaign can gain steam almost instantly; so, too, does the temptation to respond with equal speed, as there can be an overwhelming urge to do something. Even so, responding too quickly to a threatening trend on Twitter or other social platforms can be just as dangerous as responding too slowly, and if an organisation does not have a policy in place for dealing with an online media crisis, it can find itself saying exactly the wrong thing at exactly the wrong time. It is for this very reason that, in order to prepare for the unexpected, organisations should establish a proper chain of command for crisis communications, which determines who is responsible for the nature and the timing of any necessary responses. This chain should include senior communications personnel, or other managers who also have a good understanding of how social media actually works – and not just people who are skilled at spin.

Three things to remember when it's already gone bad are:

1. choose carefully (words, friends, content);
2. take a deep breath before responding; and
3. be honest, and be human.

Finally, one of the most important risk factors to consider when executing a social media strategy is who the organisation chooses to manage their social media platforms. Is it the unpaid intern, here only for the summer? Is it the already-overwhelmed communications and marketing staff? Is it an external consultant? It can be forgotten that the social media outlets used by an organisation become the voice of the organisation itself. So choosing the right people is a critical layer of risk management. Given that most people can learn how to use social media tools in a short period of time, it is not essential for a social media manager to be tech-obsessed. Still, it is very important to select someone with good writing skills, good analytical ability, a strong level of Internet awareness and (most importantly) good judgement. They should understand the character and values of their organisation, and be able to engage users as its 'voice'. They should have a sensitivity to emerging trends, and be self-directed enough to research opportunities so as to increase the influence of the organisation, and the level of engagement with its stakeholders. Additionally, and essentially, the organisation should make sure that its 'voice' has enough capacity to do well the all-important job of interacting with a growing and demanding online community.

How do we measure success?

By now, we have addressed thoroughly the notion that engaging in a social media strategy (particularly one that is service-based) requires a significant commitment of resources, such as those related to time, labour and risk. Naturally, the first question that most organisations raise after getting started comes out as something like, 'Is it worth it?'

For businesses, the question of the return on investment (ROI) in social media is more easily answered than for public and social sector organisations. For instance, ROI is calculated by measuring how well social media activity is in converting online behaviour into tangible sales and increased customer loyalty. This can, to a degree, be tracked to specific online campaigns and content. For example, a retailer that publishes a special code for a promotional rate on their Twitter feed and Facebook page can use the code itself, or a specially coded link, to track how many people used that code, and how they arrived at the purchase page. This allows the effectiveness of campaigns to be measured.

Social and public sector organisations do not have this luxury. How are organisations that are dedicated to influencing behaviours, increasing awareness or changing public policy supposed to measure the real impact of their social media campaigns? Unfortunately, many organisations decide to focus too much on the available metrics – such as page views, visitors, 'Likes', retweets and so on – as a way of determining success. These metrics only offer a very shallow view of user activity, and yield very little insight into whether the campaigns are achieving any actual success. Worse still, focusing excessively on Klout (*klout.com*) scores, numbers of followers and other metrics can create a poisonous set of incentives that lead to chasing numbers for their own sake, sometimes at the expense of the organisation's reputation or credibility. For example, in 2011, Microsoft Corporation received an extremely negative reaction when it pledged to donate $1 to victims of the Japanese earthquake and tsunami crisis for each time that a tweet from its Bing search engine was retweeted. This kind of thing happens when organisations focus more on simple metrics than on a holistic, service-oriented view of user relationships.

Instead, when engaging in a service-oriented approach to social media, the focus should be on a more qualitative analysis of the relationships that the organisation has with the users themselves. What is the interactivity like with the users? Are they commenting and retweeting? What are they saying? Is user activity generally linear in nature, steady and consistent? Or does it appear to coincide with events or certain types of content updates? What do users think? (Again, surveys and open-ended questions help here.) Have donation drives and calls-to-action been more or less successful over time? This kind of assessment model is less formal, less data-driven and less scientific. But it reflects a trial-and-error approach that is more in line with the service provider relationship – one that is human, customised and often inconsistent – than anything to do with an industrialised model that regards people as machines.

Conclusion

In summary, we are far along the path of accepting that social media has potential benefits for organisations, including any that operate for the benefit of the general populace, or the folk who are disenfranchised, downtrodden or damaged in some way, of which there are far too many in each instance, and more besides.

For public, not-for-profit and social sector organisations that strive to achieve their worthy objectives, and thus give something to the community that they aim to serve, as well as that with which it is engaged on a much broader front, it is vital that the related communications strategy is strong. Social media tools are the unavoidable key to giving any organisation the means to do so, and to know that it can make its voice heard above the hum, mumblings and noises that invade modern life.

Based on solid experience of users, it must be said that organisations engaging actively in social media through the use of a service-oriented approach will fulfil their worthy ambitions more so than can be achieved otherwise.

6

Social media in the humanitarian space

Claudia Gonzalez and Alan Rosenblatt

Abstract: When any individual or entity engages in activities for the benefit of social good, it is beneficial to use social media tools. Greater integration, especially among like-minded entities, increases information flow, as well as the global visibility of critical issues. Humanitarian missions, thereby, become more effective. This chapter provides clear guidance for communications and promotions personnel who are engaged with resolving humanitarian issues. In addition, lessons learned indicate the need for more thought in relation to engaging with the broader audience through the use of social media. This applies as much to connecting at the grass-roots level in areas requiring assistance as it does to the general public that has the capacity to provide needed support and funds. Of particular importance is for organisations in the humanitarian space to be true to their own identity before exploring ways of communicating anything to the world at large. In addition, a strategic approach to social media usage allows for direct and effective interaction with individuals and communities all over the world.

Key words: social media, humanitarian space, social good, communities, non-government organisation, civil society, networking, World Economic Forum, evolution of social media, Hindenburg, Global Fund to Fight AIDS, Tuberculosis and Malaria, Born HIV Free campaign, prevention of HIV from mother to child, World AIDS Day, civic mobilisation, crisis response, best practices.

Introduction

The definition of what exactly encompasses the so-called 'humanitarian sphere' has become blurry due to different approaches taken by related stakeholders. A specialised perspective would differentiate between what falls within the humanitarian field and that of the development sector. However, for the purpose of this chapter we will follow a more general interpretation of what is the 'humanitarian sphere', with this deemed to be the delivery of services and advocacy from individuals and organisations towards a social good.

Furthermore, although we might find diverse individuals and organisations that play a part in creating and maintaining the humanitarian sphere, in this chapter, we will focus on those that we consider are key participants, particularly in the communication process. These include media, civil society, governments and non-governmental organisations.

Governments, traditionally, as donors and recipients, are main actors in the humanitarian sphere, followed by various non-government organisations (NGOs) that emerged with specific humanitarian missions, as well as with the intention to tackle various issues more effectively and with a global perspective. Their non-governmental status helps these entities serve humanitarian needs in an otherwise politicised conflict area.

Nowadays, civil society has become a significant focus, and the NGOs promoting civil society are playing an increasingly significant role, especially given the introduction of new technologies that overcome barriers of distance and time, thereby allowing for more immediate communication, mobilisation and organisation. This has also expanded the role of the media – even what constitutes the 'media' – as an important participant that now goes beyond reporting, and on to influencing the different players, as well as creating a dynamic relationship.

Networking offline and online

The notion of connecting

In order to have a positive outcome when delivering social good, it is crucial that there is an effective relationship between all the players within the humanitarian sphere. This connection between individuals and organisations creates communities formed around a common goal. Therefore, enhancing the flow of information across the globe to allied organisations, and similarly aligned individuals, offers ever-greater opportunities to create robust humanitarian efforts that are sustainable and, perhaps, even achieving related outcomes with less resources than were required in the past.

With the emergence of social media technology, robust networking is possible today and more than ever. Once, traditional offline networks were limited to relatively small geographic regions, utilising sporadic and narrow-bandwidth interactions with allies across the globe. Now, social media technology is creating long and wide bridges that enable a constant flow of communication from offline communities to online communities, and back again. As a direct result, communities are larger, fewer of them feel isolated, and more resources are able to flow throughout these social webs.

Among the implications of this deeper and wider social graph, knitting the humanitarian world together is generating greater global attention in relation to a wider range of humanitarian concerns. Historically, concerns for a humanitarian crisis in one country would capture the world's attention, while similar crises in neighbouring nations were left unattended. Today, we can easily see and tie together the plight of several countries that share the same predicament. By doing so, we can keep the full scope of the associated crises in front of the global audience. Thus, issues of genocide in Sudan lay the foundation for a global awareness and mobilisation for combating genocide across the African continent, instead of just focusing on Sudan.

Even where global communities are forming to address a single crisis, communities doing the same to address similar crises in other countries quite easily and naturally connect with each other. This sense of an integrated, global community allows for greater information sharing and, thus, facilitates the development and delivery of more effective solutions to the humanitarian issues at hand.

Also, within the world of social media technology, we see the benefits of these meta-integrations. In the early days of social media, different countries and regions embraced different social media platforms, furthering the separateness of the communities addressing humanitarian concerns within those countries and regions. In recent years, the combination of cross-social media platform integration, and the growth of mega-social networks (e.g. Facebook), is breaking down organisational and communal silos online as well as offline.

Clearly, greater interconnection leads to positive outcomes. While Facebook quickly approaches a billion users, that application (as well as other social network platforms, and even ordinary websites) is developing

they were able to spread related details via word of mouth. But in those days, literally, word of mouth was the process of people talking to each other. Today, once people hear a story of such great import or even of no import at all, they are able to use social media technology as their own personal broadcast channel to spread the word-of-mouth message to their networks online. In essence, every member of the audience has become a potential re-broadcaster. Also, unlike the days of radio, the buzz about a story bounces back and forth in a multitude of simultaneous conversations, rather than just a stream of one-way transmissions.

With each generation of new communications-related technology, obstacles to building global communities around humanitarian issues stop working. Early breakthroughs in broadcast technology (such as radio and television) not only overcame the barriers of time and distance, but, because these vehicles had massive penetration into the home, the delivered information was pushed into everyone's living room.

Telephones added the ability for people to share information with their friends interactively, albeit via one-to-one conversations. With the advent of email, individuals were able to share with larger groups of people the information that they had acquired and do so on an interactive and simultaneous basis. Essentially, both telephones and email have enhanced the ability of individuals and organisations to share information with more people, thereby engaging audiences in the conversation; but both methods of communication were fundamentally limited to closed networks. For instance, conversations via phone and email can only take place among people who are already connected to each other. Also, that conversation takes place in a private space.

Social media changes all of that. Social media applications allow people to share information that they acquire with larger personal networks than was possible via email, and certainly via phone. Yet the sharing takes place in a very public space. Conversations once held in the private sphere are held in such a vast public domain that Jürgen Habermas, the German sociologist and philosopher who is best known for his theory on the concepts of 'communicative rationality' and the 'public sphere', must be smiling. Certainly, Twitter, Facebook, Google+ and a host of other social media spaces play host to conversations that can become global in an instant.

For the humanitarian space, development social communications and that of social media in particular means the world can learn about crises as they are happening. Plus, it means that humanitarian crises need no longer happen in isolation. Crises of hunger, drought and disease do not need to be seen as crises with borders. Against this enthralling backdrop of rising and comprehensive global awareness, the world can now be mobilised to tackle humanitarian crises systemically, as well as in specific locales.

Using social media for social good: Born HIV Free campaign

The progressive development and use of technology has brought us to the point where global support can make an immediate and positive change. However, this can only be done if the tools are used correctly and, in this regard, it must be said that the use of social media for social good is still in the early learning stages.

One example of how social media is used to generate positive impact is the 'Born HIV Free' campaign. This was an online campaign from the Global Fund to Fight AIDS, Tuberculosis and Malaria. This campaign had two goals, specifically: putting the goal of no child being born with HIV by 2015 on national and international political agendas; and rallying support for the Global Fund's work and mission.

Launched in May 2010, the Global Fund's Born HIV Free campaign was designed as a six-month awareness and advocacy campaign that ran until 5 October 2010, which was the day when donors made their three-year (2011–2013) contribution pledge to the Global Fund.

The campaign narrative, and call-to-action, was focused on the goal of virtually ending the transmission of HIV from mother to child by 2015, with this being one of the ambitious (but achievable) goals that the Global Fund could help to realise if ample resources were available. The campaign 'ask' was simple – sign your name to the digital petition that stated your belief in that goal, and affirm your support for your government's contribution to the Global Fund.

Social media was used as a catalyst to rally supporters, drive discussions, educate followers on the issues surrounding prevention of HIV from mother to child (PMTCT), and even recruit bloggers to come and see life-saving programmes in Africa for themselves. Subsequently, the Born HIV Free campaign helped put PMTCT on the global development agenda. Facebook and its application 'Causes' proved to be useful tools to drive the narrative and support advocacy efforts. YouTube was essential for engaging the public around PMTCT issues with a variety of video content that was both educational and entertaining. Less emphasis was put into driving campaign activity with Twitter, but this still proved to be a valuable tool for creating buzz during key campaign moments.

Importantly, during the Born HIV Free campaign, the Global Fund made a conscious choice to push an issue rather than its brand. Media vehicles like YouTube, celebrities like Carla Bruni-Sarkozy, Bono and Jean Paul Gaultier, as well as grass-roots advocacy leaders like Avaaz and ONE, all helped to champion the issue. The broad elite awareness survey that was conducted following the conclusion of Born HIV Free showed two key results:

1. When prompted, one in four people made the connection between the Born HIV Free campaign and the issue of prevention of HIV from mother to child (PMTCT).
2. Those who are campaign aware are more likely to think that PMTCT is a top issue in the fight against HIV/AIDS than those who are unaware.

The discussions, debates and optimism that began with the Born HIV Free campaign have nurtured more champions than ever before. For instance, in a speech during late 2011, the US Secretary of State, Hillary Clinton, indicated that the United States is fully committed to seeing an HIV-free generation by 2015. Only one month later, on World AIDS Day, PRODUCT (RED) and ONE launched a PMTCT campaign at an event in Washington DC where President Barack Obama, along with former US Presidents Bill Clinton and George W. Bush, business leaders, and artists like Bono and Alicia Keys all came together to champion the issue of PMTCT.

Fundamentally, a movement of hope that began online with the Born HIV Free campaign has evolved into a dialogue of great historical consequence, particularly the beginning of the end of the AIDS pandemic.

Humanitarian Needs Win Over Politics: Susan G. Komen Restores Funding to Planned Parenthood for Breast Cancer Screening

We write this chapter fresh on the heels of a powerful example of how social media helps humanitarian concerns trump politics. Within a span of less than a week, a social media uprising forced 'Susan G. Komen for the Cure', a major funder of efforts to detect and cure breast cancer, to reverse its decision to defund Planned Parenthood's early breast cancer screening services for low-income communities. The online campaign also forced the resignation of Karen Handel, the Senior Vice President, who was the driving force behind the decision to defund.

Some related details are useful at this juncture. Following an unsuccessful bid for Governor of the Commonwealth of Georgia, in which a key component of her platform was to stop state funding of Planned Parenthood, Karen Handel was hired to be Senior Vice President for Public Policy by the Dallas-based Susan G. Komen for the Cure foundation. In her position at Komen, Handel pushed to change the rules for funding women's clinics across the United States in a way that would disqualify Planned Parenthood.[1] The rule change prohibited funding of organisations that were the subject of investigations for illegal activities.[2]

Since the rules only required an organisation be under investigation, rather than be convicted for illegal activities, the rule opened the door for politically charged investigations to trigger defunding. Given Planned Parenthood's other activities in providing birth control and abortion services, it was a lightning rod for such investigations.

In response to Komen's decision to defund Planned Parenthood's breast cancer screening services under this new rule, there was a nearly instant uproar on social media.[3] In the first 24 hours, more than 4000 people posted protest messages on Susan G. Komen's Facebook page and Planned Parenthood raised over $400 000 from more than 6000 donors. Also, by that week's end, it had raised over $3 million.[4]

Meanwhile, across the social media landscape, a cry went up for Karen Handel to resign. Twitter petitions,[5] a constant flow of posts on Komen's Facebook page and other online petitions were added to by tens of thousands of angry activists, with all of that culminating in Handel's resignation.

It must also be said that the response to Komen's decision to defund Planned Parenthood was so fast that it took everyone by surprise – everyone except those who had been watching the spread of the women's movement across social media. Long before this controversy erupted, the women's movement in the United States had coalesced on social media. Communities that grew out of popular blogs like BlogHer.com and Momocrats.com gathered some of the most social media-savvy women in the country. In addition, conferences (and resulting communities) like Feminism 2.0 (*www.Fem2pt0.com*) connected the tech-savvy feminists with the movement's old guard. These social networks were so well entrenched prior to the Komen decision that it was inevitable many people would rise up as one to force Komen to reverse course.

Social media as 'central' to the humanitarian sphere

Social media, in many ways, is an ideal tool for the humanitarian sphere. The Internet is recognised as unique media, whereby all the parties involved (organisations, businesses or individuals) have the opportunity to interact with one another, and create a one-on-one level of communication. This way, all the actors realise the power of connecting directly with individuals, and doing that without needing an intermediary.

As stands to reason, the idea of global interaction to tackle social problems is not new; guidelines were already put into place with the Cluetrain Manifesto that enlisted a series of behaviours in order to have a two-way conversation (between organisations and individuals) online. This evolution of the relationship between the different actors in business can be applied to the humanitarian sector. There, no longer do the traditional actors – such as governments and large organisations – only give information to the general public, but the audience can have an active role and let the traditional actors know what their specific needs are, thus enriching the anticipated results.

In effect, social media has been mainstream within the humanitarian sphere since about 2007. From that time, organisations have experimented with the associated tools, individuals have learned how to create online communities around social causes and all the related actors have used these means as a way to connect with each other.

Of course, the need for non-profit organisations to use social media is being widely recognised. Once this need was detected, the market tried to fill the recognised void with numerous products and services. Consequently, we can now find books, seminars, toolkits and more that are selling how to implement social media in this niche market. The need to introduce social media to non-profit organisations is such that it is becoming a business in itself.

Uses of social media in the humanitarian space: from conversation to action

Civic mobilisation and crisis response

As indicated earlier, social media is widely used to empower individuals by turning them into communities, to amplify the voices of civil society movements and to make change bubble up from the masses at the grassroots level. In the humanitarian field, there are two main ways that this is taking place: civic mobilisation and crisis response.

As has become apparent, individuals are taking matters into their own hands and are becoming part of the anticipated solution by working with organisations that are trying to address humanitarian crises. That the beneficiaries are the ones assessing their own needs, instead of being reliant upon external parties, makes the process even more effective.

An organisation that needs a quick crisis response in order to function properly is the International Committee of the Red Cross. Previously, that entity conducted all needs assessments by relying on knowledge of the organisation. But soon enough, key people in that organisation realised that there is the possibility to get more accurate knowledge on the ground with tools like social media. This approach has a positive impact on the efficiency of relief (since it can be done faster) and effectiveness (since the local needs are met with more accuracy).

However, in order for this information flow to work, such efforts must engage 'crowds' that are willing and able to collaborate with organisations. Consider the next example.

Ushahidi is an NGO based in Kenya that allows you to send online coordinates, data and photos to local organisations for different humanitarian purposes. The service was used in situations like the tsunami in Japan, after the earthquake in Haiti, and in African countries to collect data about stock in government pharmacies or to document voting patterns. The potential for this type of service is great, but it requires active engagement of the population in order to create civic mobilisation. The organisation knows this and is trying to reach a larger audience; they have made it accessible through different apps, such as SMS, Twitter and email. All of this is in addition to reaching out to local institutions in order to build trust in the service. Through concerted effort, Ushahidi has proven to be an effective new way to use knowledge on the ground to make a difference. This particular NGO understands its potential, and so does the private sector. Now, all that remains is for them to find their larger crowd.

Information and data gathering

Thanks to new technologies and social media, there are tools readily available that allow information to be gathered and used towards a social goal. Individuals and organisations can collaborate with relevant information flows, and sources of these, and move forward on the crucial step of data gathering in the humanitarian sphere.

A good case in point is the organisation Refugees United, which is an online network that acts as a database to help locate refugees all over the world and reconnect them with their families and friends. This organisation has explored the potential of digitalisation in finding missing persons and, thereby, realises the importance of collecting information for a humanitarian purpose. Furthermore, companies like IKEA, Maersk and Danfoss are supporting the network, and this gives it a wider reach in terms of audience and partnerships.

Other uses that involve data gathering are mapping, information sharing and disaster relief. The first one is used by organisations like the UNHCR (United Nations High Commissioner for Refugees) in order to effectively locate and plan the different refugee camps; this tool helps to build sustainable villages since it allows locating the various resources, then deciding how to grow the camps, determine how many families are in each one of the camps and make better use of the space.

It is noteworthy that information sharing through social media goes beyond the regular online exchange when it has a targeted focus on social good. A good example of this is Text4baby, an organisation that tries to tackle the health challenges of pregnancy and delivery by sending timely information to pregnant women through SMS.

Finally, there is the use of information for disaster relief efforts. For instance, when you can gather all the needs assessments made in the field, you can be more effective in helping to locate the needs of the beneficiaries. Better yet, this approach gives companies, governments and individuals an immediate point of contact to avoid duplicating relief efforts, so ensuring the efficient and effective delivery of goods and services.

Communication

Most humanitarian organisations use social media as part of their communication strategy. Unlike the previous examples, this is mostly a top-down approach that is initiated by a traditional actor, rather than by individuals at the grass-roots level. Non-profit organisations have always had the need to create awareness of their cause, as well as create a community of supporters and raise funds to maintain operations. This is why most organisations are using social media as a communications tool.

Social media seems like the ideal platform to deliver a message and reach your audience – just think about the millions of users that

Facebook or Twitter has and that you could target. The reality is not that simple. Although there is power in numbers, and a great potential audience, actually, the challenge is to do with reaching a portion of that audience and getting your message across.

One of the most interesting uses of social media for the humanitarian sphere is fund-raising. Having your fund-raising efforts in social media represent a low-cost, high-impact strategy. Still, this will only be true if you have a great and committed network, in addition to a good fund-raising strategy, and the resources to make that happen.

There are successful examples of fund-raising through social media, and one of them is PRODUCT (RED). This is an initiative that partners with different companies, such as American Express and Nike, to develop 'red' products and donate part of their revenue to the Global Fund to Fight AIDS, Tuberculosis and Malaria. PRODUCT (RED) has a very strong presence in platforms, like Facebook and Twitter, which has allowed PRODUCT (RED) to engage the community, doing so to the point of making their products trendy and supporting the Global Fund too.

Another success story is that of the American Red Cross where Twitter is used to run a fund-raising campaign. However, with the use of new technologies come new challenges, like those experienced by that particular organisation. There was an incident when the person running the Twitter campaign accidentally tweeted a personal message on the organisation's account; that specific tweet mentioned drinking a certain brand of beer. This *faux pas* could have brought about a significant amount of negative attention to the organisation. However, the American Red Cross did successful damage control by responding quickly, and with humour about that rogue tweet. A surprisingly positive response came from that mistake, to the point that the beer company mentioned in the wayward tweet picked it up and joined the fund-raising efforts on their own social media platforms.

Besides fund-raising, large organisations use social media as a key part of their communication strategy. An example is the UNHCR, which joined efforts with Google to create awareness for the situation of refugees. Since UNHCR personnel were already using Google Earth to map the refugee camps, they decided to repackage the information and add different Google Earth layers, including a video and stories from the refugees. By doing this, the UNHCR was the first organisation to allow members of the public to come in direct contact with their humanitarian efforts, plus engaging the community while educating them on their mission.

Lessons learned: where are we going?

Best practices

Without a doubt, social media is a great tool for the humanitarian sector. Nevertheless, in order to take full advantage of its potential, we must follow certain guidelines that have proven to be successful in the past. For instance, realise that content leads the conversation, engage with your audience, remain authentic and always pursue a long-term relationship with the public.

First of all, you need to be aware that social media is just a tool, and by this we mean that it doesn't matter if you are in every platform available if you don't have something to say. Organisations that want to use social media need to restructure themselves in order to allow the production of quality content; this means reallocating staff for that purpose, changing the chain of content production, creating synergies between different teams and so on. A harsh reality is that international organisations are not good at telling their own stories, even though there are great ones to tell. The general trend among organisations is just to compile content from different sources instead of creating their own. Of course, this is easier, and it requires fewer resources. But it won't get you the results that you could achieve if paying more attention to the task. You need to be compelling, know the strengths of the organisation and build upon them to showcase quality content.

It has been only a couple of years since humanitarian organisations became involved in a real two-way conversation. This has to do with their own nature, since their particular mindset is not accommodating enough to allow for such an open dialogue. Whether it is because they are concerned with the safety of their beneficiaries, or because their leadership is still too traditional, the reality is that it has taken these organisations much too long to be more involved, and some are still reluctant to do so. A two-way conversation requires taking risks, changing the mindset of those involved and putting a human face to the organisation in order to incite a response and prompt an actual dialogue. If done well, all this could transform the organisation into an open entity.

We've discussed the importance of content and creating a conversation; while doing both, it is essential that you remain authentic. The first step before any communication occurs is knowing who you are and, although social media may be a new way to engage with your audience, it is important to be true to your own identity. You need to showcase what makes you unique and, therefore, what makes you stand out among all other humanitarian causes. This will get you more followers and additional committed ones too.

When using social media, you are looking to engage with your audience; this means building a relationship between the humanitarian actor and the public. Like any relationship, you need to nurture it and aim for a long-term relationship in order for it to work. There are many organisations that have a presence in the social media space. But, often, these entities only address their public when they have a specific ask, such as a particular fund-raising campaign. This way of doing things won't give them a favourable response. Basically, humanitarian actors need to be constant in order to get their message across and also engage with the public in any opportunity. That way, when it's time to call for action, your audience will have a clear idea of who you are and will be more prompt to react, since you've already made a connection.

Just as the aforementioned practices will deliver to you a better result in social media, there are certain practices that you must avoid. Although online activism might trigger offline action towards the humanitarian mission, you must be careful since there is also a portion of the audience that is attracted by the simplicity of engaging online (just a click, a retweet or a like away), can stay in a superficial interaction and never move towards a higher level of commitment.

In order to avoid the superficial online interaction that only gives the illusion of social engagement, the humanitarian actor needs to be clear, and use that simplicity to make a bigger change. When there is no clear call to action, it doesn't matter how many users are reached, or how engaged they are willing to be, since they won't know what is the next step to take towards that anticipated social change.

Unfortunately, many organisations have failed to set up such a clear message for their audience. This can be as a result of disjointed efforts within the organisation itself, that in the aim to be active in social media, communications personnel in the organisation have forgotten that you require – as with any other media – a cohesive strategy in order to be consistent, and to move forward with your message.

Social media trends that will impact the humanitarian sphere

Social media is constantly evolving. New tools and platforms are launching all the time. Existing tools and platforms are upgraded frequently. Against this ever-changing backdrop, it can seem daunting to humanitarian organisations that are trying to keep pace.

As these new opportunities emerge, we must take note of who is using the new tools and what they can do to enhance the humanitarian mission. If a new social network is able to reach people in need, or get in touch with people who can help, we need to embrace it. If new social media tools provide functional opportunities that will enhance the delivery of aid, or the mobilisation of people, we need to use them.

There are two emerging trends in social media of particular note. The first is the rise of mobile access to social media, including geo-location services. The second is the increased capacity for visualising information.

Mobile access to the Internet generally, and social media specifically, is a real game-changer. Especially in regions where hard wires simply do not exist, mobile access to the Internet enables anyone with a phone, tablet or wireless laptop to connect with social networks and all the opportunities that these present.

Even in areas where electricity is scarce, solar batteries can be used to charge mobile devices. Hand-crank powered devices are also available. This means that we can steadily extend the reach of social media into areas that once were inaccessible. For example, in the hills of northern Sudan, mobile, wireless devices make it possible for embedded reporters and rebels to keep the world informed about their struggles against violent oppression inflicted by the government.

Even in cities where electricity has been cut by oppressive governments, such as in Syria, mobile access to the Net allows information to flow out to the rest of the world. It is with this information that humanitarian responses can be mobilised more effectively.

Geo-location services permit us to create more accurate maps, with this allowing for more effective delivery of humanitarian aid. By crowd-sourcing the collection of geo-data points, detailed maps of vast expanses of land can be created with relative ease. Even in areas where there are few smartphones, consider that SMS text messaging that essentially works on every mobile phone allows for the quick flow of information that is vital to the delivery of humanitarian aid.

The second emerging trend is all about visualisation of information. Tools that map the connections between and among blogs and social networks allow us to see who is talking to whom. Mapping out these links within a country gives us advanced warnings of emerging political coalitions.

Satellites feeding data to social networks, like the Satellite Sentinel project (see *www.satsentinel.org*), give us real-time visual information that can detect imminent attacks on villages, and also help us to find mass graves. With this information, we can save lives and bring justice down on those committing crimes against humanity.

On a much simpler level, new social networks, like Pinterest and Tumblr, facilitate the sharing of visual images. These rapidly growing social networks[6] will make it much easier to share images from humanitarian crises, allowing for crowd-sourcing and real-time distribution across the globe. Also, with more images coming from the crises, it will be easier to mobilise an international response.

Clearly, in terms of better methods of communication, the seeds have been planted. Communication around the world is easier and faster, as allows for communities to come together like never before. Social media has great potential. It gives humanitarian actors what they have been waiting for, such as an easy, low-cost, mass distribution of messages, as well as organising and mobilisation tools, thus allowing direct and effective interaction with individuals and communities all over the world.

For any who seek to strengthen their effectiveness in addressing humanitarian issues, and resolving them, we must take the next step forward and take full advantage of the tools and networks that available. It is no longer enough just to recognise the existence of the tools, nor to use them as a secondary part of the communication strategy. In order to learn, grow and obtain results, it is necessary to turn online conversations into key actions that will, for the better, transform the humanitarian sphere as we now know it.

Notes

1. *www.huffingtonpost.com/2012/02/05/karen-handel-susan-g-komen-decision-defund-planned-parenthood_n_1255948.html?ref=mostpopular*
2. *www.latimes.com/health/boostershots/la-heb-karen-handel-susan-komen-planned-parenthood-fox-20120207,0,3421931.story*
3. *www.huffingtonpost.com/arianna-huffington/komen-planned-parenthood_b_1260631.html*
4. *http://articles.cnn.com/2012-02-03/politics/politics_planned-parenthood-komen-foundation_1_planned-parenthood-komen-foundation-susan-g-komen?_s=PM:POLITICS*
5. *http://act.ly/5ib*
6. *http://agbeat.com/real-estate-technology-new-media/pinterest-now-drives-as-much-web-traffic-as-twitter*

7

Social media: the new tool in business education

Susan Bandias and Anthony Gilding

Abstract: The use of social media, such as Facebook, Twitter, blogs, web conferencing and LinkedIn, has become a pervasive and popular form of communication. For many organisations, social media is a business tool of choice. The social capital that can be accrued through the use of social media is reported to have positive benefits across a range of areas, including educational outcomes, business activities and the public reputation of individuals, groups and organisations. In recent years, social media has also gained acceptance in academia as an important teaching and learning tool. Increasingly, the adoption of social media in business education is also driven by the need to mirror its contemporary use in the world of work.

Key words: social media, tool, business education, communication, social capital, social networks, curriculum, pedagogy.

Introduction

Online social networks, such as Facebook and Twitter, have become a common part of many people's lives. It is estimated that Facebook will break the billion user barrier in 2012, and Twitter already claims to have over 100 million users (Head, 2011). Logging on to a personal Facebook page, or leaving a comment on the 'wall' of a friend, or of family members, is a daily activity for many people, especially those of the younger generations. Essentially, the use of social media has become so pervasive that it is not unusual to see Twitter messages, links to Facebook pages and blogs displayed during live television broadcasts. In addition, computer-mediated engagement is so prevalent that we are now entering what has been described as 'the era of social networking, collective intelligence, participation, collaborative creation, and borderless distribution' (Warr, 2008:1).

As has become apparent, the use of social media has added a new dimension to the old adage: 'Who you know is often more important than what you know.' Also, networking with current and prospective clients, colleagues and stakeholders via Internet-based Web 2.0 applications is rapidly becoming a business tool of choice. For instance, Web-based applications that support the creation and exchange of user-generated content have become an integral aspect of the way business is conducted, and how professional contacts are created and maintained. As Kinzey (2010) pointed out, the social capital accrued through the use of social media can enhance business activities, as well as the public reputation of individuals, groups and organisations.

Universities have also been enthusiastic adopters of Facebook and other social media tools. In this educational environment, social media is used to reach current, former and prospective students, plus engage and inform the broader community of university activity. The use of social media is also making inroads into the traditional curricula of many disciplines. Consequently, and rapidly, it is becoming an integral aspect of the business and commerce curricula in many higher education institutions.

Social capital and social media

Social capital is an elusive concept, and there is considerable debate as to what actually is meant by the term. According to Stone and Hughes (2000), the essence of social capital is quality social relations. Winter (2000:1) suggests that social capital encompasses 'social relations of mutual benefit characterised by norms of trust and reciprocity'. Social capital, according to Grootaert (1998:1), is 'the glue that holds societies together and without which there can be no economic growth or human well-being'. Putnam (1995) identifies social capital as the features of social life that enable participants to act together more effectively to pursue shared objectives. The Australian Bureau of Statistics (ABS, 2004:5) and the Organisation for Economic Cooperation and Development (OECD, 2001:1) define social capital as 'networks, together with shared norms, values and understandings which facilitate cooperation within or among groups'. According to the ABS (2004), the OECD definition of social capital is emerging as a common basis for international comparability. Consequently, this paper has also adopted the ABS and OECD definition.

The positive benefits of quality social relations that constitute social capital are reported to have implications for a range of areas, including education, social and economic development, as well as social and civic stability (Bandias, 2010; Cox, 1996; Fukuyuma, 1999; Putnam, 1995). Social capital has also been linked to outcomes, such as broadening business and employment opportunities (Benson et al., 2010:21; Warr, 2008).

It is noteworthy that the relationship between information and communications technology (ICT) and social capital is widely acknowledged (European Commission, 2004; Huijboom, 2007; Lee and Lee, 2010; Sinanan, 2008; Uslaner, 2000). As noted by the European Commission (2004:9), 'the use of ICT can bring [about] fundamental changes to civil society and, therefore, social capital. In fact, we are already witnessing new emerging forms of ... organisations that would simply not exist without ICT.' In a business context, the growth of online social media, for instance, is becoming an important means of job seeking, connecting with consumers, building business intelligence, marketing new and existing products, and engaging consumers on a personal level.

There are numerous definitions of social media. Broadly defined, social media is the term used to describe a range of online tools that facilitate individuals and groups of people to connect and interact, create and share (Chrisg.com, 2011; Odden, 2011; Schottmuller, 2011). The related tools include Twitter, blogs, wikis, discussion forums, online conferencing software, YouTube and social networking sites, such as Facebook and LinkedIn. In an academic context, social media may also include (but is not limited to) synchronous online classrooms, wikis, blogs, discussion forums and file sharing.

While social capital is a theoretical construct, and social media is a term used to describe a range on online networking tools, the two frameworks overlap, and the nexus is in building relationships of mutual benefit. Even so, despite the relative 'newness' of social media, its intrinsic social appeal has sparked a rapid evolution and relatively widespread adoption. Social media, for example, is employed across a range of areas, including recreation, public relations, marketing and commerce. It is also gaining rapid acceptance in academia, both as a teaching and learning tool, and as part of the mainstream curricula. As Mackay (2010) acknowledged:

Students entering university studies today have grown up with access to computers and the Internet and have years of experience in using online social networks to make connections and share information. Now that businesses are realizing the commercial potential of these social media networks, the universities need to teach their students how to turn their knowledge of these new media channels to profitable use.

Social networks within business

Historically, the adoption of new technologies has had a profound influence on business practices (Wilson, 2008). As Subramoniam (2008) noted, tapping the advantages of developments in ICT has become the main agenda for the re-engineering of business processes. In recent years, the advantages of using social media in organisational processes has been reported to include 'shared understanding of organisational roles, increased sense of group cohesiveness, improved work processes, and improved professional and personal ties among employees' (Sinanan, 2008:4). The increased use of teams in organisations has also been encouraged by computer-mediated communication technologies. Thereby, virtual or networked teams have changed how organisational members collect and distribute data, as well as altering the dynamics and relationships between organisational members (Berry, 2011).

Consider, for example, the use of social media to leverage consumer sentiment, and gain brand and market insights, can also provide corporations with a valuable competitive edge. From a customer perspective, consumer-generated media, according to Blackshaw (2011:209), is:

> ... the new currency of relationships between business and consumers. The relationship is reflected in an endless stream of comments, opinions, emotions, and personal stories about any and every company, product, service, or brand.

As is apparent, consumers are no longer passive observers in today's marketplace of ideas and commerce. Armed with a suite of tools, resources and technologies, including the aforementioned Facebook, Twitter, discussion forums and blogs, consumers are participating in, and reshaping, the business landscape and marketplace.

Certainly, the inherent networking nature of social media assists in the development of relationships between people and organisations. Social networks allow people to construct an awareness of others, and engage in a dialogue. In a commercial sense, social media facilitates the establishment of trust in others and with organisations. However, the concepts of information access, sharing, awareness, trust and engagement apply not only to so-called 'good' business practices, but also to 'effective' learning. The skills required to use social media overlap with and expand on the skills required in social situations, in the workplace and in the learning environment.

Social media in the curriculum

The online learning environment is reported to be the fastest-growing educational context for adult learners (Rossi, 2010:3). Consequently, for a significant number of students, their learner–learner interaction and knowledge construction occurs in a context that includes the use of social media. Online learning environments offer an educational domain that is unique in terms of the potential for interaction, participation and collaboration. Among the benefits to be derived from collaborative learning is the development of critical and problem-solving skills in a social atmosphere where learners can share, consider and challenge one another's ideas (Rossi, 2010:4).

It is widely acknowledged that students have different expectations of higher education, different learning styles and study practices (Baird and Fisher, 2005:5; Van Raaij and Schepers, 2008). Today, students use the web to create 'self-paced, customised, on-demand learning pathways that includes multiple forms of interactive, social, and self-publishing media tools' (Baird and Fisher, 2005:5). The use of social media can also create a unique learning experience by enabling students to engage in networks that extend beyond the traditional confines of the classroom.

Technology tools, such as conferencing software, blogs, Really Simple Syndication (RSS) feeds, podcasts and wikis, provide simple-to-use web-based tools for asynchronous and synchronous collaboration and interaction. Interaction, or shared events between learners and teaching staff, is a decisive factor in improving the quality of both online and traditional learning. As Head (2011) noted, the use of social media to improve the student learning experience is the key driver of its adoption by the higher education sector.

Research indicates that social media is used as an instructional tool across a range of education disciplines. The integration of social media in communication, media and literacy studies (Hull and Stornaiuolo, 2010), as well as disciplines as diverse as library studies, medicine, commerce and technology (Cain, 2011; Gilman and Turner, 2001; Morley, 2011), is a reflection of the pervasiveness of social media in contemporary society, and the growing acceptance of its veracity as an important pedagogical tool.

In the area of business education, the adoption of social media in the curriculum is also driven by the need to mirror its contemporary use in the world of work. While social media has an obvious role in the teaching and learning of marketing, its ubiquitous application and widespread adoption in the workplace has increased its relevance and use in the areas of management, accounting, hospitality, tourism and economics. According to Mackay (2010), the increasing use of social media in business has created a strong demand at the hiring end for candidates skilled in its use. Consequently:

> ... several top business schools [have] incorporate[ed] courses on social networks into their M.B.A. curriculums. These include Harvard Business School; London Business School; Insead, the international business school based in Fontainebleau, France; and the École des Hautes Études Commerciales, known as H.E.C., in Paris.
>
> Mackay, 2010

Social media in business education

The most common forms of social media used in business education include wikis, discussion forums, blogs, Twitter and synchronous collaborative learning environments. Each of these social media tools differ in their intent, their level of interaction and their pedagogical application. However, they all assist in the development of work-readiness skills, technological competence, communication skills, online literacy skills and collaboration skills, as well as the skills necessary for managing information and communications technology.

The use of online discussion forums is one of the 'older' applications of educational technology. 'Bulletin boards', as they were called in the early 1990s when first used in education, have become a popular and widely applied learning tool. As a mature technology their use 'has informed online learning and development practice across many levels from school pupils to postgraduate research students, and especially in online and blended learning in higher and professional education' (Salmon et al., 2010:170). Over time, bulletin boards have evolved to incorporate the use of graphics, audio, images and video. They have also become a forum to promote discussion, debate, the exchange of ideas and collaboration. Research indicates that the use of online discussion forums can have a positive impact on student motivation, student socialisation, information exchange, the construction of knowledge, and access to lectures and peers (Salmon et al., 2010).

The term 'wiki', derived from the Hawaiian word *wiki*, meaning fast or quick, provides a simple system for collaboration. Essentially, a wiki is a database for creating, browsing and searching through information. A wiki allows for non-linear, evolving, complex and networked discussion and interaction. The most well-known example of a wiki is Wikipedia, with this being an online encyclopaedia written and maintained by the collective contributors.

It is widely acknowledged that wikis embody the social constructivist principles of learning (Caverly and Ward, 2008; Moskaliuk et al., 2009; Su and Beaumont, 2010). In the development of a wiki, a group of users jointly create a digital artefact and, in the process, become active participants in the construction of their own knowledge. From an epistemological perspective, the use of wikis assists in the acquisition of digital literacy, the formation of complex concepts, as well as collaboration and research skills (Caverly and Ward, 2008; Karasavvidis, 2010; Su and Beaumont, 2010).

Blogs are broadly defined as online public journals or diaries (Tien-Chi et al., 2011). So wikis, discussion forums and blogs are forms of social media that are asynchronous. Although interaction in an asynchronous environment does not occur in real time, most good-quality blogs allow visitors to leave comments, and even message each other via widgets on the blogs. This interactivity distinguishes blogs from other static websites. In an educational context, blogs facilitate the publication of knowledge, offer opportunities for subsequent reflection and analysis, and assist learners to understand the relational and contextual basis of knowledge construction and meaning making. According to research conducted by Saeed et al. (2009:105), students also use blogging for community building, resource consolidation, the sharing of ideas or as a personal journal.

Micro-blogging is a relatively recent extension of blogging, and works in similar ways to text messaging. As a form of expression, micro-blogging has gained considerable momentum over the past few years. The high uptake of mobile Internet technologies and smartphones has provided much of the impetus for that growth. Twitter is the most popular version of micro-blogging, and is an effective communication tool for concise messages and news items. University libraries have been very quick to realise the potential of applications, such as Twitter. Its reported use, in this context, has been one of information dissemination. As indicated by Weaver (2010), Twitter is used successfully by library staff as a news service to inform students of events, catalogue additions and library loans. Micro-blogging is also evolving to be a very powerful networking tool for educators. The immediacy of information, and the capacity to access a vast range of resources through micro-blogs, has inherent appeal for academics. However, as a relatively new technology, its application in education is still evolving and, to date, there has been limited research on its use in the curriculum.

In recent years, the use of web conferencing technology to facilitate online learning in a synchronous classroom has become part of the mainstream curricula of many higher education disciplines. Such synchronous classrooms are a 'virtual' room where participants meet online, and in real time. Virtual classrooms are becoming a common and popular method of educational delivery, particularly in distance education. As McBrien and Jones (2009) have noted, virtual classrooms have also proven to be popular among students for reasons that include convenience and equal opportunity.

There are a number of software applications that support synchronous learning. Commercial learning products such as Wimba, Skype, Collaborate and Elluminate share several interactive characteristics. These applications can incorporate the use of audio, video, text, graphics and file sharing to enable students to participate in a learning experience that is aimed to replicate the face-to-face environment. The reported benefits of synchronous learning include enhanced communication, greater social interaction, improved group cohesion and higher levels of course satisfaction (McBrien and Jones, 2009).

Social media and pedagogical issues

The incorporation of social media into the curriculum and teaching practices provides opportunities and challenges. It is argued that Web 2.0 technologies enhance the social construction of knowledge, support learner autonomy and provide an opportunity for increased participation (McBrien and Jones, 2009; Siragusa et al., 2007). Learning activities that are no longer time-bound by the constraints of the traditional face-to-face settings also provide the opportunity for reflection, and the development of deeper learning. According to Naeem (2011:65), social media has allowed greater access, flexibility and choices for both students and lecturers in the tertiary environment, as well as providing mobility, variety, a global perspective and opportunities to experiment with new tools for teaching.

To realise the potential of social media in the curriculum, effective teaching strategies are required to support its use. As Harsell (2010:66) pointed out, when social media is used as an educational tool, well-designed and appropriate teaching methodologies are required to ensure effective learning outcomes. It has also been argued that, while educators have utilised the web to develop formal e-learning platforms, many are struggling to unleash its power as an educational tool (Harsell, 2010; Lewis et al., 2010).

Research also indicates that a limited understanding of learners' characteristics is a major obstacle for the practice of web-based instruction in the curriculum (Saeed et al., 2009; Yang and Tsai, 2008). In addition, the success of educational programmes involving web-based technologies depends to a considerable extent on students' acceptance and use of these technologies (Van Raaij and Schepers, 2008). Therefore, students' learning styles and technology preferences should be taken into account in order to incorporate, effectively, emerging web technologies into course design. Cognitive overload (due to exposure to an excess of online resources over a short time), technology issues and bandwidth can also have an impact on the effectiveness of social media as an instructional tool. As Lorenzo et al. (2006) stated, 'today's students are not just the traditional-age net generation, nor have they all had the benefit of state-of-the-art, ubiquitous technology. Higher education comprises a highly diverse and growing student body with a wide variety of information literacy capabilities.'

Educational institutions also face several challenges when attempting to connect the 'informal' learning that occurs in 'open' social networks with the 'formal' learning provided in a 'closed' networks of a university course. In part, this is due to perceived difficulties in integrating emergent forms of social media into the highly structured university learning environment (Lewis et al., 2010). As McCarthy (2010:730) noted, Facebook and other Web 2.0 technologies are not always appropriate or successful vehicles for formal teaching and learning activities. The ways in which students use technologies in their everyday interactions with family and friends might often be different from their preferences for the use of technology in formal learning settings (McCarthy, 2010).

However, both social capital and social media have the potential to be powerful tools in the social construction of knowledge, and in the development of work-readiness skills. Research has indicated that the appropriate use of social media as an instructional technology can have a positive influence on academic performance (Saeed et al., 2009). Consequently, as new forms of social media emerge, and become embedded in mainstream communications, higher educational institutions must also be open to new media, new pedagogical approaches and also new ways in which students interact and construct meaning.

Conclusion

The use of social media, such as Facebook, Twitter, blogs, web conferencing and LinkedIn, has become a pervasive and popular form of communication and information access. The inherent networking nature of social media assists in the development of relationships, the dissemination of information, collaboration and engagement. The social capital that can be accrued through the use of social media is reported to have positive benefits across a range of areas, including educational outcomes, business activities and the public reputation of individuals, groups and organisations.

For many organisations, social media has become a business tool of choice. Building social capital, such as with current and prospective clients, colleagues and stakeholders via Internet-based Web 2.0 applications, is an integral aspect of the way professional contacts are created and maintained. It is apparent that the ubiquitous nature of social media is reshaping not only the business landscape but also the way in which business is conducted. Social media is used to harness customer sentiment, brand awareness and market insights. Through the use of social media, consumers are no longer passive observers in the marketplace.

In recent years, social media has also gained acceptance in academia as a powerful teaching and learning tool. A wide range of disciplines now use social media to enhance and support the students' learning experience. Increasingly, the adoption of social media in the curriculum is also driven by the need to mirror its contemporary use in the world of work.

In this regard, the role of social media in business education has important pedagogical implications. Course-related networks can also serve as a 'practice field' in which students experience the conditions that are conducive to acquiring new knowledge, as well as gaining social and technological skills. The incorporation of social media in the curricula also enables students to bridge, or to make connections between, their acquired knowledge and skills and the work environment. Here, the role of pedagogy is critical to both functions.

However, designing courses that broaden business curricula to include practices that capitalise on social capital and the media that supports its construction, development and maintenance is a significant challenge. In addition, the challenge for any dedicated university lecturer is to use social networks to support more collaborative engagement and deeper learning for and among students. If these challenges can be met, the potential for social media to enhance student learning experience is considerable.

References

ABS (2004) *Information Paper Measuring Social Capital An Australian Framework and Indicators*. Canberra: Australian Bureau of Statistics.

Baird, D. and Fisher, M. (2005) Neomillennial user experience design strategies: Utilizing social networking media to support '*Always on*' learning styles. *Journal of Educational Technology Systems*, 34(1), 5–21.

Bandias, S. (2010) Building Indigenous Social Capital in an Online World. *Journal of Media and Communication, ANZCA Special Edition* (April), 38–51.

Benson, V., Filippaios, F. and Morgan, S. (2010) Changing the face of business education and career planning. *International Journal of E-Business Management 4.1*, 20.

Berry, G. (2011) Enhancing Effectiveness on Virtual Teams – Understanding Why Traditional Team Skills Are Insufficient. *Journal of Business Communication*, 48(2), 186–206.

Blackshaw, P. (2011) User-Generated Content In Context. *Journal of Advertising Research*, 51, 108–11.

Cain, J. (2011) Social media in health care: The case for organizational policy and employee education. *American Journal of Health-System Pharmacy*, 68(11), 1036–40.

Caverly, D. and Ward, A. (2008) Techtalk: Wikis and Collaborative Knowledge Construction. *Journal of Developmental Education*, 32(2), 36–7.

Chrisg.com (Producer) (2011) The Business of Blogging and New Media. Retrieved from *www.chrisg.com* (29 October).

Cox, E. (1996) Beyond economics: the building of social capital. *Refractory Girl* (50), 52–3.

European Commission (2004) *ICTs and Social Capital in the Knowledge Society.* Spain.

Fukuyuma, F. (1999) *Social Capital and Civil Society.* Paper presented at the IMF Conference on Second Generation Reforms (1 October).

Gilman, S. and Turner, J. (2001) Media Richness and Social Information Processing: Rationale for Multifocal Continuing Medical. *Journal of Continuing Education in the Health Professions*, 21(3), 134.

Grootaert, C. (1998) Social Capital: The missing link. *Social Development Family Environmentally and Socially Sustainable Development Network.* Washington, DC 20433, USA: World Bank.

Harsell, D. (2010) Wikis in the Classroom: Faculty and Student Perspective. *Journal of Political Science Education*, 6(3), 310–4.

Head, B. (2011) Putting on your best social face. *Campus review*, 21, 11 (November).

Huijboom, N. (2007) Social capital and ICT adoption in the public sector. *Proceedings of the 8th annual international conference on digital government research: bridging disciplines & domains* (pp. 140–147). Philadelphia, Pennsylvania Digital Government Society of North America.

Hull, G. and Stornaiuolo, A. (2010) Literate Arts in a Global World: Reframing Social Networking as Cosmopolitan Practice. *Journal of Adolescent & Adult Literacy*, 54(2), 85–97.

Karasavvidis, I. (2010) Wiki uses in higher education: exploring barriers to successful implementation. *Interactive Learning Environments*, 18(3), 219–31.

Kinzey, R. (2010) Managing Your Online Reputation. *Professional Safety*, 55(1), 53.

Lee, J. and Lee, H. (2010) The computer-mediated communication network: exploring the linkage between the online community and social capital. *New Media & Society*, 12(5), 711–27.

Lewis, S., Pea, R. and Rosen, J. (2010) Beyond participation to co-creation of meaning: mobile social media in generative learning communities. *Social Science Information*, 49(3), 1–19.

Lorenzo, G., Oblinger, D. and Dziuban, C. (2006) How choice, co-creation, and culture are changing what it means to be net savvy. *EDUCAUSE Quarterly*, 30(1).

Mackay, F. (2010) Business Schools Respond to Demand for Use of Social Media. *New York Times*. Retrieved from *www.nytimes.com/2010/03/31/education/31iht-riedmba.html?pagewanted=all*

McBrien, J. and Jones, P. (2009) Virtual Spaces: Employing a Synchronous Online Classroom to Facilitate Student Engagement. *The International Review of Research in Open and Distance Learning*, 10(3). Retrieved from *www.irrodl.org/index.php/irrodl/article/view/605/1264*

McCarthy, J. (2010) Blended learning environments: Using social networking sites to enhance the first year experiencesites to enhance the first year experience. *The University of Adelaide Australasian Journal of Educational Technology*, 26(6), 729–40.

Morley, D. (2011) All in it Together. *Nursing Standard*, 25(43), 61.

Moskaliuk, J., Kimmerle, J. and Cress, U. (2009) Wiki-supported learning and knowledge building: effects of incongruity between knowledge and information. *Journal of Computer Assisted Learning*, 25(6), 549–61.

Naeem, J. (2011) How to Better Prepare Students for E-Learning and Avoid Common Pitfalls: Online Learning and its Impacts. *Journal of Australian and NewZealand Student Services Association 37*, 65–9.

Odden, L. (Producer) (2011) Top Ranked – Online Marketing Blog. Retrieved from *www.toprankblog.com/category/social-media* (29 October).

OECD (2001) *The Wellbeing of Nations: The Role of Human and Social Capital, Education and Skills.* Paris: OECD Centre for Educational Research and Innovation.

Putnam, R. (1995) Tuning in, tuning out: the strange disappearance of social capital in America. *Political Science & Politics*, 28(4), 664–83.

Rossi, D. (2010) Learning relationships in online contexts : an educational response to declining rates of participation and a means of support for undergraduate students. *Studies in Learning, Evaluation, Innovation and Development*, 7(3), 1–17.

Saeed, N., Yang, Y. and Sinnappan, S. (2009) Emerging Web Technologies in Higher Education: A Case of Incorporating Blogs, Podcasts and Social Bookmarks in a Web Programming Course based on Students' Learning Styles and Technology Preferences. *Educational Technology and Society*, 12(4), 98–109.

Salmon, G., Nie, M. and Edirisingha, P. (2010) Developing a five-stage model of learning in Second Life. *Educational Research*, 52(2), 169–82.

Schottmuller, A. (Producer) (2011) Actionable Marketing Expert. Retrieved from *http://heidicohen.com/social-media-definition*

Sinanan, J. (2008) Social tools and social capital: reading mobile phone usage in rural indigenous communities. *Proceedings of the 20th Australasian Conference on Computer-Human Interaction: Designing for Habitus and Habitat* (pp. 267–70). Cairns, Australia ACM.

Siragusa, L., Dixon, K. and Dixon, R. (2007) *Designing quality e-learning environments in higher education.* Paper presented at the ascilite Singapore 2007, Singapore.

Stone, W. and Hughes, J. (2000) What role for social capital in family policy – and how does it measure up? *7th Australian Institute of Family Studies Conference* (Sydney).

Su, F. and Beaumont, C. (2010) Evaluating the use of a wiki for collaborative learning. *Innovations in Education & Teaching International*, 47(4), 417–31.

Subramoniam, S. (2008) Commanding the Internet era. *Industrial Engineer*, 40(10), 44–8.

Tien-Chi, H., Yueh-Min, H. and Fu-Yun, Y. (2011) Cooperative Weblog Learning in Higher Education: Its Facilitating Effects on Social Interaction, Time Lag, and Cognitive Load. *Journal of Educational Technology & Society*, 14(1), 95–106.

Uslaner, E. (2000) Social capital and the net. *Association for Computing Machinery*, 43(12), 60–4.

Van Raaij, E. and Schepers, J. (2008) The Acceptance and Use of a Virtual Learning Environment in China. *Computers and Education*, 50(3), 838–52.

Warr, W. (2008) Social software: fun and games, or business tools? *Journal of Information Science*, 34(4), 591–604.

Weaver, A. (2010) Twitter for teachers, librarians and teacher librarians. *Access*, 24(2), 16–20.

Wilson, R. (2008) 'The machine should fit the work': Organisation and Method and British approaches to new technology in business. *History & Technology*, 24(4), 321–33.

Winter, I. (2000) *Towards a Theorised Understanding of Family Life and Social Capital*. Melbourne: Australian Institute of Family Studies.

Yang, F. and Tsai, C. (2008) Investigating university student preferences and beliefs about learning in the web-based context. *Computers and Education*, 50(4), 1284–303.

8

Social media: does it generate the continuum of transparency in organisations?

Andrew Creed and Ambika Zutshi

Abstract: Transparency in the workplace is better than the opposite. Positive results can come in the form of more ethical behaviour, better organisational communication patterns, and the avoidance of discriminatory and other unacceptable practices, with these sometimes bordering on illegal behaviour. But is transparency always good? The potential negative effect of transparency on individuals, and subsequently on the functioning of organisations, has received little attention. New social media is fundamentally altering the communication patterns in organisations, thus giving transparency a new energy. Specifically, it is easier, exponentially, to expose and share information through the interconnected networks inside and beyond an organisation boundary. By polarising transparency, and exploring the positive and negative aspects of it in context with examples, this chapter sounds a timely warning about being too complacent in the midst of the constant wash of technological changes. The good effects of social media on positive transparency are acknowledged, but the negative impacts are also highlighted and illustrated. The findings are that thoughtless spruiking (public speaking) and intentional abuse are human pastimes that can have deleterious effects on the individuals involved, and these are magnified through the new media networks. If managers and staff in organisations could adhere to more balanced applications of transparency policy, then more ethical and effective work situations will be the beneficial result.

Key words: social media, transparency, workplace, organisation, communication, privacy, control, mobbing, civility, etiquette, benefits, challenges, social network.

negative elements, all of which is overviewed in the following sections of this chapter. Unless otherwise stated, please note that the concepts of transparency and privacy in this chapter are mentioned in the context of work or professional settings.

The positive and negative continuum of transparency

Transparency is broadly defined and analysed in organisational contexts, especially as corporate collapses, breaches of fiduciary trust and large economic events, such as the global financial crisis, have unfolded (Roth, 2009; Crotty, 2011). Most researchers focusing upon transparency begin with a simple dictionary definition, then move to more detailed contextual alignment. For example, the Oxford English Dictionary, quoted in Westphal (1986:312), defines transparency as 'having the property of transmitting light so as to render bodies lying beyond it completely visible, so that it can be seen through'. In this chapter, some qualification of that definition must occur, with this depending on which resources a reader might be considering. For example, finance, production data, staffing information, strategic planning and other variants require different levels of 'visibility' for different audiences. Further to this, the effects resulting from certain types of people knowing particular types of information in an organisation can either be helpful or harmful to individuals or the organisation overall.

While the good effects of transparency in organisations in relation to financial management and information disclosure are well documented (Williams, 2005; Bandsuch et al., 2008; Williams, 2008), limited attention is given in that literature to the possible downside of being transparent (Pratt, 2005; Ball, 2009). In the field of corporate governance, through the notion of privacy, some of the negative aspects of transparency are considered. Nonetheless, emphasis on the notion of freedom of information highlights that the benefits of transparency often outweigh the remnant concerns that people may have about the loss of privacy (Rodan, 2000). It is our view that both the good (positive) and the bad (negative) aspects of transparency need a clearer distinction. There is no denying that transparency is here to stay and, hence, it is imperative for managers to consider the ramifications of implementing and reinforcing transparency policies and initiatives in their organisations. As information technology advances, so too do the opportunities for information transparency through access to copied, or stored, data increase. These then place a further imperative on managers to act appropriately in the interests of their organisations, as well as each group of stakeholders. We need to remember that the actions of managers at various levels, in addition to their peers and subordinates, all contribute towards the ethical culture of an organisation.

Positive transparency is when information disclosure leads to the better functioning of an organisation that benefits all stakeholders equitably. In effect, positive transparency operates on the principle of mutual knowledge (Lee, 2001) and is essentially a post-modern approach to ensure that patterns of power, as well as control over knowledge, do not become entrenched and abusive (Koall, 2011). It is quite common, however, for people in organisations to have mutual knowledge of a type that, in some way, diminishes the status of one or more of the people who are subjects of the knowledge (Braxton, 2010). For instance, when information is spread that harms or unfairly embarrasses individuals, we have negative transparency. This is a situation that may lead to shame and humiliation, plus instances of inequity and various other degrees of abuses of power (Namie and Namie, 2011). The useful distinction between positive and negative outcomes of information disclosure is illustrated in Figure 8.1. It is a timely reminder, as information-sharing tools continue to fill our organisational and private lives, that both the advantages and the pitfalls of transparency policies and practices must be considered.

A feature of Figure 8.1 is that some elements of every person are always held outside of the shared field of transparency. The outer crescents of each circle denote these mutually exclusive realms. Personal information that, possibly, is perceived as socially embarrassing is always guarded by people. In essence, there is a personal and private boundary to every individual that is probably best left unravelled by any policy of transparency.

Consider that negative transparency, as it is portrayed on the right side of the top of Figure 8.1, has a distorting effect on the individual, mainly when privacy is breached or when power-control relationships are imbalanced. The person who has certain private information exposed will suffer embarrassment, or a taint to their reputation. A complication comes when the information that is exposed is distorted and misrepresentative of what is happening in reality. So, not only can true and sensitive private information be exposed in negative transparency situations, but false information can also be circulated, thus leading to embarrassment. The elliptical shape of Person A in Figure 8.1 portrays the distortion of shame, embarrassment or discrimination that comes

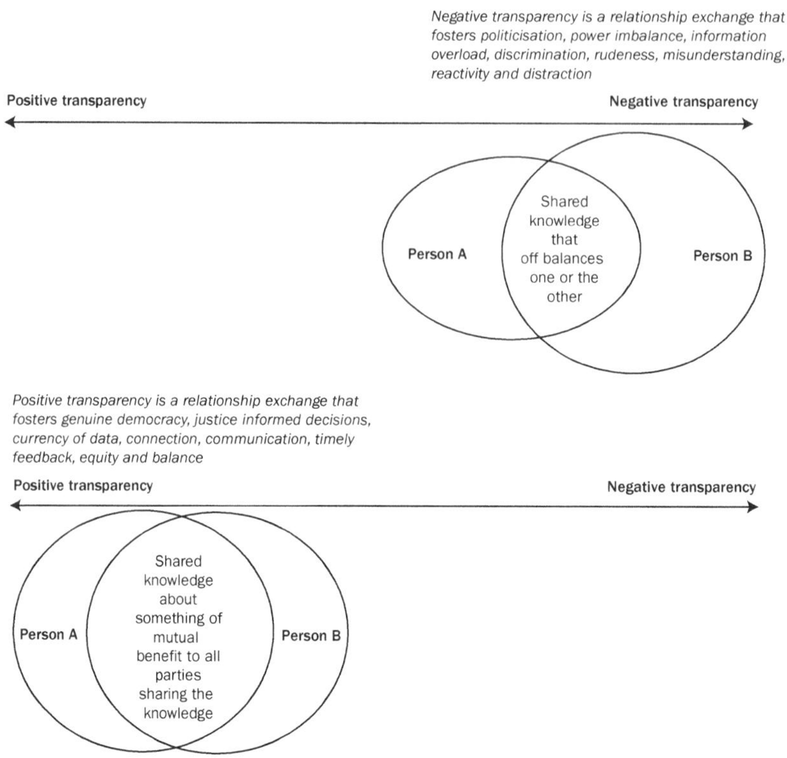

Figure 8.1 **The continuum of transparency**

Source: Authors' own composition

from negative transparency. The relationship effectively drags Person A from the left to the right of the continuum. It reveals the natural desire of a shamed or embarrassed individual to return to a more positive state. In addition, the people enmeshed in the negative transparency situation may or may not be conscious of what is happening, effectively suggesting that intentional as well as unintentional harm can result. Person A's inner balance can be disturbed with or without them realising, and Person B can either consciously or accidentally expose sensitive information that causes the problem.

The bottom right of Figure 8.1 displays the positive aspects of transparency and helps explain why some managers have sought to implement policies supportive of greater transparency. There are many good economic and relational reasons why democratic, open, fair, current, equitable and balanced communication should be encouraged in all kinds of organisations. The trouble is that, without thoughtfulness, transparency can become an ethically slippery slope (Krotosky, 2010; Rosenberg, 2010; Bannister and Connolly, 2011). The person initiating a tactic of transparency must bear in mind the motives that lead to the information being exposed, the truthfulness of the information and the potential for embarrassing another person(s). Intentional embarrassment is among the purposes of the principle of fiduciary transparency. For instance, it is the fear of embarrassment and socio-legal reprimands that discourages people from defrauding an organisation. But when the power offered by the opportunity to intentionally embarrass seduces an individual to apply it indiscriminately and dishonestly to someone they actively dislike or, unthinkingly, to someone who is not perceived to be socially significant, a situation of negative transparency will occur. Racism, sexism, ageism and other kinds of discrimination in social settings are variations of negative transparency, especially via the misrepresentation of personal information that normally should have no relevance to organisational or other kinds of relationships (Epstein, 2008). This is the territory in which managers find themselves when a seemingly innocuous policy is implemented that has the focus of making them more transparent with their employees, or other stakeholders. Yes, decisions and actions that lead to positive transparency are to be applauded, but negative transparency is to be avoided. This is why an understanding of the subtle differences in the concepts is important. When the development of new, powerful communication applications are added to the mix, we have an especially challenging set of circumstances to consider. For instance, race- or gender-specific communications, trade secrets, strategic knowledge and sensitive financial data might all be spread much further than anticipated through websites and messaging technologies if users are not very careful in following correct protocols.

Transparency as control through social media

Transparency is justified in organisations as a way of encouraging equity and fair resource allocation. But that same transparency can be turned upon staff as a mechanism of control and strategic embarrassment that can lead to the same kinds of inequities and unfairness it was intended to avoid. Email circulations, Facebook, Twitter, blog postings and mass media exposures can all be widely used as control devices, but the question is: do they achieve much more than satisfying the need of people to engage in gossip (and pursue darker motives), or as an aspect of social control?

Managers and colleagues do need to consider that gossip has the potential to hurt, rather than help, individuals and the organisation. There is anecdotal and case-based evidence of embarrassing gossip in many workplaces that (unintentionally or purposefully) is directed toward controlling the behaviour of people (Sutton, 2010; Seidler, 2011). When embarrassing gossip is spread using the powerful magnifying effects of social media, the most insidious kind of bullying can emerge. People's words and reactions can be fanned and inflamed by social media, in addition to the usual communication modes of meetings, corridor discussions and drinks after work. Accordingly, there are many opportunities for intentional and accidental public humiliation. Recently, in higher education workplaces, this practice has been referred to as 'academic mobbing' (Leymann, 1996; Tigrel and Kokalan, 2009; Khoo, 2010), and the negative health effects are also noted. Wider studies of mobbing, or bullying, in the workplace arrive at similar conclusions about health issues (Rodríguez-Carballeira et al., 2010; Soylu, 2011; Hershcovis, 2011). With social media now in the mix, such mobbing can become more pervasive.

Consider this scenario: a group of academics teaching an online subject communicate with each other regularly by email and teleconferencing. In addition, their student engagement activities are mutually observable via the online learning management system through a collection of social media tools, including discussion threads, blogs, wikis and web conferencing applications. One day, the team leader asks members of the teaching team to complete a data-gathering task that is not core to the teaching policies of the associated faculty or school. One member of the team does not complete the task within the time that it is requested by the leader, although it is completed later after the core teaching duties are finalised. Subsequently, the team leader becomes frustrated with that particular team member for not doing as told and when told (regardless of the fact that key objectives and policies are still met subsequently). Without discussing the reasoning behind the delay directly with the team member, the leader circulates an email stating the feeling of frustration to a number of senior managers in the school.

Discussion thread postings are also made by the team leader inside the learning management system, with this implying to students that the team member is not undertaking their required duties. All of this activity by the leader makes an internal team issue a matter of strategic embarrassment for the team member in the eyes of the team, the senior managers and the students. The matter is also not resolved in an open manner by the senior people who are copied on the email. Requests by the affected team member to senior managers for negotiation assistance are left unanswered.

The abovementioned scenario describes behaviour and outcomes that are adapted from a real experience and shows how negative transparency, as an effort to control someone, was generated by the team leader's actions. Note that the team member was in a subordinate position, and that the associated power relationships were asymmetrical. Furthermore, the team leader was a senior staff member, and the aforementioned email was copied to other managers who outranked the team member and leader, respectively. When students were also involved in the miscommunication, the feelings of humiliation for the team member became worse. A perception of mobbing was generated and feelings of uncertainty, or being scrutinised for any possible slip-up in future work, filled the team member's mind in the months that followed. What made this situation more stressful and increasingly complicated was that necessary discussion between the team member and the head of the school occurred two months after the initial incident.

From our perspective, this situation could have been turned around at three key points.

1. The team leader should have discussed any delay with the team member prior to going up the so-called chain of command.
2. The team leader should not have posted a double-barrelled message to students with access to the online learning management system.
3. Senior managers who had been copied in the email of complaint by the team leader should have intervened in a timely manner after observing that the matter was unresolved.

The role of civility and etiquette

As is increasingly evident, bullying, mobbing and discrimination are dramatic examples of the effects of negative transparency. However, there is a more subtle disruption in the transparency continuum that comes from a lack of civility and etiquette in communications that spreads outward and onward, just like a ripple in a pond (Mullen et al., 2011). Now, with emoticons as well as SMS and Twitter abbreviations proliferating in online language, the potential has grown for breaches of etiquette and misinterpretation leading to misunderstandings of communication intentions (Farina and Lyddy, 2011; Thurlow and Mroczek, 2011). Obviously, there are diverse perceptions as to what should be civil behaviour and proper approaches to communication at work (Bryant and Sias, 2011). In this context, give thought to cultural differences, in addition to variations in socialised expectations and behaviours, which are common in workplaces (Figiel, 2011; Witte, 2011). Nevertheless, communication policies can be generated that explicitly define the range of behaviours, words and activities that would constitute appropriate etiquette in various media. For instance, workplaces have been quick to recognise the social changes happening through online applications, such as Facebook and Twitter, but workplaces have been limited in the extent of their associated response. Policy initiatives related to social media usage have tended to be reactive to perceived breaches of privacy, or are a response to claims of bullying or discrimination among some staff members (IBM, 2011). Unfortunately (and commonly), such policies are ignored, or not prioritised. For example, it can seem pedantic for a manager to insist on everybody in their area of responsibility being trained in how to compose electronic messages in a certain style; so much depends on the literacy, mood and professionalism of a communicator. Yet, practically, so little can be done to motivate diligent attention to foster continuous improvement of communication styles and habits.

The social media companies themselves are having to respond to community feedback on issues of etiquette and other genuine concerns linked with privacy versus transparency. Facebook, for instance, introduced a real-time ticker in 2011 that shows what friends are currently talking about and, as a direct result, there was an instant reaction as people realised that they might have lost a little control over how they communicated in their online space (Halliday, 2011). Also, the sensitivities of making changes to social media are closely allied with the usual dynamics of human relationships. Users of social media, therefore, like to have clarity and transparency offered by service providers, but not at the expense of personal control and privacy. Nevertheless, by no account are we dismissing the use of social media to communicate, as this would be unrealistic and unachievable in this digital age. However, we urge the users of social media to be aware of the benefits and challenges from our perspective for organisations and individuals as highlighted in Table 8.1.

As social media proliferates, a number of the resultant disadvantages have been overlooked or misinterpreted. The benefits are strong enough to encourage proponents to continue the spread of the technology. However, there is enough history available at present to demonstrate the need for caution, as the boundaries between positive and negative transparency have become more fluid.

Table 8.1 **Benefits and challenges of transparency via social media**

Positive changes associated with social media	Challenges for organisations and individuals with social media
▪ Increased awareness and facilitation of grass-roots democracy on important social issues ▪ Speeding up of processes possibly leading to better justice in some individual and group disputes ▪ More informed decision making ▪ Instant updates on matter significant to individual ▪ Connectivity and networks across the globe ▪ Receiving feedback from people and your discipline irrespective of geographical and time boundaries	▪ Instant politicisation of issues that become transparent and are discussed through the networks ▪ Swift changes to the power balances in organisations leading to instability and uncertainty over leadership and tenure ▪ Deluge of information, much of it potentially irrelevant or distracting from making good decisions ▪ Proliferation of opportunities to invoke negative transparency to marginalise and discriminate against individuals ▪ Relative ease of slipping into breaches of communication etiquette ▪ Potential of misunderstandings due to lack of body language ▪ Temptation to reply reactively to a message without being reflective on the content or control of emotions ▪ Distraction from core work responsibility to check for updates across various social mediums such as Facebook and LinkedIn

Source: Authors' own composition

Transparency tensions in the organisational social network: The next step

Information contains power of different polarities. Positive transparency is a policy that seeks to balance informational and positional power. In comparison, negative transparency tends to put individuals and organisations off-balance on the basis of so-called 'dirt', or distorted innuendo. Broadly, it can be understood that a political scene emerges out of these tensions (Shirky, 2011). For instance, the traditional status divide between management and workers, in part, is defined by the level of access to information and the extent of any transparency. Often, workers' unions have campaigned for greater management transparency as part of the fight against various inequalities in workplaces and other business settings. Conversely, unions have also come under criticism for not being transparent enough about their own activities. In the analysis of the decline of traditional unionism in countries such as Australia, it is noted that the need for people to band together in order to push back against oppressive situations is not diminished and, in fact, it is through social media networks that this need is arguably finding fresh expression. People will email, text and tweet readily about their abusive boss. Yet these folk are more reticent about invoking action through a traditional union that is perceived to be increasingly expensive, slow to respond to individual situations and focused on larger political negotiations that are often well beyond immediate organisational concerns. Remarkably, there have also been cases of management choosing to use Facebook to sack employees, rather than handle the matter person to person (Gettler, 2010).

As presented in Figure 8.1, positive transparency is an expression of balanced mutual knowledge, as forms the basis of the sorts of revolutions that improve organisational functioning. In this regard, social media networks are found to be facilitative of positive transparency and have been identified as possibly crucial in recent political upheavals at the country level, such as during the Arab Spring (Harb, 2011; Khondker, 2011; Tapas, 2011). When everybody in a social network begins to know that everybody else agrees with their point of view (for instance, that a dictator should be deposed), this new transparency diminishes the fear that would otherwise serve to prevent any possible revolution. The same mechanism applies at the organisational level. Leadership of an organisation depends upon follower support; positive transparency, therefore, is an important way to identify the levels of support circulating through the network of communications. The 'elephant in the room' for leaders is how to handle negative transparency if, and when, it emerges. The social network can just as easily connect everybody in an organisation through private and innuendo-based knowledge that upsets any existing power balance and, thereby, can spark a revolution that need not happen. Intentional debasing of people, or just clumsy, inaccurate undermining, can occur through negative transparency. Abuses of power are still very possible and can in fact be magnified through new media, thus making the basic principle of a worker union still highly relevant. But the social mechanism for how people come together to communicate has changed irrevocably.

While proponents of social media technology readily point to the positive benefits of changes being wrought by the proliferating networked applications of Twitter, Facebook, Google+ and more, it is timely to highlight the potential downside. Organisations and individuals might need technological change and social innovation to remain competitive and sustainable; still, the reality of change is closely allied with power bases and political tensions. Harm to individuals and groups can just as easily be the result, as can expected improvement. The emergence of social media guidelines and similar communication policies is indicative of the growing awareness of the possible abuses that can be promulgated through social media. Accordingly, more empirical research is required across different sectors and organisational sizes to identify if, and how, various organisations have accepted and responded to the new forms of social media in order to communicate effectively and appropriately with their employees and other stakeholders. In addition, consideration must be given where any necessary bans are put in place to restrict the use of workplace assets and resources (including access to the Internet) as relate to social media usage by employees. The penalties implemented in the latter case also need to be publicised and further discussed, especially in light of our next generation of employees who have been born and brought up in the digital age, with all the attitudes toward transparency and online behaviour that this entails.

References

Ball, C. (2009) What Is Transparency? *Public Integrity*, 11(4), 293–308.

Bandsuch, M., Pate, L. and Thies, J. (2008) Rebuilding Stakeholder Trust in Business: An Examination of Principle-Centered Leadership and Organizational Transparency in Corporate Governance. *Business and Society Review*, 113(1), 99–127.

Bannister, F. and Connolly, R. (2011) The Trouble with Transparency: A Critical Review of Openness in e-Government. *Policy & Internet*, 3(1), 1–13.

Braxton, E. (2010) Healing the Wounded Organization: The Role of Leadership in Creating the Path to Social Justice. *Tamara Journal for Critical Organization Inquiry*, 8(3), 89–118.

Bryant, E. and Sias, P. (2011) Sensemaking and Relational Consequences of Peer Co-worker Deception. *Communication Monographs*, 78(1), 115–37.

Crotty, J. (2011) Structural Causes of the Global Financial Crisis: A Critical Assessment of the 'New Financial Architecture'. *Cambridge Journal of Economics*, 33(4), 563–80.

Epstein, D. (2008) Have I Been Googled: Character and Fitness in the Age of Google, Facebook, and YouTube. *Georgetown Journal of Legal Ethics*, 21(1), 715–28.

Eriksson, J. (2011) Privacy Is Dead: Long Live Surveillance Symmetry. *Internet Computing, IEEE*, 15(1), 81–3.

Farina, F. and Lyddy, F. (2011) The Language of Text Messaging: 'Linguistic Ruin' or Resource? *The Irish Psychologist*, 37(6), 145–9.

Figiel, V. (2011) Culture: National, Organizational And Occupational: The Case Of Honda Of America Manufacturing, Inc. *Journal of Business & Economics Research*, 1(12), 65–72.

Gardels, N. (2011) WikiLeaks and the Perils of Extreme Glasnost. *New Perspectives Quarterly*, 28(1), 6–11.

Gettler, L. (2010) Facebook Sackings. *The Age*, 17 November. Available at *www.theage.com.au/executive-style/management/blogs/management-line/facebook-sackings-20101113-17rny.html*

Halliday, J. (2011) Facebook Changes See the Social Network Trying to be More Social. *The Guardian*, 21 September. Available at *www.guardian.co.uk/technology/pda/2011/sep/21/facebook-changes-social-network*

Harb, Z. (2011) *Arab Revolutions and the Social Media Effect*. M/C Journal, 14(2). Available at *http://journal.media-culture.org.au/index.php/mcjournal/article/view/364*

Haufler, V. (2010) Disclosure as Governance: The Extractive Industries Transparency Initiative and Resource Management in the Developing World. *Global Environmental Politics*, 10(3), 53–73.

Hershcovis, M. (2011) Incivility, Social Undermining, Bullying… Oh My!: A Call to Reconcile Constructs Within Workplace Aggression Research. *Journal of Organizational Behavior*, 32(1), 499–519.

IBM (2011) *IBM Social Computing Guidelines: Blogs, Wikis, Social Networks, Virtual Worlds and Social Media*. Available at *www.ibm.com/blogs/zz/en/guidelines.html*

Khondker, H. (2011) Role of the New Media in the Arab Spring. *Globalizations*, 8(5), 675–9.

Khoo, S. (2010) Academic Mobbing: Hidden Health Hazard at Workplace. *Malaysian Family Physician*, 5(2), 61–7.

Koall, I. (2011) Managing Complexity: Using Ambivalence and Contingency to Support Diversity in Organizations. *Equality Diversity and Inclusion: An International Journal*, 30(7), 572–88.

Krotosky, A. (2010) Introduction to the Special Issue: Research Ethics in Online Communities. *International Journal of Internet Research Ethics*, 3(12), 1–6.

Lee, B. (2001) Mutual Knowledge, Background Knowledge and Shared Beliefs: Their Roles in Establishing Common Ground. *Journal of Pragmatics*, 33(1), 21–44.

Lewis, D. (2011) Whistleblowing in a changing legal climate: Is it time to revisit our approach to trust and loyalty at the workplace? *Business Ethics: A European Review*, 20(1), 71–87.

Leymann, H. (1996) The Content and Development of Mobbing at Work. *European Journal of Work and Organizational Psychology*, 5(2), 65–184.

Marwick, A. and Boyd, D. (2011) I Tweet Honestly, I Tweet Passionately: Twitter Users, Context Collapse, and the Imagined Audience. *New Media & Society*, 13(1), 114–33.

Morozov, E. (2011) WikiLeaks and the New Language of Diplomacy. *New Perspectives Quarterly*, 28(1), 7–11.

Mullen, C., Bettez, S. and Wilson, C. (2011) Fostering Community Life and Human Civility in Academic Departments Through Covenant Practice. *Educational Studies*, 47(3), 280–305.

Namie, G. and Namie, R. (2011) *The Bully-Free Workplace: Stop Jerks, Weasels, and Snakes from Killing your Organization.* Hoboken, NJ: John Wiley & Sons Inc.

Overbaugh, J. (2011) 24/7 Isn't the Only Way: A Healthy Work–Life Balance Can Enhance Research. *Nature,* 477(7362), –27–28.

Palackal, A., Mbatia, P., Dzorgbo, D., Duque, R., Ynalvez, M. and Shrum, W. (2011) Are Mobile Phones Changing Social Networks? A Longitudinal Study of Core Networks in Kerala. *New Media & Society*, March 2011, 1–20.

Pratt, A. (2005) The Wrong Kind of Transparency. *The American Economic Review*, 95(3), 862–77.

Rodan, G. (2000) Asian Crisis, Transparency and the International Media in Singapore. *The Pacific Review*, 13(2), 217–42.

Rodríguez-Carballeira, Á., Escartín Solanelles, J., Visauta Vinacua, B., Porrúa García, C. and Martín-Peña, J. (2010) Categorization and Hierarchy of Workplace Bullying Strategies: A Delphi Survey. *The Spanish Journal of Psychology*, 13(1), 297–308.

Rosenberg, A. (2010) Virtual World Research Ethics and the Private/Public Distinction. *International Journal of Internet Research Ethics*, 3(12), 23–37.

Roth, F. (2009) The Effect of the Financial Crisis on Systemic Trust. *Intereconomics*, 44(4), 203–8.

Seidler, J. (2011) As Social Network News Goes Viral, Who's Doing Any Work? *The Sydney Morning Herald*, 18 March. Available at *www.smh.com.au/opinion/society-and-culture/as-social-network-news-goes-viral-whos-doing-any-work-20110318-1bzt9.html*

Shirky, C. (2011) The Political Power of Social Media. *Foreign Affairs*, January/February, 1–9.

Soylu, S. (2011) Creating a Family or Loyalty-Based Framework: The Effects of Paternalistic Leadership on Workplace Bullying. *Journal of Business Ethics*, 99(2), 217–31.

Sutton, R. (2010) *The No Asshole Rule: Building a Civilised Workplace and Surviving One That Isn't*. London: Piatkus.

Tapas, R. (2011) The 'Story' of Digital Excess in Revolutions of the Arab Spring. *Journal of Media Practice*, 12(2), 189–96.

Thierer, A. (2011) *Public Interest Comment on Federal Trade Commission Report, Protecting Consumer Privacy in an Era of Rapid Change*, 17 February. Available at *http://ssrn.com/abstract=1763398*

Thurlow, C. and Mroczek, K.R. (2011) *Digital Discourse: Language in the New Media*. Oxford: Oxford University Press.

Tigrel, E. and Kokalan, O. (2009) Academic Mobbing in Turkey. *World Academy of Science, Engineering and Technology*, 55(1), 963–71.

Tschannen-Moran, M. and Hoy, W. (2000) A multidisciplinary analysis of the nature, meaning and measurement of trust. *Review of Educational Research*, 70(4), 547–93.

Veil, S., Buehner, T. and Palenchar, M. (2011) A Work-In-Process Literature Review: Incorporating Social Media in Risk and Crisis Communication. *Journal of Contingencies and Crisis Management*, 19(2), 110–22.

Westphal, J. (1986) White. *Mind*, 95(379), 311–28.

Williams, C. (2005) Trust Diffusion: The Effect of Interpersonal Trust on Structure, Function, and Organizational Transparency. *Business Society*, 44(3), 357–68.

Williams, C. (2008) Toward a Taxonomy of Corporate Reporting Strategies. *Journal of Business Communication*, 45(3), 232–64.

Witte, A. (2011) Making the Case for a Post-National Cultural Analysis of Organizations. *Journal of Management Inquiry*, 20(4), 1–19.

Yoo, C. (2011) Modeling Audience Interactivity as the Gratification-Seeking Process in Online Newspapers. *Communication Theory*, 21(1), 67–89.

9

Social media: blessing or curse? – a business perspective

Richard Messik

Abstract: With the immense popularity of social media comes an increasing understanding that it has a valuable application for business users too. Essentially, social media can become an intra-organisational communications tool, as well as one that connects with the world at large. For reasons of immense practicality, social media has the ability to replace email, as is already the case for wise and wary people who prefer a certain form of communication that is without issues caused by the sending of ill-thought-out messages. Even so, care must be taken when any online posting takes place to ensure that the right message is delivered to the right audience, and for the right reasons. If this is not done, significant problems can arise, as will be magnified by the effectiveness of social media in reaching out to an increasingly interconnected, international population.

Key words: social media, business perspective, communication, audience, growth, enterprise, social network, tool, marketing.

Introduction

Ever since ancient civilisations recorded events on stone tablets (if not earlier), the ability to disseminate information has played a pivotal role in the development and intellectual growth of the human race. The invention of the printing press was a seminal enhancement in the method of transmitting knowledge to a wider audience and, arguably, the growth of the Internet has played no less a part in the history of communication – fundamentally changing the way that we impart and gain information, as well as communicate with each other.

Whereas the Internet was a late twentieth-century innovation, social media in all its forms is a twenty-first-century pivotal progression in the science of communication.

Seemingly, it came out of nowhere, developed by bored university students (if popular myth is to be believed) and struck a chord with the younger generation – and, probably, has saved a generation of parents a fortune in telecom charges as their children no longer needed to spend hours on the telephone to impart the latest and most important gossip of the day.

As with all innovations, many different social media brands have sprung up. Some have continued to flourish, while others withered on the vine of popular acceptance. However, those that survived have gained followers in hitherto unbelievable numbers.

It has grown exponentially in the last five years as the following would indicate:

- One in every nine people on Earth is on Facebook (calculated by dividing the planets 6.94 billion people by Facebook's 800 million users).
- People spend 700 billion minutes per month on Facebook.
- Each Facebook user spends on average 15 hours and 33 minutes a month on the site.
- More than 250 million people access Facebook through their mobile devices.
- More than 2.5 million websites have integrated with Facebook.
- 30 billion pieces of content is shared on Facebook each month.
- 300 000 users helped translate Facebook into 70 languages.
- People on Facebook install 20 million apps every day.
- YouTube has 490 million unique users who visit every month (as of February 2011).
- YouTube generates 92 billion page views per month. (These YouTube stats don't include videos viewed on phones and embedded in websites.)
- Users on YouTube spend a total of 2.9 billion hours per month (326 294 years).

- Wikipedia hosts 17 million articles.
- Wikipedia authors total over 91 000 contributors.
- People upload 3000 images to Flickr (the photo-sharing social media site) every minute.
- Flickr hosts over 5 billion images.
- 190 million average tweets per day occur on Twitter (as of May 2011).
- Twitter is handling 1.6 billion queries per day.
- Twitter is adding nearly 500 000 users a day.
- Google+ has more than 25 million users.
- Google+ was the fastest social network to reach 10 million users, at 16 days (Twitter took 780 days and Facebook 852 days).

Source: www.searchenginejournal.com/the-growth-of-social-media-an-infographic/32788

Psychologists have had a field day in attempting to outdo each other by providing explanations as to why those of the generation of today wish to share their experiences and thoughts (however banal) with – almost literally – the whole world, and why, indeed, others want to know about them.

A rather tongue-in-cheek way of explaining the various brands of social media is provided in Table 9.1.

Table 9.1 **Social media apps and their descriptions**

Social media app	Description
Twitter	*I'm eating a doughnut*
Facebook	*I like doughnuts*
Foursquare	*This is where I eat doughnuts*
YouTube	*Here I am eating a doughnut*
LinkedIn	*My skills include doughnut eating*
G+	*I'm a Google employee who eats doughnuts*

Source: Various

Perhaps those are a little unfair; but, it does give the general idea. Of course, there are other brands of social media, but those shown in Table 9.1 above are arguably the most popular.

So given the growth of social media, and its ever-increasing popularity, does it have a role in the business environment? Can it become the

Social media as a marketing tool

A few years ago, marketing was a much simpler affair. Companies advertised their products, claiming how wonderful they were. People bought the product or didn't, as the case may be. Some people might have passed the message on to others, but essentially this was a one-way communication process: company to consumer – one to one.

A few happy (or disgruntled) customers can affect the success of a brand, although that can happen with some notable exceptions. In the past, communicating to a wide audience was a complicated business, and well beyond the ability of most individuals. Mistakes, or bad service, could be localised and isolated. Damage to a brand was limited.

Social media has changed this concept completely. Do something right, and one person might mention it – do it wrong, and they tell the world. Modern marketing must recognise this – after all, that old adage might well have been coined for the world of social media. As a mode of complaint, social media has no equal.

In his aforementioned article, Justin Webb quotes the experience of Qantas, the Australian airline, when it launched a social media campaign to improve its brand image after a damaging strike. The airline used social media to ask people to name their 'dream luxury flight experience' and offered prizes for the best suggestions. The Twitter reaction was devastating.... no one was interested in the prize, but it provided the perfect forum to complain about Qantas!

Another example relates to a well-known magazine that sent out subscription offers with the additional incentive of a substantial supply of chocolate to those who subscribed. A reader responded to the promotion and, sure enough, received a confirmation for the new subscription – but, surprise, surprise, no chocolate. A number of emails to the marketing department prompted a response stating that, had the reader looked at the small print more closely, she would have seen that the offer only applied to the first 500 subscribers... in other words – tough!

A few years ago, probably, that would have been the end of it. However, in the new world of instant response and a worldwide audience, this particular incident for that solitary subscriber was like the proverbial red rag to a bull. The affected reader immediately tweeted about the magazine's poor customer service, with this quickly becoming an issue that was taken up and retweeted by numerous others. The result? The magazine's marketing department became aware of the

Twitter traffic and sent out a tweeted response that additional supplies of the chocolate had been resourced; honour was satisfied.

Of course, the principal feature of social media is that it is a medium that enables communication by one to many – as opposed to email that, usually, is one to one (unless, of course, you hit the 'Reply to all' button inadvertently – as many have discovered to their detriment).

This is fine when the message or comment is directed at the world at large – and, as has been discussed above, there is nothing more efficient than internationally connected, electronic communication. However, its strength is also its major weakness.

LinkedIn is a site that has grown in popularity in recent years and is now the *de facto* source of professional information – very much a public CV. It is so much so, that this can say more about someone whose details are not on LinkedIn than those folk who are. Normally, this is fine – a great resource for finding information on contacts, enabling people to know who they are dealing with when they first get in touch.

However, as with ill-considered comments on Twitter, many have come unstuck when they publish, for example, that they are looking for new employment. It is great that the world at large can discover that they are available – although not so great if their current employer can also see that they are about to lose a principal member of the team.

Can social media generate new business?

At a recent seminar, the following question was posed: does social media work for professionals?

The gist of the argument was that while many professionals now use social media, did they benefit from so doing? Apart from the overriding (and not unimportant) consideration that it is fun. (As is often said, 'If it ain't fun, don't do it.') It was an interesting point.

As many professionals will agree, networking in its many forms is an essential component of business generation and, over the years, this has become more popular and widespread.

In many respects, this is what social media is – being another form of networking in getting your name out to a wider world, and expressing views and opinions which might not be heard otherwise. Importantly, those who will be reading your online comments and so on are users of social media themselves and, if they are looking for an accountant or professional advisor, they are possibly more likely to choose one who is social media-savvy.

It is obvious to the millions of daily users that social media is an excellent medium for getting your name and message heard by a larger audience. Yet will it generate new business? Well, like chicken soup, it probably won't hurt!

As with most media, when used sensibly, it can be a great asset; used carelessly, it can be an absolute disaster.

10

Improving the customer experience: how social media can make a difference

Urs E. Gattiker

Abstract: By early 2012, Google+ had 90 million users and was growing fast, but still far behind Facebook. This chapter outlines what these numbers could mean for your business. Specifically, we suggest four steps to ensuring effective social media use. In addition, we explain how quality management with actionable metrics and key performance indicators (KPIs) can help you better engage with your fans or readers. We end this chapter with several practical implications, and possible trends, to watch out for.

Key words: actionable metrics, key performance indicators, trends, define objectives, sales, trust, assess, create, target audience, added value, listening, monitoring, engagement, key drivers, corporate strategy, monitor quality, measure performance.

Introduction

You may likely share with me the belief that customer loyalty and retention are critical to the survival and growth of any business. The two-way conversation resulting from the addition of social media to the equation is the new kid in town that plays an increasingly important role in customer relationship management. Even so, making an impact in social media does not necessitate redefining the role of customer loyalty and retention. However, we all need to be aware that the quality of any related experience and service is the most important branding exercise. Basically, customers' opinions matter in most companies, regardless of whom you talk to in the organisation.

Social media encompasses any tool or service that uses telecommunication technology, including digital media, to facilitate the production and exchange of information and action. Of course, how social media is used is influenced by context, such as your business' industry and culture (e.g. language), as well as other factors such as gender and users' age. For instance, female teenagers use social media differently than their male peers. To make matters easier, social media is often described using examples, such as:

- Facebook, where people connect with friends and family, and share images, videos and status updates;
- LinkedIn or Xing, both networks where professionals connect;
- Twitter, a micro-blogging platform that allows people to share ideas in up to 140 characters at a time with their followers;
- a corporate blog, where employees post information; and
- another platform, such as Orkut/Google in Pakistan and Brazil or Bebo in the UK.

We can discuss if a company *should* use social media, although that seems beyond the scope of this chapter. However, if a company wants to use social media *effectively*, it must evaluate its current position with the help of a social media audit (Gattiker, 2012). The resultant data can then be used to serve target audiences better with content they value.

Research based on 400 million Facebook fans indicates that only 3.5 to 7.49 per cent see your status update and only 0.25 to 0.90 per cent interact with the status update (Parker and Brian, 21 June 2011). To put this in email campaign terms, only 3 to 7 per cent open the message. Moreover, less than 1 per cent click-through on one of the links you provide in your email newsletter. Therefore, 50 000 Facebook fans (or email newsletter subscribers) represent just 3750 active Facebook likes (or newsletter subscribers). The rest is deadweight: fake user accounts or robots that certainly are not potential clients.

Does this suggest that we are producing content that represents added value for the client? It sounds more like a nightmare for any marketer, and implies that email campaigns and Facebook status updates are akin to broadcasting to an empty stadium. This chapter helps you to take these numbers with a grain of salt and proceed cautiously while crafting a strategy that best fits your organisation's circumstances.

Define what you want to do and why

Remember the last time you purchased shoes? If you wanted stiletto heels you probably wanted to look taller and sexier. Accordingly, you would probably wear them for a night out on the town, but going for a countryside walk in them is unlikely. Similarly, the purpose social media has for you is the single most important factor that influences whatever you do with it.

For instance, you may want to use it to help improve the customer experience regarding the product, interacting with your company or brand, as well as getting help when needed. Therefore, this overriding purpose will drive how you use social media (see Figure 10.1 below). Yes, spreading your name, building brand recognition and so forth is important and helps. Nevertheless, the single most important factor is helping your customers.

So what tracks, connects and helps your customers? Regardless of how we go about outlining this, it absolutely must be defined, beginning with Figure 10.1 and pages 156–7. Figure 10.1 shows three facets of the process for using social media to facilitate a better customer experience. In most cases, a company's interactions comprise a bit of all three types.

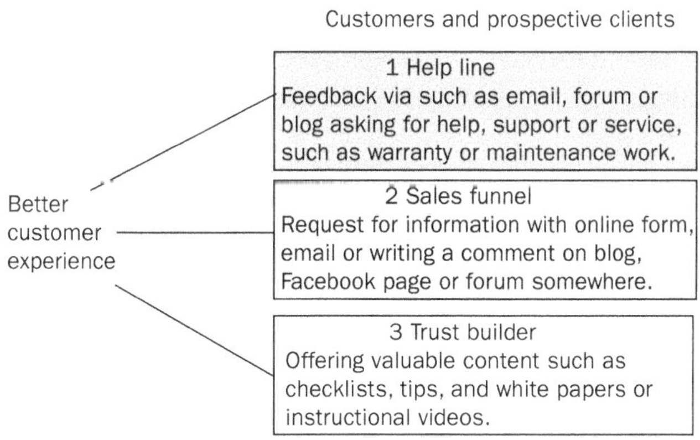

Figure 10.1 **Social media offers various ways to engage with the targeted audience for a better customer experience**

Source: CyTRAP Labs GmbH

Note: Added value means additional benefits for the client (e.g. learning, fun, instructional). Content with added value might be an instructional video, blog entry or research study that can be downloaded as a PDF file.

Such content helps grab the client's attention, which is the most valuable and difficult commodity to acquire on the Internet, because most cannot keep up with the information flow as they risk data overload.

For those who believe customer experience is not critical, let us review. When compared to a dissatisfied customer, a satisfied one:

- is about six times as likely to recommend the product, service or company to another person or to make a repeat purchase; and
- speaks with about five people about their 'great' experience, deal or service.

In comparison, a dissatisfied client:

- discusses their dissatisfaction with about nine people (word-of-mouth marketing at its worst); and
- rarely tells us they are dissatisfied – only about 4 per cent of dissatisfied customers tell us so (e.g. by email, online comment, phone or letter).

This illustrates that focusing on improving the customer experience before, during and after the sale is critical to attaining and maintaining a brand's desired reputation and image.

Help line

The help line can be described as various channels through which people can obtain support. For instance, I can visit coffee machine manufacturer Jura's website (*www.jura.com*). Beyond a Facebook Like button, it offers little in terms of social media, but it does offer the opportunity to fill out an online email form. If I do so with a problem pertaining to one of their products, an agent will call the same day or early the next morning at the latest. The competent agent will have your coffee maker's details, including repair records, on their screen. If necessary, they may ask you to stand in front of your machine and possibly help you fix the problem right then. If this works, I save time and money for the repairs I just avoided.

Other approaches are also feasible. For instance, fashion brand ASOS offers the ASOS Here to Help Facebook page. Its sole purpose is to ensure customer issues and requests for help or service stay off the main ASOS Facebook page (see *www.facebook.com/ComMetrics/posts/166548693451713*). However, 99 per cent of all companies in the EU have 250 or fewer employees. In the US, 96 per cent have 100 or fewer employees (see *http://commetrics.com/?p=16*). For such a small or medium-sized enterprise (SME), maintaining two Facebook pages is not on the cards.

Sales funnel

The sales funnel is a systematic approach to selling products or services. ASOS's main Facebook page keeps its customers informed about upcoming sales, incorporating social media into the sales funnel.

By contrast, Helsana, the Swiss health insurer, decided to establish a community on its homepage for clients to ask questions or discuss issues with others (*http://forum.helsana.ch*).

Another company may choose to offer a newsletter to which people can subscribe via email. Its monthly content might inform subscribers about new offerings, and how its products can be used more effectively. There are numerous options available, but considering staff time, costs and so forth, you must choose what is best for your organisation. Most important is that you are present where your clients wish to engage with you.

Trust builder

According to Figure 10.1, the last area we must address for improving the customer experience is to build trust with our audience. One way to do that is to offer content that is very useful, and valuable, to the target audience. For instance, a moving company such as North American Van Lines can offer an online checklist to help potential clients get ready for their move (see *www.northamerican.com/household-moving/residential moving-company-process.aspx*).

For a software company, it might be a blog that addresses issues of interest to its clients, and those who might still become customers. It could also offer slides or videos of recent presentations given by its experts at industry conferences (see also Gattiker, 6 October 2010).

Of course, it is best if a person signs up to get their blog content or newsletter via email, because it represents an opt-in, whereby the client agrees to receive your content (remember privacy and data protection laws). However, abusing such trust by sending sales-related material may result in a backlash, so stay focused on content that is of value to your target audience, such as industry trends, regulations, upcoming law changes, tools and so forth.

Define, assess and create

Figure 10.1 outlined how to achieve a better customer experience by using social media:

1. to provide help and support;
2. to apply it as a sales funnel; and/or
3. as a trust builder with those consuming the content you provide.

Depending on context, most companies use each of these approaches. For instance, providing an insightful answer in a discussion forum helps build your reputation. Somebody might approach you based on your visibility in a group.

Put differently, it is extremely hard to determine what actions are critical for encouraging your customer to complete a purchase. You might give a speech, or write a chapter as I did here, which can result in a person wanting to connect with you on LinkedIn, sending you an email, or downloading a white paper you wrote. Some call such behaviour 'micro-conversions' or 'actions' that could eventually result in a sale. But remember what goes around comes around – you must treat everybody's request with respect. This means that you must make the effort to acknowledge as well as reply to emails, comments on your Facebook page or a Twitter reply (an example of what not to do from Migros: *www.flickr.com/photos/cytrap/6724819869*). Now, we address additional challenges.

Who is my target audience?

If your focus is on a better customer experience, whatever clients need and prefer plays a key role. This means that you have to talk to your client to find out what content they would be interested in consuming, or what type of support would help them.

For instance, if I have a problem making an online payment using my bank's software, I probably need the answer right now so I can finish the payment process. However, if I need cosmetic surgery, things are a bit different. Sending an email and getting an answer within 24 hours might be fast enough.

In addition, it is important to be and remain aware of the fact that once the purchase is completed at a clothing store, such as H&M or Target, the cycle begins anew: the person moves back to the pre-sales stage and a repeat sale might happen if the customer experience continues to be satisfactory (for example, how easy it is to get warranty work done on appliances).

What content represents added value for my target audience?

The more narrow the definition of your target audience (for instance, breast cancer patients), the easier it is to provide value for that particular group. Whatever definition you use, it is advisable to consider five things:

1. **Share insights or help solve problems:** Do not shill/push your product, but make sure that the content is helpful to your reader, such as by providing a checklist.
2. **Show and tell:** With the help of graphics, images and/or short videos, explain how the product can be better applied, or how surgery will reduce the pain, for example.
3. **Surprise your audience:** Do something unexpected to grab your audience's attention.
4. **Create wings and roots:** Children need to see things in context to understand better. For instance, show the number of views for a video to get social validation, or explain how things relate to your corporate mission or strategy.
5. **Re-imagine – create five new things from one:** Do not recycle content, such as retweeting the same research paper on three different Twitter accounts over ten days. Instead, make a video about the research paper, pull audio from it and offer that as a podcast. Plus, write transcripts of podcasts and/or videos and post them to the web, or publish a blog post about the video, and embed the media files within it, and so on.

The challenge is that even if people subscribe to your content, it does not mean they actually consume it (remember our Facebook example – less than 1 per cent of your fans read and click on your status update). Getting people's attention on the web is the most important and valuable commodity you can get from social media users (see also Figure 10.2 below). So use your social media activity wisely to gain your audience's attention and keep it over the long haul.

A good example of value-added content is when it was discovered in late 2011 that women who had received breast implants from French manufacturer PIP could face a possible health risk. In response, many clinics and hospitals posted information on their blogs about this issue, which female patients eagerly sought out to learn whether their surgeon had used PIP implants or others (see *http://mem.to/t/g/28hjXi311*).

Where does our target audience want to engage with us?

As the above section outlines, our target audience wants content that is of value to them. If we are certain our content meets the criteria outlined on page 159, the next challenge is how we can get people to engage. To succeed, we must answer the following questions:

1. When does our client want to talk to us?
2. When does anyone interested in our product need to engage with us?

Often, people want to talk to you when they have a problem with your product (remember the e-banking example above). Twitter has become the agony aunt for disgruntled customers who take to the medium to complain about negative experiences. Of course, sometimes using a micro-blogging service (such as Identi.ca, Naijapulse.com or Twitter) is a last resort to get the supplier or seller to reply and rectify any problem (see also Figure 10.2 below).

As shown in Figure 10.2, attention is the most valuable commodity on social media because clients never have enough time to keep up with the flow of status updates from their friends and foes. Accordingly, one might click the Like button on a brand's Facebook page to be eligible for the sweepstakes, or a discount coupon. Nevertheless, after having participated, or receiving the discount voucher, some people most likely will not come back to read content, or view a video.

And just because 50 per cent of your clients are on Facebook does not mean they want to engage with you that way. Instead, they might want to share Kodak moments with their friends, or family members. Others want to chat with friends or update their Facebook wall with gibberish.

In short, you must figure out where your clients will want to engage with you. It could be that they prefer to comment on one of your blog entries, instead of leaving a comment or clicking on the Like button on your Facebook page. Talk to your clients and find out where they want to meet for a conversation using social media tools. Do this before

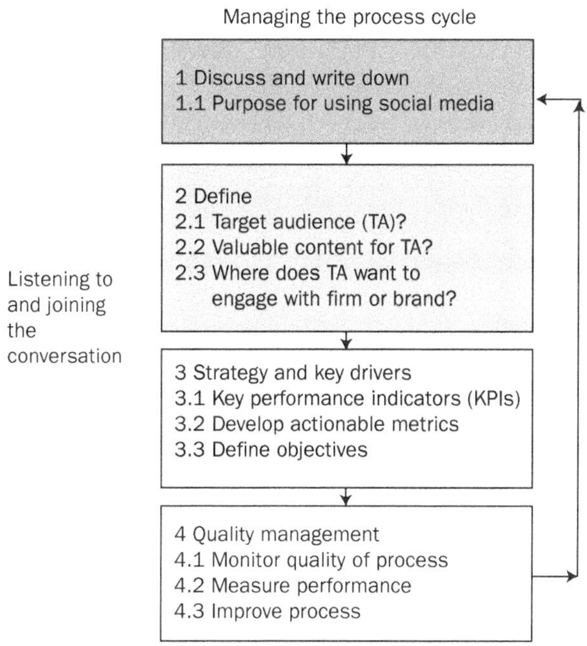

Figure 10.2 **Listening means monitoring what people say about you and what is happening on social media. The conversation about your organisation or brand happens with or without your participation**

Source: CyTRAP Labs GmbH

Note: Joining the conversation means that you reply to comments on your blog, tweets mentioning your brand, or emails sent to you. Guide the person requesting information to those who can provide the required help. All this improves the customer experience.

spending a lot of resources on, for example, Facebook, only to find that your clients want to engage on Google+ – or worse, neither.

By the way, some people simply do not want to be friends with their sock, butter or soft drink manufacturer.

Link key drivers to corporate strategy

Unless you understand what your target audience values regarding content and services, it is difficult to engage them with the help of social media. To illustrate, by now many of us who travel a bit are members of several loyalty programmes airlines offer their customers. It took airlines a while to discover that their most valued customers – people who travel a lot in business class – are those least likely to appreciate getting free flights. In response, airlines offered people the opportunity to redeem miles for merchandise, such as travel luggage. Just as with a frequent flyer programme, we must have a clear strategy spelling out what we want to accomplish. Obviously, easyJet's strategy is different than Ryanair's and both differ from Emirates' road map. Accordingly, these issues need to be addressed when developing a strategy for your organisation, regardless of whether it is for profit or not (see also Figure 10.2).

Strategy is the process of specifying an organisation's objectives, developing policies and plans to achieve these objectives, and allocating resources to get there. It can be for the outcome of the organisation as a whole, in which case we call it corporate strategy, or it might be for the outcome of using a particular resource, such as the IT, innovation or social media strategy.

Every strategy might state something to the effect that the company wants to be a leader in its industry, and take 20 per cent market share in some key markets. In turn, we need the operational goal that may point out that we plan to increase sales by 14 per cent and profits by 17 per cent this year, when compared to last year.

Now we must determine the key drivers that influence higher sales, lower customer returns, less warranty work, lower absenteeism and so on. Of course, social media will not affect your bottom line directly, but it can support your efforts to improve key drivers that do affect the bottom line.

Set up some key performance indicators (KPIs)

Once you have completed all of the abovementioned tasks, how are you supposed to score this to assess whether your performance is satisfactory? You do not want to end up 'data rich and information poor'. In addition, we need to know what high-quality data helps us to improve our understanding at the customer level about where your performance makes money (not just generating revenue). Furthermore, we will want to know where we can forge new relationships, change our price structure and redirect marketing campaigns.

As we read about how well people are doing in terms of linking, and increasing traffic to their website or blog, we often tend to forget that some of these experts produce content as the vehicle by which to generate revenue from such things as Google advertising. For most companies, however, producing content is just one of several ways used to help improve the customer experience. Of course, attracting prospects is a desirable outcome, but so is producing and offering content that is valued by targeted users.

While traffic may be important, it cannot be the sole purpose of this exercise. Many companies also talk about KPIs, or high-level metrics, such as customer satisfaction, revenue growth and profitability. Typically, KPIs rely upon smaller metrics that relate to business processes. For instance, if an e-commerce company has a KPI of 'percentage of repeat customers', it will need to measure metrics related to:

- customer complaints;
- merchandise returns;
- website performance; and
- shipping performance.

This allows the company to understand the KPI measure better. It is ideal if KPIs come from the top down, reflecting company-wide goals but, typically, KPIs come up from ground level; sometimes, the act of measuring something in one department filters up to the top.

Corporate objectives are not always clear, or shared across the employee base, and such a lack of insight can slow the process. Unfortunately, unless something is part of (or linked to) the overall strategy, it is unlikely to be worth measuring. Accordingly, if 20 000 comments and Likes are set as a target for the Facebook page, this needs to be linked to the top-level goals, such as increasing sales by 14 per cent this year.

To illustrate this further, if an HR department initiates a metrics programme, its goals might include improving employee performance and reducing attrition. Those goals then link to a corporate-level KPI, such as revenue generated per employee. You must find the same purpose for your social media efforts within your own organisation.

Develop actionable metrics

KPIs include actionable metrics that help you measure social media activities in ways that trigger actions. Hopefully, those actions will help to improve operating metrics, such as customer complaints or returns.

Actionable metrics provide you with data that helps you understand the 'why' behind a result, while supporting your efforts to reach higher performance targets. Such metrics are the little heroes of the data world, because they deliver actionable insights to help you make smart decisions that positively affect your bottom line.

No matter what metric you develop, unless there is a link between it and some key drivers/operating metrics, such as calls to your client hotline, why should top management care?

The beauty of metrics is in the eye of the beholder – whatever you decide to use, you must use what is most important to you and your stakeholders while ensuring your stakeholders understand it all.

Watching the trends is your best bet, but not necessarily by financial year quarters. Comparing July 2010 with October 2010 makes little sense in the northern hemisphere, because most people vacation during the former time, meaning your traffic will drop. Instead, comparing July 2010 with July 2011 and July 2012 shows whether a particular trend is moving in the right direction. Since the trend is what matters, do not forget to look ahead.

Primarily using traffic or volume to measure potential success might not result in profits. When it comes to success or failure, it is critical to understand the most important drivers or operating metrics. Accordingly, you must address what contribution(s) for achieving the company's operating metrics, such as higher customer retention, will come from social media efforts.

For example, a restaurant's Twitter followers might receive a daily code at around 10:30. If the code is used before 11:30, or after 13:30, to order lunch, a 10 per cent discount is given. Here, the idea is to satisfy regulars while enticing them to come before or after the lunch rush. The result is not waiting to be seated. In turn, lunch hour walk-ins have a better chance of getting seated right away. Accordingly, the percentage of clients who are forced to wait before getting a table during lunchtime – an important operating metric – is lowered.

Another example is business brochures: most businesses need a brochure to explain their products, services and/or mission. To reduce costs – an operating metric – a smaller number is printed. In one case, we found that beyond the 1000 print brochures, another 600 (a fictitious number) were downloaded from the Internet. Here, social media not only helped save costs, but it also increased diffusion of the information, resulting in more people looking at the product through downloads.

We can take a final example from advisory services. Many businesses start groups on social networks, such as LinkedIn, Xing or even Facebook. Unfortunately, building the membership of a social networking group, while supporting the company's brand and reputation, takes time – as much as a few months to build a following, and hard work each week to provide valuable content that keeps the group alive and kicking.

As a consultant, one needs contracts (an operating metric), and social media can help to increase opportunities by increasing one's visibility. However, rarely does one get a call from a group member to be invited to bid for a job. Often, it starts with meeting offline at a conference or networking event. These offline events facilitate building a better rapport that might ultimately result in the chance to bid for a job, or foster another subscription for one of our services.

Define objectives

As the third rectangle in Figure 10.2 suggests, once we have our actionable metrics, we need to do some more work. In fact, we need to develop **SMART** metrics that help guide us so that we reach our performance targets faster. SMART metrics are **Specific**, **Manageable**, **Actionable**, **Relevant** and **Trending**, making them ideal for creating a system to benchmark blogs and other social media efforts, such as Facebook or Google+ pages. However, these can also be used to evaluate social media analytics, and media metrics systems that you might purchase.

SMART metrics include goals that provide a set of measurable objectives, such as that overall attendance of a cancer support group's monthly meeting should increase from about 10 people in Q1 2011 to about 20 by Q1 2012. Of these newcomers, five to ten will be followers of our Facebook page.

This objective might raise a second, 'so what?' question before recommendations for action are made, and that is fine. However, if we get more than two or three 'so what?' responses in succession, we have the wrong metric and should therefore kill it.

Manage the process

You defined your target audience, know what kind of content they value and are sure where they want to interact with you (e.g. Facebook versus Google+ or Twitter). Moreover, you developed a sensible corporate strategy, set up the KPIs and developed actionable metrics backed up with SMART objectives. Then it is time to consider issues regarding the managing of the process and quality assurance (also see Figure 10.2 above).

In this section, we address the issue regarding monitoring the quality of the process (see also part 4 of Figure 10.2). Accordingly, the focus is on finding out how to measure performance, and if our SMART metrics were accomplished or not. It is most important to use this collected data to improve performance in subsequent quarters (Gattiker, 2012).

Monitor quality of process

There are different ways to monitor the quality of the process and, for the sake of brevity, we provide here just two short examples to illustrate how this works in practice.

Quality exit survey on the web

In human resource management (HRM), the exit survey is sometimes used to find out from people leaving the company what they liked and disliked. Similarly, one can do an exit survey with visitors to one's blog, or website. For instance, ask up to five short questions of every fiftieth website visitor, doing so just before they want to leave and with their browser window still open. Some will answer, and others will not. One question that must be asked is whether they found the information they sought.

For *http://ComMetrics.com* we do this to see what people might like and dislike. Of course, this information is just one indicator, but it can be very helpful. With all its limitations, it still tells you if the visit met expectations and what was great, as well as what (if anything) should and could be improved.

However, because a person answered anonymously and was selected at random (i.e. by chance), an exit survey does not allow us to reply, so beyond a 'thank you' at the end of the survey, there is little we can do to show our appreciation.

Follow up with email

Clearly, if someone unsubscribes from your email newsletter or blog, you should follow up, either more or less formally. In my experience, anywhere from 40 to 70 per cent of those who receive my less formal email when asking for help will respond with a reply. Mailed surveys and telephone interviews often generate a 10 to 25 per cent response rate. The rest of those who are sent the survey do not reply, or refuse to speak to the interviewer. Sometimes, the reply might be that they just had to change emails, or jobs, and unsubscribed only to subscribe again with another address. However, if the feedback suggests we post stuff that does not help our readers do better, we have a problem and need to reassess the situation.

Measure performance

As the fourth part in Figure 10.2 suggests, we have to measure our performance. There are three strategic reasons for measuring performance:

1. **Assess whether objectives are reached.** Know where you are, and know where you are going. Benchmark ratios are inherently measurable and comparable. They help you to focus your attention on the most controllable aspects of your online and social media activities (such as blogging for results). Success and failure can be evaluated clearly.
2. **Monitor your performance.** Keep your eye on the ball. Benchmark ratios provide an objective standard by which to measure your website or blog's performance. By tracking key measurements at regular intervals, you can pay closer attention to those key factors that affect your firm's performance. Follow the numbers, and the numbers will set you free.
3. **Share the results.** You should communicate your results internally and externally. Benchmark ratios enable your investors, owners and clients to evaluate objectively your online media efforts and positioning (as per branding). Clients and business associates can use them to understand better your strengths and weaknesses when it comes to social media and the web. Use your ratios to manage your online efforts better, securing your annual marketing budget, while spending it more wisely to improve your bottom line.

All of the above is done because we cannot just make buzz, we must make meaning – make money, not just web traffic.

Improve process and performance

In some ways, this is easy because all we need to do is appreciate the client, and acknowledge that they are important to us. But how does this work in practice? Today, the challenge is that people want to consume your content or service using whatever channel or platform they prefer, whether Facebook, Twitter, Quora or whatever. Most important is that many people expect an instantaneous answer to whatever question they might have fired off in your direction (Gattiker, 11 August 2010).

Joining the conversation means that you must carefully monitor and, most importantly, contribute to the discussions involving your company, brand or the group of which you are a member. Consider the out-of-sight, out-of-mind phenomenon. And when people take the time to share their ideas and insights on your platform, group or blog, they expect – if not demand – that you pay attention. In fact, you must show respect in terms of a polite and thoughtful reply. We illustrate this with four examples as follows.

Xing or LinkedIn

If you run a forum, please do it properly and do not misuse it for broadcasting and/or neglecting your duties as the moderator (see *www.flickr.com/photos/measure-for-impact/6105729213*). Not even those who should know better always behave in a proper way by taking the time to answer questions thoughtfully (Monster's example of how not to do it: *www.flickr.com/photos/cytrap/6311228553*).

In addition to cheering on members and ensuring everybody gets a reply, sometimes group moderators must be taskmasters and remind people of the rules (see this example from the LinkedIn group called Philips – Innovations in Health: *www.flickr.com/photos/measure-for-impact/6170495976*). Other times, it might be necessary to remind someone that posting an ad-like contribution in the forum is not the way to get a discussion going (see this Xing group regarding brands and image management: *www.flickr.com/photos/cytrap/6755127925*).

Also, as a group moderator you cannot go on a two-week business trip or holiday and be unavailable. You must designate somebody else to respond to any issues that may arise in your absence. Hence, you need a team of moderators.

Performing all of these tasks requires motivation, time and effort. It also means it is best to have several people share these duties for the company, and their job description must in turn include this responsibility. Additionally, enough time must be allocated to do it properly.

When addressing and evaluating the above issues, it is clear that you quickly get an idea of whether the group is working. Having a stream of posts without any replies means the group is used for broadcasting, not for conversation. That is not the way to use social media effectively – get it fixed!

Facebook or Google+

For a consumer brand such as ASOS, having the ASOS Here to Help Facebook page is a good way to keep customer issues and requests for help or service off their main Facebook page (see *www.facebook.com/ComMetrics/posts/166548693451713*).

In our case, we have found the Google+ page is a bit better than Facebook for our B2B (business-to-business) activities. Nevertheless, our Facebook and Google+ pages are used primarily for our own purposes – namely sharing and gaining insight into matters of direct interest. Rarely, if ever, have we had a customer ask for support through these channels. Instead, it has happened on a Xing group, our blog or via the web-based form.

In short, discover how this plays out best in your organisation. Then, think about how to improve it, simply by making it easier for clients to get in touch with you. Of course, you must provide timely and constructive feedback, as well as generous appreciation of your clients' online comments, replies and other online communications.

Twitter

US media giant Comcast was probably one of the earliest companies to start using micro-blogging service Twitter to offer customers a channel of last resort (*@ComcastCares*). Many more companies now offer a similar service, such as BankofAmericaHelp (see Gattiker, 6 October 2011). But as other examples indicate, Twitter is far from ideal for providing customer service that outscores other channels for user-friendliness and usefulness of replies (i.e. Deutsche Bahn or Swiss Federal Railways – see Gattiker, 12 February 2012).

Depending upon your Twitter account's primary objective, look at what can be improved. In our case, it is to gather intelligence from knowledgeable people whom we follow, and to share information with those that follow us. I do not advocate our using Twitter for customer service; instead, we use Google Chat (for example, commetrics [dot] voip [dot] support [at] gmail [dot] com) to accomplish this and many other objectives.

Nevertheless, we are currently trying to improve our click-through rates for shortened URLs that we send out with our tweets from about 15 per cent to over 20 per cent, but we have discovered that this is getting tougher to achieve with Twitter. This is because people follow far too many people to read carefully all the tweets that they receive each day. Just imagine following 120 people, and that each writes two tweets every day. How can you get your job done or have a life if you read them all?

Remember, between 1 and 3 per cent of a person's Twitter followers usually click on a link they tweeted. You can often check the statistics for a shortened URL by adding a + sign to the URL, such as *http://goo.gl/zsT8q+*.

Corporate blog or web page

The corporate blog and/or webpage can be used to share ideas, reviews and more with customers. However, it also requires time and effort. Customers expect you to treat them with dignity and respect. Of course, this means that you should answer their comment within 24 hours, every day of the week, including weekends (for an example of how not to do it, see *www.flickr.com/measure-for-impact/6144250565*).

Naturally, the corporate blog should be on your corporate domain, thereby making it easier for people to find. In turn, its traffic and links will contribute to the main webpage (see Gattiker, 8 July 2009). The more relevant the blog content, the more valuable the blog will become for the company. It will attract comments by readers, your replies and so on, thereby allowing you to engage with readers who might already or soon will be customers. Nevertheless, do not forget that, like building a high-quality car such as a Ferrari, building a high-quality blog post takes effort and time. Serving your customers a Happy Meal will not do (for more on what this means, check *@KarenDietz*'s comment here: *www.flickr.com/photos/measure-for-impact/6755319795*).

Relevant content lets others link to you from their website, blogs and Tumblr accounts, or include your story in their stick.it account. All these links further enhance your chances of being found by those who could become your clients.

So, how are you doing with regard to your blog's incoming links from relevant and credible websites? What about comments, resonance and much more? We have some indices and statistics that go beyond Google Analytics. You should take a look, and see how much they can help you improve accordingly (see *http://howto.commetrics.com/bang*). You will see positive changes within 30 days, guaranteed. Just use our template to track your blog and improve at *http://My.ComMetrics.com*.

Conclusion

The reality, unfortunately, is that social media measurement is a very public click-measuring competition. Worse still is that we buy it, hook, line and sinker. How else could Newt Gingrich – a Republican running to become President Obama's opponent in the November 2012 US election – allegedly not only pay to build a following that dwarfs the other candidates, but then have the audacity or naivety to brag publicly about the advantage this brings. I doubt it, and unfortunately, this illustrates how illiterate he, and others, can be regarding social media (*http://gawker.com/5826645/most-of-newt-gingrichs-twitter-followers-are-fake*).

In Figure 10.1 we graphically illustrated our need to use social media to improve the customer experience. Customers remain as important after the sale as they were before. Their sharing of how they experienced the purchase process, warranty work and after-sales support is critical. Of course, thanks to search results and people who share on the web, everybody can see when we have failed or not delivered as promised to a customer. And once it is online, there is no getting it back, no matter what 'it' is.

We believe that delighting customers does not increase loyalty to your product or service beyond average levels. However, reducing the effort required by customers to get their problem solved significantly improves loyalty. Therefore, we must act deliberately on this insight to help improve customer experiences with our product, service or brand, reducing costs and customer churn (see Dixon et al., 23 January 2012).

This chapter focused on how social media and any other technology-mediated communication can help you in your efforts to improve customer experience. Delivering the basics is the best path to do no harm, if nothing else. Providing social media services and communities that do not improve customer experience are both a waste of scarce resources and may upset the client. One fundamental action for improving customer experience is to resolve the client's issue in their favour, in such a way that the result neither takes too much time, nor is too difficult to achieve. Of course, patronising clients or making them jump through various hoops to get what they need is a sure way to cause dissatisfaction. Unfortunately, clients may choose to go public these days and let it be known among their many online friends.

Marketers currently have no standard measurement of social media success. Many believe that social media benefits their business. Often, what we come across are metrics that are easy to collect, such as social presence, as measured by the number of followers and fans on Facebook, Twitter or Google+. Unfortunately, asking how these affect the key drivers that top management cares about usually garners silence as a response. However, while we may neither like nor want to admit it, the number of Twitter followers or people putting your Google+ page in one of their circles has an impact on how your organisation will be viewed by the public. Of course, it is not a key performance indicator. Nevertheless, it is a key *popularity* indicator.

Regardless of whether your focus is getting more followers, or to be more down to earth in linking social media activities to your bottom line with the help of KPIs and key drivers, the schemata presented in Figure 10.2 will help you. Managing the quality management cycle of your social media process is a helpful tool for getting started. It enables you systematically to go through the process of improving the way you use social media for achieving a better customer experience. By methodically analysing the process, we can access data we need to gain valuable insights, allowing us to make changes that further help our clients, thus improving their bottom line as well as our own.

As a final note, let me ask: how many fans actually bother to have a conversation with brands on Facebook? One metric we can look at is Facebook's People Talking About This, the awkwardly named running count of likes, posts, comments, tags, shares and other ways a user of a social network can interact with branded pages.

A recent study used this metric as a proportion of overall fan growth of the top 200 brands on Facebook over a six-week period in October 2011. Data revealed that the proportion of overall fans who were People Talking About This was 1.3 per cent. But it gets worse: if one subtracts new likes, which only require a click (somewhat akin to TV ratings) and focuses on the forms that suggest greater interaction, one is left with only 0.45 per cent. Accordingly, less than 0.5 per cent of Facebook fans that identify themselves as 'liking' a brand actually bother to create any content with regard to it (Gattiker, 5 February 2012).

Also, Facebook fan bases skew toward heavy buyers rather than the more casual shoppers that your company has to reach in order to grow. Moreover, to expect that a Facebook page for your butter company, handyman business or bakery will change the way people interact with your company or its brand overnight is not on the cards. This means that putting a disproportionate amount of effort into engagement and strategies to get people to talk about a brand on Facebook is not the way to go. Believing that your comment or note will go viral on Facebook or Google+ is wishful thinking (ComMetrics, 25 January 2012). Instead, spend more time attracting new light buyers by giving talks at conferences, being interviewed on traditional media and having a webpage with content that your target audience values.

Good luck and be social. @*ComMetrics*

References

ComMetrics (25 January 2012) Sainsbury – customer service example goes viral on Facebook. [Google+ post] Retrieved 25 January 2012, from *https://plus.google.com/103400392486480765286/posts/Arrdw5PKVjp*

Dixon, Matthew, Ponomareff, Lara and Milgramm, Anastasia (23 January 2012) Stop trying to delight your customers: The idea in practice. [Blog post – HBR Blog Network]. Retrieved 25 January 2012, from *http://blogs.hbr.org/cs/2012/01/stop_trying_to_delight_your_cu.html*

Gattiker, Urs E. (8 July 2009) Increasing blogging effectiveness: Step 3. [Blog post – HowTo.ComMetrics]. Retrieved 15 January 2012, from *http://howto.commetrics.com/?p=79*

Gattiker, Urs E. (11 August 2010) Social media DO's and DON'Ts: 6 remedies for any emergency [Blog post – ComMetrics]. Retrieved 15 January 2012, from *http://commetrics.com/?p=9456*

Gattiker, Urs E. (6 October 2010) 4 ways to foster dialogue with corporate blogs [Blog post – ComMetrics]. Retrieved 15 January 2012, from *http://commetrics.com/?p=10356*

Gattiker, Urs E. (6 October 2011) My bank loves me NOT [Blog post – ComMetrics]. Retrieved 15 January 2012, from *http://commetrics.com/?p=16836/#comments*

Gattiker, Urs E. (5 February 2012) Facebook: Why do so many brand pages fail? Retrieved 15 February 2012, from *http://commetrics.com/?p=18203/#comments*

Gattiker, Urs E. (12 February 2012) Social CRM: Kundenservice mit Twitter (Social CRM: Customer service with Twitter)? [Blog post – CyTRAP] Retrieved 13 February 2012, from *http://info.cytrap.eu/?p=3122*

Gattiker, Urs E. (2012) Social media audit: Measuring for impact. New York: Springer more at: *http://info.cytrap.eu/?page_id=35*

Parker, Brian. (21 June 2011) SHOCKER: 3% to 7.5% of fans see your page's posts. [Blog post – All Facebook]. Retrieved 25 January 2012, from *www.allfacebook.com/shocker-3-to-7-5-of-fans-see-your-pages-posts-2011-06*

11

The uses and accuracy of social analytics data and platforms

Marshall Sponder

Abstract: While the online social media domain attracts all forms of analysis, there are lingering questions as to the actual usefulness of current methods employed to determine what issues and trends are hidden in the mass of accessible data generated by social media users. As a result, there is the useful conclusion to be drawn that commercial and non-commercial entities seeking to enhance their brand, and its reach into their relevant markets, need to be clear on what they do to grow their audience. Similarly, it is very evident that the measurement of any associated process of marketing, communication and stakeholder engagement must be accompanied, if not underpinned, by an appropriate, reliable form of social analytics to ensure that there is acceptable return on investment of necessary physical, financial and human resources that are required to make a success of any social media strategy.

Key words: social media, marketing, communication, stakeholder engagement, return on investment, ROI, measurement, strategy, public relations, branding, sales, advertising, community management.

Introduction

Social media is a means for people to communicate in a peer-to-peer fashion. While blogging has existed for close to 15 years,[1] 'social media' as it is currently understood (blogs, social networks, forums, twitter, online news sites, photo sharing sites, etc.) did not come into being until 2004. It was around that time that the first so-called social analytics platforms evolved, mostly to explore the online sentiment of audiences, and integrate social data with enterprise data platforms and tools. The goal of these and subsequent social analytics platforms is to provide actionable market research and, in some cases, information that can be tied to return on investment, commonly nicknamed 'ROI' (Return on Investment). While online marketing has embraced social media, there are serious and deep measurement issues for branding, public relations, sales and advertising that I will examine in this chapter.

Social media data and various practices

Public relations

Perhaps more than any other field, public relations (PR) has reinvented itself though adding social media, as well as social analytics, to its traditional offerings, such as crisis management, brand awareness, brand perception and event management. But there are significant challenges for agencies practising social analytics from within the communications space, including a conflict of interest between spinning a message, and measuring it (which I have written about in my book, *Social Media Analytics: Effective Tools for Building, Interpreting, and Using Metrics*).[2]

Furthermore, the disciplines and practice of social analytics, in addition to social media creation, when practised within the marketing communication (Marcom) environment, is akin to mixing oil and water; a successful emulsion of the two approaches is difficult because *there is no common lexicon*. In this chapter, I will share what it takes to set up social analytics properly in organisations that focus entirely on communication, or that have significant communications departments.

Branding

The more immediate goals are fostering brand awareness, doing so by extending digital footprints of a brand online and, thereby, growing the desired audience. As stands to reason, by increasing the audience associated with any brand, this should realise higher sales and, thus, more profit. In the case of not-for-profit (NFP) entities, audience growth equates to increased support and the prospect of further donations. Also, a common goal of branding campaigns in social media is to develop empowered fans that drive demand for branded content. However, the ultimate goals of branding, as it pertains to social media, are soft in that these are often difficult to quantify. For instance, consider measures such as increased awareness, purchase consideration, brand preference and the lead closure rate.[3]

By heightening brand awareness, associated customers tend to become more 'engaged with the brand', spending more money on the brand's products and services than would happen otherwise. Essentially, the measurement problem is determining an accurate correlation between online 'chatter' via social analytics platforms, such as Radian6, Alterian SM2, Brandwatch and the offline word-of-mouth (WOM) chatter that varies by industry and situation.[4]

Sampling issues with social data for public relations and branding

There are additional challenges with obtaining a complete sample of online conversation that is free of any platform collection bias.[5] Here, it is worthwhile to understand that a complete collection of relevant data is possible to in a point-of-sale (POS) environment, such as in a retail store. In direct contrast, when it comes to web analytics, search analytics, customer in-house analytics, database marketing and email marketing, the related social data is sampled at several levels and, as a direct consequence, a representative and unbiased sampling might not be possible to achieve.

As each social collection platform collects and processes data in its own way, the choice of platform, in itself (if that choice is not made properly), creates a potential source of concern for anyone seeking data accuracy (and that was one of the main reasons why I wrote my book on social media analytics).[6]

Sales

Research conducted by Empathica, a market research company, shows brands using social media for customer outreach are more likely to succeed in getting customers to interact with them online if a business offers free coupons and assorted promotions. According to Dr Gary Edwards, the Empathica EVP of Client Services:

> ... while many companies are adopting social media strategies, most have yet to tap the opportunities to go beyond social media adoption and engage consumers as active brand advocates. Many companies are still finding this level of engagement and nurturing tremendously challenging today.[7]

Consider that the recommendations from friends taking place on Facebook and Twitter are followed at least 33 per cent of the time, and it would appear that all of those recommendations can be tracked via social media analytics. Certainly, 'likes' and 'votes' are tracked by Radian6. In addition, InfiniGraph, a social intelligence platform, tracks the interaction level of branded content, trending content, affinity content and related trends, as well as influential factors.[8]

Businesses that desire to *monetise social media*, but are not fully prepared to track and map their social data to their sales data, all too frequently express their frustration over the lack of data that is capable of tying social media outreach and other such campaigns to measurable income. However, businesses do need to examine – perhaps using a detailed audit methodology – if they have done enough of the preparation work to enable the tracking that is necessary both on a business process level and measurement tactic level, so as to be able to follow outreach through to the cash register or (in the case of NFPs) to the collection box and related income stream. In relation to these important, if not mission-critical, issues, I developed an approach based on the concept of 'Ultraviolet Data' that brands can implement. But there are significant challenges for setting up complete tracking in most business environments.

The aforementioned problems, as per incomplete tracking, led me to found my new company, WebMetricsGuru Inc., in 2011. In so doing, I developed an approach for uncovering 'Ultraviolet Data' and enabling it, both on a social level (such as for sales) and for technological infrastructure support. This approach is now being deployed within local and international businesses in several vertical areas.[9]

Advertising

Social media data for assessing advertising effectiveness is the most accessible case for the use of social advertising, particularly with Facebook and, now, by Twitter. Facebook allows advertisers to target Facebook members (whose profile information, demographics, psychographics and behavioural data are known within Facebook) using a feature called 'profile targeting'.[10]

One example of how to use the profile approach came from Dennis Yu, CEO of Blitzlocal.com, a Facebook advertising agency, in a conversation that we had in late 2010.

> When you want to plug or pitch a new idea as part of a new business opportunity, you can present your work using neuro-marketing through Facebook profile advertising. First, decide on your audience (for example – male, 25 to 44 years of age), then set up Facebook profile targeting once you know who you want to reach in a given company/location. Perform the necessary research to find business members at the targeted company on Facebook. Finally, run Facebook advertising that that shows the results of similar work for another client to a few people in the firm you are pitching.

As a result, the people for whom a business proposal is to be presented will now be predisposed to favour your proposal based on the ad that they saw, whether that was directly or subliminally.

Analytics measurement chasms

Common lexicon and company DNA misunderstandings pervade many practices.

The public relations chasm

The practice of public relations is comprised of the effective use of spin, influencer outreach, messaging to foster free publicity, and changing public sentiment about individuals and companies. More recently, market research disciplines are included in some PR shops, with this focusing on brand sentiment, as well as brand competitors and industry-related information, with this often obtained using social media analytics tools and platforms.

Integrated marketing communications firms attract communications professionals along with editorial and business development candidates. But give thought to the fact that public relations professionals and social media analytics professionals are usually at cross purposes with each other.[11]

Analysts, for example, have a religious love for the truth, and for the real story. Also, they value data integrity. In comparison, communications professionals, for the most part, focus on messaging and creative assets. The accuracy of analytics, in and of itself, depends on finding essential truths within a situation, or in a set of situations and scenarios, which requires clear thinking, focused and extended time, along with the right set of methodologies, platforms and tools in order to provide actionable insights. Associated categorisation and filtering capabilities are still emerging. Plus the work that is involved to take social listening, and to make it useful for marketing insights, is considerable, with this often not being properly planned and staffed in PR firms.

On the other hand, PR and integrated communications firms tend to be focused on a client's reputation management, possibly with an eye to spinning the truth or, in the most positive light, putting a client's best foot forward, especially in bad circumstances. As a result of their preoccupation with spin and influencer outreach, the PR professional's notion of analytics is more akin to media research and campaign metrics, with the emphasis on media (clipping services, media placements, measured spots). Furthermore, note that most of the analytics platforms that exist for social media are not built for analysing media. Accordingly, analysts who find themselves in a PR firm often end up doing 'one-off' online media research and, usually, with not enough time or the right platforms to do it well. Social media analytics, as a research service, is a new offering in this area of investigation. But there are few 'good use' cases to predict how long most related tasks ought to take, which can complicate deliverables and keep analysts working overtime, typically needlessly.

Furthermore, while market research for a pitch or business opportunity is valuable, it is unclear how long it will take to produce the kind of research that will 'wow' a client (just as it is unclear as to what would comprise that kind of research). As a pitch has yet to produce revenue for the PR firm, the amount of time allotted for research is typically not sufficient to provide very interesting and useful results.

But the biggest problem with all of this is with varying lexicons, or ways of communicating. (For example, when a person says 'x', does the other person in the conversation hear 'y'? When people communicate, they do need to agree on common meanings. Otherwise, the conversation will lead to a bad outcome. In fact, that happens quite frequently.) As might be apparent, there are differences in vocabulary between that for PR/Marcom folks, and that for analytics people, with the two being quite far apart. It requires a bit of work and knowledge to translate effectively the output analytics platforms so as to provide anything useful from a PR perspective.

Lastly, in this part of the chapter, platforms used for 'social listening' are still immature and are not capable of providing that much in the way of useful information without a considerable amount of effort, energy and time, which can quickly burn out anyone! I've also noticed that most communications deliverables don't budget nearly enough time for setup, configuration, culling and operating in relation to gathering this conversational data, much less its delivery. Also, there is a data quality issue whereby communications professionals aren't concerned about the quality of data as much as its marketing effectiveness, while data professionals are much more focused on what the data/conversations consist of, and how to organise them properly (which, again, takes a great deal of valuable time and effort).

For me, a legitimate question arises as to where the value in the future of PR lies – shouldn't PR organisationally structure itself around the needs and support of the analyst (with this, I contend, due to the strong, an observed, notion that analytics, more and more, is driving the value of communications offerings) rather than the other way around? I will suggest that it all depends on who is asking the question.

The brand measurement chasm

One approach to increasing branding and brand awareness within companies lies with empowering authentic employee advocates, or as these people are more commonly called, 'Brand Ambassadors'. Consider the contribution to industry of Steve Rubel. He is EVP of Global Strategy and Insights for Edelman, the world's largest independent public relations firm. His concept of 'Brand All Stars' or 'Brand Ambassadors'[12] starts with a brand's employees spreading messaging to target audiences (this is more believable than corporate officers promoting the brand because, generally, few people trust CEOs). One way to do this is by internally recruiting employees who are already 'stars' within social media and, thereby, turning them into superstars, doing so by blending personal branding with corporate branding. As social media adoption becomes more widespread, what seemed like a special effort for corporate communications people a few years ago, when Steve Rubel first put forward his ideas on brand ambassadors, is much more commonplace nowadays.

It is generally held that people need to hear or see a message three to seven times before it is absorbed or believed, just as it is that 40 per cent of brand messaging gets through by means of employees promoting the brand to stakeholders, and via social media. As a result of social media outreach, there is often heightened visibility and higher rankings within search engines due to increased social content creation (by the brand ambassadors and influencers). In order to use brand ambassadors effectively, social listening has evolved to help find, select and target audiences in terms of locations, interests and activities. But creating effective messaging is not the same thing as measuring it, or fully understanding the impact of online conversations.

According to Gary Angel, CTO of Semphonic, which is a large independent analytics consultancy based in the Bay Area around San Francisco,[13] there is a real problem in using online listening tools to measure the effect of brand advocacy or to measure brand sentiment:

> ... ***One function that I'm rather skeptical of is brand sentiment monitoring as a replacement to traditional brand tracking studies.*** I haven't laid out the full case for this in any post yet, but I did, in my next post, show some of the reason for my skepticism about this AND about the use of sampled posts and human readership to classify brand sentiment. **The gist of my argument is that there are multiple levels of sampling involved in creating a social media measurement and that each of those samples had potential issues.**
>
> Listening tools sample the internet, they do not produce an exhaustive set of all verbatim (a particularly serious problem internationally). From their sample, the analyst must build a subset or sample using keyword classifications that are difficult to validate and can easily introduce significant bias. ***Most organizations give almost no thought to this step and don't realize how critical it is in achieving accurate representation of your topic-set.***
>
> Finally, if you are further subsetting verbatim for human readership, you have a sampling problem that will either introduce significant bias (if you weight by source or influence or any other variable) or severely limit analysis of key sources like traditional media.
>
> ***All this poorly controlled sampling makes me skeptical of the validity of most brand-tracking functions with social media as a true representation of consumer sentiment. I just don't think most companies have done the work to justify the data.***

The data quality issue might make social media analytics a non-starter, especially if organisations do really care about the quality of the data and its accuracy (with this being the 'substance versus hype' argument), as neither can be guaranteed in the social space, as it can be for other types of data, such as web and search analytics. On the other hand, if reaching customers and fostering conversations is the main business goal, perhaps the quality of the data in social media is not so much of an issue (but that's debatable).

Social media analytics can be used to find your audience online through platforms, like Rapleaf, that determine which social networks are prominent for target audiences. Then, a brand can dispatch empowered employees to reach out to customers in those social networks.

Rapleaf uses this data to create anonymous audience segments, such as 'Female' and 'Age 24–34', for online ad placements, then creates segments based on specific demographics requirements, as defined by clients. The Rapleaf platform places a cookie on your computer via your web browser. The Rapleaf cookie tells ad serving networks what ads will most likely be of interest to you, with this helping you to see more relevant content and helping companies to advertise their products more efficiently. Given that our segments are based on general profile data, Rapleaf cookies enhance your user experience without identifying you personally.[14]

While technology can personalise content by helping brands become more relevant, it's not able to replace primary research, such as the Edelman Trust Monitor.[15] This is due to the extent of the primary research undertaken, for instance, where Edelman's research consists of conducting several thousand 25-minute telephone interviews with people meeting certain criteria, and where respondents are chosen from a panel and statistically scored.[16] Going beyond who the survey takers are, the Edelman Trust Monitor attempts to find out 'brand health', as well as how it is perceived and trusted.

There have been attempts to create something equivalent to Edelman's Trust Monitor by using social media listening (thereby avoiding direct contact with customers) and the closest-known attempt about which I am aware is the PoliPulse project.[17] The brains behind PoliPulse are a team at Powell Tate, a leading DC-based public affairs and communications agency that is in partnership with Crimson Hexagon, which provides social media monitoring and analysis using machine learning algorithms.[18]

On the surface, it would appear that Crimson Hexagon provides a solution for many of the questions that Edelman Trust Monitor asks. Yet the level of reliability goes down due to limitations of ascertaining online identities and understanding to what extent viewpoints culled with machine learning neurolinguistic algorithms are often not proven to be representative of the way that people really think and feel.

Citing the issues from work by Wharton University in showing that there is little correlation been online and offline buzz, Gary Angel (mentioned earlier) suggests the data collected by social media listening isn't good enough to base good research on.

> '*... it turns out that Wharton's research has, at least partially, addressed an even larger issue:* ***how representative is social media chatter of word-of-mouth (WOM) conversation.*** *In other words, if you look at social media mentions, are they the same kinds of subjects and attitudes expressed by people in real conversation?*
>
> ***If social media isn't representative of word of mouth, then the whole enterprise of brand tracking is doomed, sampling be damned.***
>
> *The study Elea showed tackled this problem in classic academic fashion. They listened to a social community and they set up a Word-of-Mouth (WOM) experiment and they compared the results for two different industries.*
>
> *As you might almost expect, the results were both positive and negative. In their study, automotive social chatter correlated reasonably well with WOM.* ***Beauty-Supply chatter had zero correlation with WOM.***
>
> *In other words, if you're Ford, then if you can listen very carefully, you have some chance of using social media to measure brand sentiment.* ***If you're ProActiv, no matter how carefully you listen and sample, you're not tracking actual consumer sentiment when you listen with social media.***
>
> *And the million dollar question, of course, is what if you're neither automotive or beauty supply? How do you know if social media measurement is correlating to actual customer attitudes?*
>
> ***You don't.***[19]

So, in reality, using social analytics to track brands has significant challenges; this suggests very strongly that much work needs to be done to shore up the integrity of reporting and analysis around brands in the online space.

The sales analytics chasm

One of the more interesting developments over the last three years is a rise in use of Quick Response (QR) codes that can be scanned with mobile devices, such as smartphones, that can also be used to track sales.[20] With the automatic generation of QR codes by many URL shorteners, such as bitly and Goo.gl, it is possible to track instances when customers interact with a bottle of wine, or a menu item at a restaurant, doing so in ways that were not possible to do before now. The problem is that QR codes are not yet widely adopted and, even when they are, these do interfere with a user's experience of brand messaging (for instance, acting on QR codes involves using a mobile device in a specified, frequently awkward, way). For an example of a QR code, see Figure 11.1.

Greg Dowling, VP of Analytics for Semphonic.com, is a specialist in the area of mobile technology and he has valuable insights for how QR codes

Figure 11.1 QR code for social media analytics book summary

should be used for sales, marketing and advertising,[21] along with six of the most popular types of QR codes being used in marketing today.

Unfortunately, at this time, detailed geo-location information is usually not collected while using QR codes, though it is possible to foresee a day in the near future when all mobile devices are collecting geo-location and passing on of that information to analytics. Nevertheless, it is likely that analytics will improve for QR code data collection, especially when these codes are used more pervasively.

More likely, as I covered in my Rainbow Analytics paper[22] with Compete.com, there is a great deal of data that is 'ultraviolet' that, if made trackable, could translate directly into sales numbers, as had occurred with one of my former clients, the Havana Central Restaurant chain in New York City, where the direct measurement of social media efforts translated into sales numbers. However, the problem continues to be that social media actions are often not able to be tracked back to the cash register or the bottom line, even this correlation is expected to be in place. In that regard, consider the information contained in Figure 11.2.

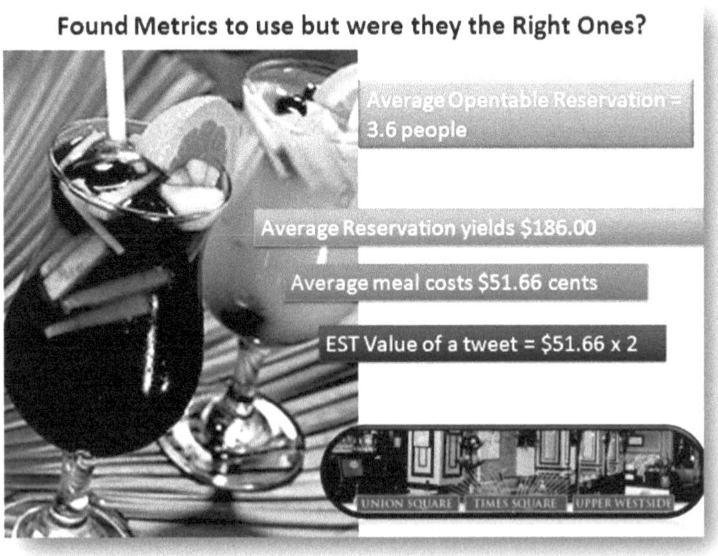

Figure 11.2 Sales information calculated by using triangulation of social media monitoring data and open-table data

Source: WebMetricsGuru Inc.

Rarely is social media a direct sales channel, according to Amber Naslund, a former community manager at Radian6:[23]

> ... Social media can increase the likelihood of sales through better targeting, more consistent touch points and availability of information, establishing affinities and relationships and all of the things that support the eventual transaction. Those are the same things we would want to do offline to nurture our prospects, but now we have more online channels to bridge those connections in both places.

The problem is that many businesses expected social media to lead to measureable sales when, in fact, they usually haven't. No doubt, in time, we'll close the loop on sales and measuring the effectiveness of social media. But meanwhile, managing stakeholder expectations seems to be the order of the day.

The social advertising chasm

Perhaps the one area where the accuracy of online measurement is not as much of a problem is with the practice of social advertising[24] where, usually, sophisticated tracking is available, especially on Facebook. Increasingly, this is also true of other applications, such as Twitter and LinkedIn. However, the issue of privacy has come up as platforms such as Facebook collect a fantastic treasure trove of user data. Understandably, the user data provides better targeting, but the effect can often feel like a *1984* scenario.

So, collecting too much social data, which conflicts with what people still believe to be their rights to privacy, might be where the chasm arises between data collectors and users. However, the Internet Advertising Bureau (IAB) has standard best practices for social advertising, although these are largely missing for the other practices examined in this chapter.[25]

What works for social media and return on investment?

With the preceding point seeming to cast a pall over social media usage, I wanted to end this chapter on a positive note by focusing on research that highlights what works when using social media, along with the measurement of it. I collected the following information from a variety of sources (and too many to list in the notes) but I'm happy to follow up with interested readers and discuss the details, if I am contacted via my WebMetricsGuru.com blog.

What works in social media for corporate stakeholders and social media return on investment?

What works for branding?

Brands are focusing on communicating directly with existing, and prospective, consumers with content placed in social media sites (such as Blendtec). Brands are abandoning other media platforms in favour of creating their own branded original content in social media channels.

My findings suggest that *brands should concentrate on the quality of their product or service* first, and let the messages spread organically. In fact, personal relationships with brands are entirely optional (and may not be what you want to promote, after all).

What works for advertising in social media?

Focusing on smaller niche communities and supporting services is where advertising should be concentrated. This is certainly the case in business-to-business (B2B) as getting people to share information in a 'safe' environment is most important.

What works for sales and social media?

The global recessions are helping to drive social media campaigns – but at this time, what is generally understood as ROI will probably come from traditional marketing channels instead of social media. In time, what we call social media today, will itself be rolled up into a traditional marketing channel, and be tracked along with the rest of the channels – but I'd give that three to five years to mature fully.

What works for marketing and social media?

Good marketers tend to be good storytellers. Social media for marketers is primarily a communications tool that sits across multiple channels to speak with customers (and listen to them) and where ROI comes from precise targeting of the right customers.

What works for retail social media?

Using customer support for retail products is the best place to find ROI in social media, and this is repeatedly shown to be the case. Having said that, using platforms such as Sprinklr, Shoutlet, Awareness Networks, Radian6 Engagement Console, Synthesio Unity and so on (being platforms that are built for engaging with customers) will be the best play here. This will amplify marketing and support efforts, along with increasing customer lifetime value.

What works for customer service and social media?

Putting a dollar value on customer service transactions is premature until we reach a consensus on the value of social media and how to measure it. Therefore, it is best to reach a consensus first. Any company or organisation can come up with an index value for a lead or customer transaction that is based on their own record keeping – and apply that to the customer service channel.

What works for customer resource management and social media?

Current customer resource management (CRM) solutions are uneven in their effectiveness, by type and segment, in reaching and recording vital transactions with the best bets being selling and ordering with customer insight that turned out to be interesting, but too hard to implement.

What works for community management and social media?

Reverse engineer whom you need to reach via community management software, such as Sprinklr, or use InfiniGraph to find the most active influencers behind the most active content being shared and acted upon.

Keep in mind that it is no longer enough to show growth of Twitter followers or Facebook fans, because social media ROI and clients are asking for qualification of how those increases translate into actual value. In fact, clients are often put off by 'fuzzy ROI' metrics, even though social media is still fuzzy in and of itself. ROI should be evaluated against certain objectives your organisation is trying to achieve and not in absolutes.

What works for business-to-business and social media?

Business-to-business (B2B) customers want to adopt social media. But C-level executives are still waiting to see hard proof from other B2B campaigns that worked before they get their feet wet. Using free gifts in email links sent to clients seems to work well by combining email and common social networks.

Also, B2B conversations need a safe place to happen. Often, a custom community portal is the best place to engage customers in this case.

What works for business-to-consumer in social media?

Again, customer support of a brand is the best place to see ROI in social media and looking at it as a marketing channel will be frustrating. It's also tempting to use listening systems to monitor customers. However, the related platforms are too immature for determining social media ROI.

What works for generating awareness using social media?

Start by creating content and sharing it via aptly named sharing tools (such as Share This); the more sharing of social media content that takes place, the more awareness will be generated – but make sure that you are generating awareness in the right circles by using an appropriate platform, such as InfiniGraph, that measures the interactions of followers of specific brands on Facebook and Twitter.

What works in moving customers from awareness to consideration?

Opinion sharing and word-of-mouth are the best ways to move potential customers from awareness to consideration in social media.

What works in moving customers from consideration to trying a product or service?

To move people to try a product or service, there should be several positive reviews that are easy to find/read/share and, in particular, it helps if their friends like the product/service.

What works in moving customers from trying a product to recommending it to friends?

Customer support from a brand may be the main motivating factor in getting customers to refer to a friend a product or service that they have tried.

What works in creating engagement using social media?

Get back to good marketing – have a compelling story with crisp messaging and artwork that appeals to smaller and well-targeted niche communities. That helps. Having complementary services that lend weight to each other can help to increase the number of engaged followers.

What works best for email marketing and social media?

Using free gifts in email links that are connected to social networks seems to work well by combining email and common social networks. Also, using personal targeting is helpful when combining social media and email.

What works best in using Facebook?

Return on Engagement (ROE) is a more reasonable measure of success than ROI – driving thousands of eyeballs to pictures/videos depicting your brand when utilising social networking services, like Twitter or Facebook, is more likely to be seen as a metric that you can put to good use without too much difficulty.

What works best in using mobile social media?

According to a Forrester research study, 75 per cent of online retailers are developing a mobile marketing strategy, and there is an increasing appetite for mobile applications in driving online retailers to speed up their mobile marketing initiatives. Product and price information, store information and coupons are among the most popular features that retailers are offering consumers. In order to realise increased ROI from mobile marketing, retailers are investing in features that support the cross-channel experience.

In addition, note that Forrester expects the worldwide online video marketing spend to explode from $1 billion in 2008 to $7 billion this year. Add to this the fact that viral commercials, movie and game trailers and social media are major online trends across the globe.

What works best for geo-location services like Foursquare and Facebook Places?

Looking at Foursquare for ROI was premature until late in 2011, where about 25 per cent of the online population was using geo-location, which was up significantly from 6 per cent only two years earlier. It is possible now, with applications such as Valuevine.com, to measure geo-location fairly well, and this level of marketing measurement should be encouraged.

Historically, businesses have used geo-location for retail locations, in relation to rewards, prizes and giveaways. But there are still too few brands and businesses using geo-location intelligently to build best practices.

What works best for blogs and blogging?

Blogging should be the hub of your social media efforts. Content creation is the best thing that one can do to create ROI. Blogging helps drive search traffic, which can be a driver of ROI and social media ROI. Usually, blogs are where opinions on products and services are posted, and these can be effective in moving people from awareness to consideration and then on to purchasing. Be a good storyteller when blogging. Note that personal blogs are ego-driven and they are either personal opinion platforms for the author, or the content is almost solely what the author chooses to write about.

What works best for content creation in social media?

Generally speaking, the more content a brand has that is search- and social media-accessible, the more likely it is to be searched for and found. But web analytics provide misleading results for social media ROI. For example, using page views fails to differentiate between segment traffic, and a loyal visitor is more valuable to a content site than someone who visited the site for the first time and will likely never come back. It's also true that page views alone fail to report the level of engagement on the pages visited.

What works best for search marketing and social media?

When people buy, they generally first do Internet research via search, then ask the related opinions of their friends.

What works bcst for cstablishing and measuring social media ROI?

Typically, results are measured in soft metrics, such as friends, followers, likes, bookmarks, retweets, reach and link tracking via Google/bitly. In addition, it is helpful to distinguish between the five types of social media ROI:

1. **Return on Engagement:** The duration of time spent either in conversation, or interacting, with social objects and, in turn, what transpired that's worthy of measurement.
2. **Return on Participation:** The metric tied to measuring and valuing the time spent participating in social media through conversations, or through the creation of social objects.

3. **Return on Involvement:** Similar to participation, marketers explore touch points for documenting states of interaction and tie metrics and potential return of each.
4. **Return on Attention:** In the attention economy, we assess the means to seize attention, hold it and measure the response.
5. **Return on Trust:** A variant on measuring customer loyalty, and the likelihood for referrals, a trust barometer establishes the state of trust that is earned in social media engagement, as well as the prospect of generating advocacy and how it affects future business.

Conclusion

There are several problems with measuring social media effectively to determine return on investment. In this chapter, I delved into the issues surrounding measurement of social media and public relations, branding, sales and advertising. In each use case, there was a different challenge and, possibly, a different solution. (I suggest you read those sections again to find out what they are.)

In closing, I gave some best practices, being recipes from what I personally found had worked in social media, which were taken from thousands of postings that I have read over several years, and up until today. Admittedly, I didn't want to leave the reader with a hopeless situation in monetising social media efforts. On the other hand, we're still missing the 'common lexicon' that allows buyer, seller, agency, vendor, customer, analyst, stakeholder, business manager, CEO/CIO/CMO and so on to understand and define the deliverables that they need. Until that 'common lexicon' evolves to a point of widespread acceptance, I must admit that all of us will need to be a bit more careful, more introspective, and more specific about our wants and needs within social media. If we don't do that, it will be just more 'garbage in – garbage out' efforts and marketing.

Consider that data, and the enablement of data, is only as valuable as a brand, customer or related stakeholder thinks it is, and what they are willing to pay. In this regard, give thought to the fact that we show what we value by how we spend our time and energies, and what we actually do, but not by what we say (or say that we do).

Anyone that wants to continue the conversation, seek me at WebMetricsGuru.com or contact me at *now.seo@gmail.com*

Notes

1. 'History of blogging', Wikipedia: *http://en.wikipedia.org/wiki/History_of_blogging*
2. Sponder, Marshall (2011) *Social Media Analytics: Effective Tools for Building, Interpreting, and Using Metrics*, McGraw-Hill.
3. 'Social Media Return on Investment (ROI)', Don Bartholomew, Fleishman-Hillard Digital Research Group, 16 June 2010: *www.usefulsocialmedia.com/assets/pdf/usm_slides/don_bartholemew.pdf*
4. 'Social Media and the Sampling Problem', Gary Angel, President of Semphonic, 10 November 2011: *http://semphonic.blogs.com/semangel/2011/11/social-media-and-the-sampling-problem.html*
5. 'Sampling and Social Media', Gary Angel, 23 October 2011: *http://semphonic.blogs.com/semangel/2011/10/sampling-and-social-media.html*
6. Sponder, Marshall (2011) *Social Media Analytics: Effective Tools for Building, Interpreting, and Using Metrics*, McGraw-Hill, Chapter 10, 'The Limits of What We Can Collect'.
7. 'Coupons and Trusted Friends Drive Users' Social Media Brand Engagement', Neil Glassman, SocialTimes, 8 December 2010: *www.socialtimes.com/2010/12/coupons-trust-socialmedia-brands-empathica*
8. 'Attending Digiday Video and New York Area IBM Business Analytics Users Group Meeting plus a romp with Infinigraph and Anthony Gemma', Marshall Sponder, WebMetricsGuru, 8 November 2011: *www.webmetricsguru.com/archives/2011/11/attending-digiday-video-and-new-york-area-ibm-business-analytics-users-group-meeting-plus-a-romp-with-infinigraph-and-anthony-gemma*
9. 'Tracking Social Media ROI using Spectrum Analytics', Marshall Sponder: *www.scribd.com/doc/38176762/Tracking-Social-Media-ROI-using-Spectrum-Analytics*
10. 'The Most Powerful Secret in Facebook Ads', Dennis Yu, AllFacebook, 22 June 2012: *www.allfacebook.com/facebook-ads-secret-2010-06*
11. 'What is Public Relations?', wiseGEEK: *www.wisegeek.com/what-is-public-relations.htm*
12. 'Using Social Media to promote your brand – Steve Rubel (Brand All Stars)', Marshall Sponder, WebMetricsGuru, 3 June 2009: *www.webmetricsguru.com/archives/2009/06/using-social-media-to-promote-your-brand-steve-rubel-brand-all-stars*
13. 'Social Media and the Sampling Problem', Gary Angel, 10 November 2011: *http://semphonic.blogs.com/semangel/2011/11/social-media-and-the-sampling-problem.html*
14. RapLeaf: *www.rapleaf.com*
15. '2010 Edelman Trust Barometer': *www.edelman.com/trust/2010*
16. *Ibid.*
17. 'PoliPulse and the Power of Opinion Monitoring from Crimson Hexagon', Marshall Sponder, WebMetrics Guru 3 November 2010: *www.webmetricsguru.com/archives/2010/11/polipulse-and-the-power-of-opinion-monitoring-from-crimson-hexagon*

18. PoliPulse: *www.polipulse.com*
19. 'Social Media and the Sampling Problem', Gary Angel, 10 November 2011: *http://semphonic.blogs.com/semangel/2011/11/social-media-and-the-sampling-problem.html*
20. 'QR Codes and Analytics Tracking', Marshall Sponder, WebMetricsGuru, 12 November 2010: *www.webmetricsguru.com/archives/2010/11/qr-codes-and-analytics-tracking*
21. 'Tracking QR Code Performance', Gary Angel, 7 January 2011: *http://dowling.typepad.com/dowling/2011/01/tracking-qr-code-performance.html*
22. 'Tracking Social Media ROI using Spectrum Analytics', Marshall Sponder: *www.scribd.com/doc/38176762/Tracking-Social-Media-ROI-using-Spectrum-Analytics*
23. 'Social Media, Sales, And How They Work Together', Amber Naslund, Radian6, 7 December 2010: *www.radian6.com/blog/2010/12/social-media-sales-and-how-they-work-together*
24. 'Facebook aDs 101 – How to Set up and Track Facebook Ads': *http://subliminalpixels.com/facebook/how-to-set-up-and-track-facebook-ads*
25. 'Guidelines, Standards & Best Practices', Interactive Advertising Bureau (IAB): *www.iab.net/iab_products_and_industry_services*

12

Altruism – a valuable dimension of the digital age

Russell Yardley

Abstract: Social media applications provide the opportunity for people to connect with others, as well as to record their various activities on a digital canvas that is for all to see. As such, skills and virtues are developed and displayed. Thereby, individual reputations unfold, and this can prompt deeper links between people who pursue selfless benefits. In effect, members of emerging online communities have an increased capacity to share ideas that are more for the common good than for personal gain, as well as determine which people should be invited to participate. As a direct result, what unfolds is a greater likelihood that evolving projects, and related outcomes, will address any number of issues and opportunities related to the public interest than would have been possible otherwise.

Key words: social media, social discourse, altruism, digital age, networking, collaboration, cooperation, building trust, exchanging value, copyright laws.

Introduction

People are becoming more important, not less. This is because, in the digital age, greater connectivity is driving collaboration. In turn, this is fanning innovation and creating new ways of working, learning and living. That will result in increased productivity, which will provide a higher standard of living. What distinguishes the digital age is the connection between people and things, which is driven by the ubiquitous nature of the Internet. Given that the Internet connects billions of people and trillions of devices, and that everything is connected with everything else, this modern phenomenon will change how people relate, altering those relationships in ways that we have not seen before. These changes will come from increasing levels of trust that will provide individuals, firms and nations with a powerful competitive advantage. This will also come about because connected people will realise that they are accountable for their deeds and that will motivate them to become better people.

As has already become apparent, changes brought about by the digital economy will increase our dependency on others. For instance, the fall of Lehman Brothers caused financial pain even in remote and rural locations far from business centres in capital cities. Also, drought in one food bowl now causes food riots on the other side of the world. In addition, the essence of power will change as networks become more important than individual people, companies or nation states, and this change will resurrect the intimacy of the village because, in trusted groups, valuable collaborative behaviours will flourish and relationships will not just be driven by self-interest – for instance, 'I help you in exchange for you helping me.' But further change in modern society will be driven by people wanting to do the right thing to help others for rewards in reputation, respect and munificence. This is due to altruism, whereby that principle and practice is fostered by technological innovation in social media applications.

Still, there is a dire need to address current obstacles, so that people attain and maintain ready access to ideas in fomenting innovativeness, and yielding all the benefits. Copyright laws, developed centuries ago, are not suited to today's technology, and a new balance is needed between private incentives for innovation and mutual benefits for society.

Facebook, Bebo, YouTube and LinkedIn emerged from a plethora of innovators, such as MySpace, Friendster and many others, to assist pre-existing social networks improve how they operated, as well as providing tools for members to form new networks around an unlimited set of social attributes.

The culture evolving in Facebook is different from that of LinkedIn that, again, is different from Google+. This is because social mores evolve and gain acceptance across the member base and, importantly, the associated functionality, culture and social pressure changes member behaviour. Consider that printing in the fifteenth century, especially the use of movable type and the invention of Gutenberg's press, encouraged consistency in spelling and that, together with improved visual clarity of words printed on the page, this obviated the need for reading out loud. Thereby, silent reading permitted the reader to apply their own thoughts to those of the author and that very element of human development eventually changed political structures and organisations. Just as printing presses changed politics, so too are the social media tools changing society.

Social Networking Sites (SNS) and the available social media tools assist people to create a public or controlled access profile that they can use to connect, communicate and collaborate with their networks of people. This online environment varies substantially from a traditional network in that connections of personal or business contacts can be traversed, as well as being used to expand dramatically both one's own network and the understanding of who is connected to whom. Established networks of people can use a SNS to operate more effectively, to enhance the depth, ease and speed of communication and collaboration. But groups that have physical as well as virtual connections usually build trust more easily. Particularly, networks of people that are established online will require additional functionality and engagement to establish the trust that is required to conduct desired, effective online collaboration or communication. For a more detailed academic discussion of SNS, see *http://onlinelibrary.wiley.com/doi/10.1111/j.1083-6101.2007.00393.x/full*

Prior to the Internet, savvy political operators in large organisations had the ability to notice who was connected to whom, and how to penetrate those people networks for their own advantage. What SNS, particularly LinkedIn, have done is to make those people connections more transparent and obvious to a larger number of people.

With hundreds of millions of people signed up to the major SNS, the potential for understanding both constructive and destructive behaviour is enormous. Without breaching general expectations of privacy, these sites could aggregate information and connection patterns to identify and harvest productive practices, as well as design relevant tools to accelerate outcomes. Today, techniques to hunt for new connections and to farm existing ones are pretty basic. Generally, LinkedIn is seen as the preserve of recruitment companies and sales people. However, as the power of collaborating with people networks is established in most people's minds, many more people will see the value of such services. Tools to define interests, opportunities and ventures to encourage valuable connections while protecting a member from unwanted, annoying approaches are clearly in their infancy.

Traditional networking behaviour

Dale Carnegie's iconic book *How to Win Friends and Influence People*, which has sold more than 15 million copies since it was first released in 1937, is recognised as one of the most successful self-help books ever published. As a direct consequence, that title and Carnegie's name became synonymous with the power of business networking, and the development of useful connections to create valuable business relationships. Basically, he was the first to define traditional business networking skills covering fundamental techniques in handling people, how to make people like you, winning people over to your way of thinking and being a leader.

Traditional social interactions relied on participants' social skills to uncover common interests, shared contacts, shared knowledge and complementary skills among acquaintances. Hence, Dale Carnegie became such a household name in the 1930s by helping people to master these important skills. However, as might stand to reason, different types of people with different skills play different roles in this process, as Malcolm Gladwell points out in *The Tipping Point*. Mavens, or experts, have an uncanny habit of being at the centre of important events and thus providing an essential role in connecting people both with other people, and with relevant information. They learn how to be in the right place at the right time. Social media technology leverages these different roles to improve the networking process by providing facilities to push or pull social and connecting information in bringing to the surface people connections across any given network, so as to create value more quickly than can be achieved in traditional situations. This makes it much easier to identify people, interests and connections to shape opportunities and to create related value.

The 'middleman' was once able to charge a fee or, in economic parlance, charge a rent just for being a facilitator. There was no demand for adding value because the other parties were 'in the dark'. But as communications improved, light was shone into those dark places and 'middlemen' either became valuable or were soon eradicated. This is happening to retailers today. Any physical retailer that provides the same service and role as an online e-commerce retailer must also provide the same range of goods, cost of delivery and price. Without providing a better service, a stronger relationship or a more trusted brand, modern retailers cannot charge a price higher than their online competitors.

Traditionally, businesses saw any other business providing the same services, or selling the same goods, as a competitor. However, as small businesses were outgunned by the buying power and market position of very large businesses, they soon formed buying groups and associations to address the comparative deficiencies. IGA (Independent Grocers of Australia) is a good example where small businesses joined forces to compete with the major supermarket chains. Companies in these groups networked either to increase revenues (through cooperative advertising campaigns) or to decrease costs (by bulk buying of stock). Any cost of doing business that could be divided by more than one entity can add dollars to the bottom line by sharing costs appropriately. In this way, competitors competed, and cooperated, in the marketplace. More efficient and effective online communications accelerates this process. As ideas and knowledge became more important to delivering a differentiated service, amortising the cost of creating the ideas and knowledge across more customers had significant impact on the applicable business and pricing models. New Internet-based communication and collaboration applications again accelerated this process.

Collaboration and cooperation

Businesses must think very differently in a digitally enabled economy. Just as Marmite, Promite and Vegemite were created from a waste product in the process of brewing beer, value can be created from by-products in the digital economy. Luis von Ahn at Carnegie Mellon University brought to the world the squiggly graphic challenge that is used to distinguish a real person from a computer program trying to access a website. This is a very useful security service where automated systems could inappropriately access services directed at real people, and has become extremely popular, with hundreds of millions of challenges issued every day. Von Ahn recognised an opportunity here to utilise the 'wasted' time of these people wanting access to a website by using the security challenge to interpret scans of old books. He did this by modifying the challenge so that two separate squiggly graphics are simultaneously presented to the user, with one known to the security application and the other being a graphic taken from a scanned book. The known graphic determined if the user was a computer or real person and, when ten real users consistently interpreted the other graphic, their answer to the challenge was added to the text file of the scanned book. This service is translating 100 million words per day, or 2.5 million books per year. At that rate, the cost of paying interpreters, even from a low-cost economy, would exceed $1 million per day. If these low-cost salaries were cut in half, they still cannot compete against a service that has no cost of labour at all.

Using the above example, can you think of other potential digital economy by-products that could replace traditional services? Louis von Ahn has. He is developing *www.duolingo.com* to offer free foreign language lessons while translating the web by presenting sentences from web pages to language students, then combining (so-called wisdom of crowds) translations validated by proven performance of a large numbers of students to deliver translation of those web pages into any number of foreign languages. The ambitious yet achievable aim of this project is to translate the bulk of the web into every major language.

This process has been described as collaborative production of goods or services, and the same concept can be applied to consumption. Airbnb.com has used this collaborative consumption model to take a resource that would otherwise go unused (such as an empty bed) and connect the owner of that resource to someone who is prepared to pay for using it (say, a bed for the night). To make this system work, sufficient trust must be created for the provider and user of the resource to be comfortable in undertaking the transaction. Traditional babysitting clubs have now been extended with substantial online services, like *www.findababysitter.com.au*, which illustrates how communities can share goods and time that are in surplus of requirements, either for a fee or the reward of giving.

Online collaboration can go beyond production and consumption of goods and services to share using what American writer and advisor Clay Shirky has termed 'cognitive surplus', in his 2010 book of the same name, to create things of community value. That is to say, your surplus brain cycles, when not applied to earning a living or entertaining yourself, can be applied, together with those of others, to create valuable things altruistically. Wikipedia is a fine example.

You may not be able to design a digital process to generate your desired service for free. But there may be ways to reduce the cost significantly by more effective collaboration. In every industry, and in every market around the world, big companies and small are paying large numbers of people to do very similar tasks. These tasks could be as simple as evaluating products or services, creating induction programmes, a wide range of training modules used in everyday business or more complex projects, like planning to open an office in Beijing. If it were possible to find a similar company or person who was also planning to do the same or very similar task, and efficiently establish sufficient trust to help one another with ideas and knowledge and, most importantly, to share the workload and save resources, considerable productivity increases could be achieved.

This approach to collaboration and cooperation has not just suddenly appeared. It has evolved over the past couple of decades. In 1995, Acumentum (web applications), Cambridge Consulting (recruitment), Campaign Palace (advertising), FHA (branding), Geyer Design (interior architects), Invetech (product design), Mann Judd (accounting/advisory), Quantum Market Research and Royce Communications (Public Relations) became part of a business network they named the Australian Retail Solutions Group. At first, the aim was to incorporate and establish an entity that would bring together all the capabilities of members to better market the companies to larger companies and much larger projects. That approach was not successful. Even so, it did deliver significant business to the collaborative network through sharing business intelligence, work in progress and discussing ideas whereby various combinations of the members won tens of millions of dollars' worth of business. The network remained active for almost a decade and it did not lose momentum until owners of the various businesses began selling their interests a few years ago.

Similar, small trusted networks continue to appear and organisations like the Hub Melbourne (*www.hubmelbourne.com*), a professional member community that drives innovation through collaboration, and the Creative Performance Exchange (*www.meetup.com/The-CPX*) an open community to exchange creative ideas and methods, help to show the way for applying new collaborative technologies and inventing new ways of working, learning and living.

Consider that the ubiquitous Internet has extended the geographic scope and improved the efficiency of finding the right collaborative partners, doing so while providing a 'digital village' environment where good behaviour can be rewarded and bad behaviour is discouraged. Motivation to participate in this digital village is driven by substantial increases in productivity as well as reputation, respect and munificence. Having spent three months developing a marketing plan to penetrate the 79 local government councils in Victoria, Australia, a web design company could be quite content with new business generated from some of those councils, or it could share the ideas, information and knowledge in their marketing plan with a non-competitive collaborator so that, with far less investment of money and time than they had to invest, their collaborative partner could also be rewarded with new business from the same 79 councils. In the collaborative digital economy, businesses are learning that it is not just their products and services that can be traded online. This can also apply to their trusted relationships, ideas, knowledge and tools developed by them over many years, and these can be traded for valuable consideration, which is not always just money.

Social media in the emerging digital economy

Every new communication technology breakthrough, from radio to television to computers, caused experts to become overly excited about the potential to revolutionise education, entertainment or business. Visions of replacing expensive people with cheaper machines in these people-dominated economic segments were mostly dashed and the early excitement quickly dissipated. Cinema has not replaced theatre, computers have not replaced teachers and, while computers are everywhere in business, people still like doing business with people. Where technologies have brought people closer together, they have been embraced, and where technologies have come between people, such as in interactive voice response systems, they were much less successful.

It is often felt that we are at a dawn of a new age, and that this moment has a significance unlike most others. Tom Stoppard wrote in *Arcadia*, 'A door like this has cracked open five or six times since we got up on our hind legs', and he goes on to highlight that relativity and quantum mechanics have yet to provide A Theory for Everything.

Will the excitement for Internet technologies transforming human relationships and driving massive increases in productivity come to very little? Or is this the door that will open to a new way of living? What has to be done to avoid disappointment? How do we achieve trusted valuable online communications and collaborations? The great successes in take-up of modern technologies have shown that these must fit the established behaviour and existing mental models of people, not the other way round. Steve Jobs knew this, and Apple products have become the benchmark of usability, as they are built from the inside out. For instance, the success of iTunes came from a deep understanding of all the required ingredients: accessibility, efficiency, engagement, persuasion, sales and delivery. Apple was successful in selling music to an audience who were all too aware they could rip CDs or access free downloads of their favourite music from a BitTorrent site, because Apple painstakingly attended to every tiny detail to make the process a better experience than any alternative, even when the alternative was free.

Now, contemplate the social media space. Facebook, LinkedIn and other SNS are beginning to recognise the need for a trusted, simple, yet powerful way for communities to do more than just connect, communicate and collaborate, and so provide an environment to conduct our lives more effectively. This means that we live in a very different economy to our parents. It no longer makes sense to talk about the digital economy being separate from the real economy because these online connected facilities are impacting the whole economy. Everyone is beginning to work, learn and live using a digital canvas, and those nations that provide the trust, integrity and safety in their digital environment will create more productive economies than those that do not.

What must be addressed in economic and public policy to meet this challenge? In order to build trust, and integrity, as well as provide a safe digital canvas for our society, we need a frictionless, trusted, safe payment system; also, we need to feel in control of our personal information, so we will need appropriate privacy and security. In addition, as this digital canvas is all about creating, enhancing and utilising ideas and knowledge, we need to fix our busted intellectual property (IP) system.

Building trust

Building trust in the connected economy will have important economic and moral benefits. Figure 12.1 maps trust against GDP per capita and is from a dated, although still very relevant, 1996 study that asked 'generally speaking would you say that most people can be trusted?' (Zac P J 2003 Trust. *The Journal of Financial Transformations*, CAPCO Institute 17–24); it is worth reviewing the key components that are presented in Figure 12.1.

The conclusion is that high trust leads to economic cooperation, which leads to prosperity, which enhances trust in a *virtuous circle*. Low trust leads to low cooperation, leading to poverty and further eroding trust in a *vicious circle*.

Distrustful economies in the lower left are in stark contrast to the successful economies in the top right. We should all be very afraid if the online world is moving us down to the lower left corner where there is

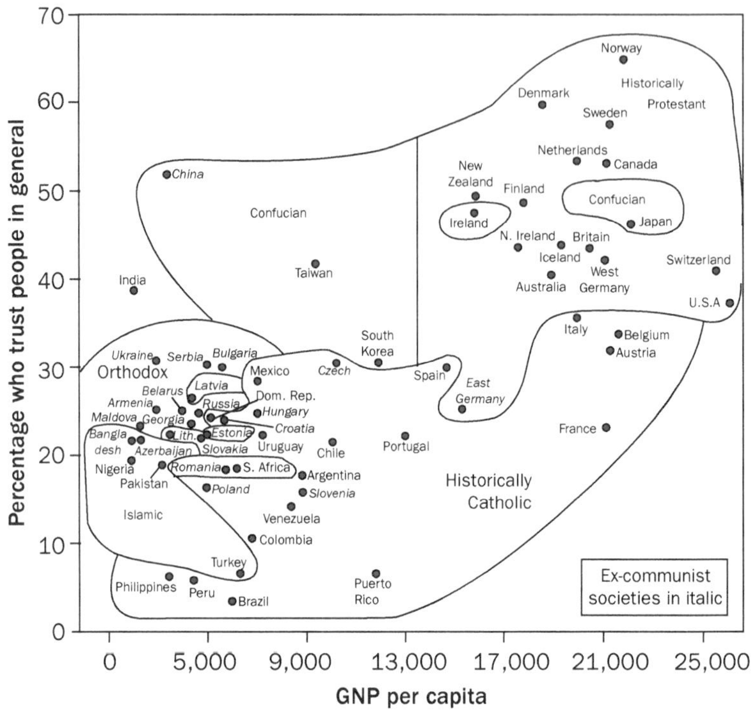

Figure 12.1 **The relationship between trust and economic performance**

low trust and lower GDP per capita. It doesn't have to be this way. To protect our economy, we must question very seriously the fundamental lack of trust inherent in the World Wide Web. I accept that there is a place on the web for anonymity, freedom of movement, freedom of speech and freedom of association. Nevertheless, with the web becoming the very foundation of our connected economy, there is an essential need for identity and reputation. Also, we need to retain the trust that was, and is, fundamental to economic success.

Trust and collaboration

The striking patterns in most SNS are that these are built on how humans communicate and behave. Social networks can use social technologies to magnify communications and behaviours. Some people knit the people around them together to become friends, whereas others do not.

One pattern of carbon atoms creates graphite and another diamonds, graphite being soft and dark, while diamonds are clear and hard. The differences are created by the way that the same atoms are linked together. Similarly, the way that people are linked together in social networks can produce radically different outcomes. It is the ties between people that make the whole greater than the sum of the parts.

SNS have the potential to use social technologies to establish reliable identities and reputations for collaboration within groups. But groups are not better at everything. Would you want everything in your world to be designed by a committee? Too often today, we give tasks to individuals when groups would achieve more, and we give tasks to groups where individuals would do better. There is a mantra in much of the online culture that collectives make the best stuff, but that is patently not true. When you have everyone collaborating on everything, you generate a dull, average outcome in all things. You do not get innovation, and you never get accountability.

Do you really think that a crowd could have painted the *Mona Lisa*? Or composed *Rhapsody in Blue*? Jazz bands benefit from individual solo performances and group collaboration. Individuals, like Lennon and McCartney, or Rogers and Hammerstein, often worked better in pairs. The ubiquitous, massively connected web gives us choice, and we need to become better at making these choices. When all creative things are subject to mass collaboration, there is no accountability and no greatness. Isolation can starve ideas. With the dictatorship of the majority there is palpable horror.

Exchanging value

Unfortunately, today, the web is straddled with a very uncompetitive payments system dominated by banks guarding their monopoly. We need a frictionless, ubiquitous payments system to exchange value efficiently as we communicate and collaborate with our networks, and with no additional charge for moving money internationally, nor with long delays in processing transactions.

The banks and credit card companies have built a proprietary, locked-down system for which, despite substantially lower costs for computing, storage and communications, they are charging similar fees as they did 50 years ago. Now, consider that Daniel Roth at *Wired* warned the banks, ‘It’s safe to say that the payment industry is going to change dramatically. As money becomes completely digitised, infinitely transferable, and friction-free, it will again revolutionise how we think about our economy.'

People expect governments to protect consumers with a sound and just legal system. The nineteenth-century scammers and snake oil salesman were slowly shut down by consumer protection legislation. The system continues to work today because offenders can be exposed by the trashy, but popular, current affairs programmes. While most of our economy was not conducted online, we might have tolerated an unregulated, unenforceable, 'buyer beware' online commercial environment – but not now!

Not only must a payments system be safe, secure and trusted, it must also be extremely easy to use. Digital payments need to use a device that people are already carrying, such as a smart card that replaces all credit cards, or a mobile phone.

Today, credit cards could display a number that changes every 30 seconds so that your credit card identity can never be stolen. Effective online consumer protection is available now, but it may take government regulation to make the banks responsible for the protection of transactions and the identity of their customers.

Just as child protection laws provide safety for children, and consumer protection laws create a safe and reliable place for commerce, we should look to our governments to provide the same in the online space because, without feeling safe and secure, there will be no trust, and without trust, we will not achieve the potential productivity gains that are necessary to attain the potential benefits from a digital canvas whereby we can create better ways of working, learning and living.

Our copyright laws are a mess

Having raised the importance of trust, payments systems and security, it is important to address the most fundamental challenge of the digital world – copyright. How often have you heard, 'Copyright is dead, it's an outmoded concept destroyed by students all over the world who refuse to pay for any digital content, especially music'? The conclusion to this discussion usually goes, 'Like drug laws, copyright laws just turn students into criminals, and won't stop downloading, so they are irrelevant and should be abolished.' This expresses a widely held view, but this attacks the fundamental and essential core of any successful knowledge economy.

In the US, in the 1920s, there was a widespread disrespect for the law because of the failure of prohibition. Literature of the time, including *The Great Gatsby*, celebrated economic predators. Similarly, today, we all know a significant number of people who illegally download copyrighted entertainment, and there is a widespread disrespect for copyright law.

When US legislation provides for greater damages for downloading two songs in breach of copyright than it does for the medical negligence by a surgeon who removes the wrong limb in an operation, it is easy to argue that copyright laws are inequitable. When the Recording Industry Association of America can sue Jesse Jordan, a freshman university student, for $15 million dollars because his search engine technology enabled other students to illegally download music files, and his lawyers had to advise him to settle because, if he won, he would not recover any of his estimated $250 000 legal expenses. When the chance of a moral victory is coupled with sending your family bankrupt, then US copyright legislation is unconscionable. These cases are not an argument for or an incitement to break the law; they are remarkable evidence that these inequitable and unwarranted laws must be fixed.

While we have been ripping off music, and cheering as software and news became free, the work we were doing every day increasingly relied upon respect for, and valuing of, IP. But just as free software, music and news have undermined the value of IP, we have undermined the very basis for our emerging knowledge economy.

When Google takes the advertising revenue streams for our major newspapers because they can place their ads freely alongside any newspaper content, then who will pay the salary of the investigative journalist working on the next Watergate break-in? It is not the sensational story that is important; it is the need for constant enquiry into the power and politics of every nation that keeps our institutions honest and operating with some level of accountability to the people. That is important.

Chris Anderson, the great advocate of *Free*, argues in his book of the same name that 'Everyone can use a Free business model, but concedes all too typically only the number one company can get really rich with it.' It is not surprising that the two major advocates for *Free*, Google and Apple, are also the most guarded and proprietary about their core revenue-generating digital assets, and benefit greatly from others providing digital assets freely.

This is not a formula for an economy to create better ways of working, learning and living for all. It is a formula for turning all of us into digitally enabled itinerant workers never achieving Jefferson's dream of 'life, liberty and the pursuit of happiness'. This demonetised result for most digitised ideas will render the inventor all the poorer for their clever efforts. After all, there are only a few writers and musicians who actually make a decent living in the new digital utopia.

It is blindingly obvious that a knowledge-based economy must protect IP and build an efficient value exchange system for earning money from collaborating and communicating our ideas and inventions because, in the longer term, technology will just become better and better.

The advertising model is effective when a third party is prepared to pay for advertising in gaining market access to sell their product to your audience, but it is inefficient and ineffective in many areas, particularly when the value of that access is low, or when such access distracts your audience from the use of the product that assembled the audience in the first place.

This model worked well for the media industry, and brilliantly for Google. There are also excellent variations. Construction Data Management (CDM) applied this model to the construction industry by collecting building plans from architects without cost in exchange for providing the architects with costing data by region. CDM, in turn, built a revenue stream from manufacturers by charging them for access to information on building projects to help their sales teams in selling building products to construction projects.

Contorting this model to apply to everything, as the aforementioned Chris Anderson has done, is nonsense and will reduce economic efficiency when the total fees from third parties are less than the cost of the products provided. Put another way, the total costs within the economy must be met by someone, and a more efficient system with lower total costs and less 'wastage' will provide a higher growth in GDP and, ultimately, a high standard of living for its citizens.

If there ever was a paradox, then copyright is one. At a superficial level it is easy to agree with both sides of this argument. When an author labours for a lifetime, and produces a substantial body of work, why should the ownership of that work vaporise 70 years after their death? If the author had chosen to apply their labour to build physical objects, then their heirs could enjoy that value for an unlimited time.

Alternatively, why should a company that freely utilised the ideas from earlier stories involving animals and fairy tales strictly control the use of a mouse, or a rabbit or a deer in all film and television forever? If Christopher Marlowe and Thomas Kyd, both Elizabethan dramatists, had been given the same copyright protection in 1590 as Disney has been given for Mickey Mouse, would the works of William Shakespeare have achieved the same recognition 500 years later? For, in the words of Sir Isaac Newton, William Shakespeare stood on the shoulders of giants and, in Shakespeare's case, the giants were Marlowe and Kyd.

If you want to quote Tom Peters from his seminal *In Search of Excellence*, there is no requirement to pay a copyright fee, nor do you need his permission to do so. With all the multimedia tools available today, rather than quote his text, it would have much greater effect if you inserted a short video of Tom making the point. But, because *and only* because you have changed medium, you are not only required to pay a copyright fee, you are also required to negotiate permissions first. Why is it that a learned speech is free to quote, but quoting with modern tools is now against the law?

At the turn of the last century, when the Wright Brothers first flew an aeroplane, American law held that a property owner owned not just the surface of his land, but all that lay below, through to the centre of the earth, as well as all the space above to an indefinite extent upwards. If American property owners were allowed by the courts to keep those rights, the airline industry would never have left the ground.

The connected digital economy, similarly, requires the associated law to change. If it does not change, then digital inventors of the future will be grounded because they will be negotiating with every digital property owner beneath every digital flight path that they wish to take.

There are many other examples where a new technology has changed the law. If the courts had decided that photographers required the permission of property owners to take photographs of their property, what a difference that would have made to photography. Imagine how much music radio stations would play if they were required to request permission from copyright holders before a song could be played.

The greatest advocates for the current copyright laws are the Hollywood film studios, and it was these film studios that took on iiNet in the Australian Federal Court by charging iiNet with authorising their customers' illegal downloading of music files. One wit described this as an argument to charge road transport authorities with aiding and abetting every armed robbery because the robbers use roads to escape.

The irony here is that Hollywood was created by film producers escaping to the West Coast of the US to avoid paying royalties to Edison back on the East Coast, because he held patents on film cameras. The even greater irony is that the USA, being the copyright police of the world, was itself built on piracy of IP from the Old World. Clearly, self-interest is king, and the kings of self-interest have deep pockets. We therefore need politicians with great foresight and enormous integrity to withstand the certain onslaught from those vested interests.

What must change

The copyright system for digitally connected economies of the twenty-first century requires a radical overhaul. The complexity of this challenge *is* daunting. Those who create new things, whether that is music, memes, stories or services, and also establish valuable trust, should be rewarded by society. To do this, we need to give our innovators and inventors the power to control their innovations and inventions, to set their price and the conditions that apply to their creations. Modern technology gives us almost unlimited choices in how we might design such a system.

In his wonderful book, *Free Culture*, Lawrence Lessig argues that creators of IP rely on the ideas and knowledge that went before them, and that innovation requires access to those ideas and knowledge to be in the public domain. If the law causes, or at least permits, the public domain to become barren, innovation will be diminished. Consequently we need to protect IP to reward creation, and do so while building a public domain of knowledge and ideas.

Ponder the following. Harvard law professor William Fisher has suggested that all content capable of digital transmission should be marked with a digital watermark, and that governments should regulate a system, but have it developed by entrepreneurs to measure usage and collect payments based on this watermark.

I see the solution as an online automated system that:

- allows digital files to be loaned, just as we currently loan a paper book using an iPod/Pad/Phone or Kindle by suspending access to a file on one device for a preset period while it is active on another device;
- allows digital files to be transferred permanently (sold) to another device;
- allows copyright holders to set their fees for permitting permanent transfer (selling), or temporary transfer (lending), of files;
- sets 'fair use' permissions for limited extracts of file content, and that those extracts are secured with a digital watermark;

- sets a 'fair use' fee structure by copyright holder at publication;
- lodges and registers a digital work so that copyright can be claimed;
- ensures the copyright owner renews their registration, say, every ten years, and failing to do so renders that copyright to the public domain.

This system would remove the need for private detectives, and the investment of large amounts of time and money in hunting down the ownership of digital assets; it will also remove a major barrier to innovation and invention, which is damaging to our economy.

This system would also stop the likes of Larrikin Music demanding royalties in the order of 60 per cent of millions of dollars, as already earned by the real creative people, for a four-second, rather vague reference in a musical riff in a hit song by Men At Work to the children's song *Kookaburra* because a deal of that size could never be done before a song was released.

The US Congress and other parliaments have extended copyright protection for authors since 1908, taking it from 14 years to an author's lifetime plus 70 years, or 95 years for a corporation. If this continues, as it is likely to do, we are operating under permanent copyright protection by stealth.

To simplify the system, we need to strengthen copyright. To reduce the high legal fees involved in current copyright cases, we need to make copyright narrow and clearly defined. Derivatives from a copyright work should be separated from the rights of the work itself and should be limited to a very short term – perhaps as little as ten years.

That is, where a film is made based on a book, or a musical is created from music, innovators will be free to create new works from existing works ten years after publication. But fees for exact reuse of existing works will require payment of a fee forever. It is justified in restricting the broader rights by providing permanent copyright in exchange for the narrower rights.

Conclusion

Listen to obituaries at funerals, and you will hear that society values what people do for each other, and with each other. Stories of joining together to achieve valuable outcomes, and of sharing the experience, are the focus of most eulogies. Wise counsel is to pay attention to the relationships that you have, and improve the quality of those experiences. Life is about communication and collaboration around common goals and aspirations.

SNS and technologies have evolved to become everyday tools that are used to paint our lives on a digital canvas with people congregating with others who have similar values, interests and ambitions. As in the village of old, your community knows your true character. In contrast, in the emerging digital village, it is difficult to pretend to be what you are not. Your past deeds are a permanent exhibition on your digital canvas and your reputation, respect and munificence the substantial currency of the digital age.

The immediacy and ubiquity of this connected world accelerates activity and relationships so that the communities formed are able to achieve so much more in far less time. Achievement, and the shared experience in those communities, will expand our feelings of self-worth through trusted relationships extending further around the globe than was possible in the past. Whether this is a superior way of working, learning and living will be determined by the efficacy of what is achieved with all our resources now at our fingertips, and must be pursued vigorously if we are to see the altruistic aspects of our emerging society blossom, and yield fruit.

References

Anderson, C. (2009) *Free: the future of a radical price*. Hyperion.

Fisher, W. (2004) *Promises to keep: technology, law, and the future of entertainment*. Stanford University Press.

Gladwell, M. (2000) *The tipping point: how little things can make a big difference*. Little Brown and Company.

Lessig, L. (2004) *Free culture*. Penguin Group.

Index

Kolibri 360 GmbH
Ferdinand-Jühlke-Straße 7
99095 Erfurt, Deutschland
produktsicherheit@kolibri360.de